Material Culture
and Mass Consumption

Social Archaeology

General Editor
Ian Hodder, University of Cambridge

Advisory Editors
Margaret Conkey, University of California at Berkeley
Mark Leone, University of Maryland
Alain Schnapp, U.E.R. d'Art et d'Archéologie, Paris
Stephen Shennan, University of Southampton
Bruce Trigger, McGill University, Montreal

Published

FRAGMENTS FROM ANTIQUITY
An Archaeology of Social Life in Britain, 2900–1200 BC
John C. Barrett

ENGENDERING ARCHAEOLOGY
Edited by Joan M. Gero and Margaret W. Conkey

EXPLANATION IN ARCHAEOLOGY
Guy Gibbon

IRON-AGE SOCIETIES
Lotte Hedeager

THE DOMESTICATION OF EUROPE
Ian Hodder

THE ARCHAEOLOGY OF INEQUALITY
Edited by Randall H. McGuire and Robert Paynter

MATERIAL CULTURE AND MASS CONSUMPTION
Daniel Miller

READING MATERIAL CULTURE
Edited by Christopher Tilley

In preparation

THE RISE OF MESO-AMERICA
Elizabeth Brumfiel

SOCIAL THEORY AND SOCIAL CHANGE
Christopher Gosden

AN ARCHAEOLOGY OF CAPITALISM
Matthew Johnson

THE ARCHAEOLOGY OF DEMOCRACY
Ian Morris

READING ARCHAEOLOGY
Christopher W. Tilley

FEMINIST ARCHAEOLOGY
Alison Wylie

Material Culture
and Mass Consumption

Daniel Miller

BLACKWELL
Oxford UK & Cambridge USA

First published 1987
First published in paperback 1991
Reprinted 1992, 1993
Reprinted 1994 with new epilogue

Blackwell Publishers
108 Cowley Road, Oxford OX4 1JF, UK

238 Main Street
Cambridge, Massachusetts 02142, USA

British Library Cataloguing in Publication Data

A CIP catalogue record for this book is available from the British Library.

Library of Congress Cataloging in Publication Data

A CIP catalogue record for this book is available from the Library of Congress.
ISBN 0–631–18001–X (pbk.)

Typeset in 10$^1/_2$ on 12 pt Garamond
by OPUS, Oxford
Printed in Great Britain by T. J. Press (Padstow) Ltd

This book is printed on acid-free paper

Contents

Preface   vii

Part I   Objectification   1
1   Introduction   3
2   Hegel and Objectification   19
3   Marx: Objectification as Rupture   34
4   Munn: Objectification as Culture   50
5   Simmel: Objectification as Modernity   68

Part II   Material Culture   83
6   The Humility of Objects   85
7   Artefacts in their Contexts   109

Part III   Mass Consumption   131
8   The Study of Consumption   133
9   Object Domains, Ideology and Interests   158
10   Towards a Theory of Consumption   178

Epilogue, 1993: From Theory to Ethnography to Politics in
Consumption Studies   218

References   229
Index   243

For Rachel

Preface

Several factors have influenced the writing of this book, an awareness of which may assist the reader in transcending the intentions of the author. First, my perspective evolved during the course of lecturing within the framework of 'Material Culture Studies'. This category may have had a coherent focus in the nineteenth century, under the influence of evolutionary studies in anthropology, but it has since become something of a residual box, housing otherwise 'homeless' interests such as the links between archaeology and social anthropology, or cross-cultural studies in the arts and technology. This lack of clear disciplinary allegiance has, however, afforded me the perhaps rare freedom to range over several disciplines in my discussion and to draw together threads which might otherwise have remained unconnected. Furthermore, the category may gain a new integrity as a basis for tackling topics such as mass consumption which have been neglected because they also happen to lie outside the particular emphases of the various branches of the social sciences as they have arisen historically.

The second influence dates back to my years as a graduate student. In attending interesting-sounding courses – whether in geography, architecture or psychology – I found that the chances were that the lecture would actually be on Habermas and a set of propositions which were very much the academic fashion of the time. Of these, the one which has best maintained its original impact is the denial of the fact–value dichotomy and the insistence that all academic work is informed by, and in turn contributes to, the moral and political climate within which it is conducted. In the present work I have attempted to address directly the relationship between my critical accounts of earlier writers and the models of possible future or ideal societies which lie implicit within such criticisms.

A third influence has been the experience of conducting fieldwork in several developing countries. I suspect that I am not alone in having found that my first period of fieldwork reinforced the initial propensity in much anthropological enquiry to romanticize the place under investigation as idealized 'other', a perspective which focuses almost exclusively on its attractive features. This vision tends to fall away with subsequent studies and is, at least in part, replaced by a growing awareness of the constraints of poverty, close kin relations, and the generally limited possibilities available to people within non-industrial societies such as the archetypal peasant community. Experience of these constraints has curbed any tendency to indulge in easy nostalgia for assumed ancestral roots, and social life in earlier times. It has therefore seemed to me important to distinguish between a conflation of criticisms of the inequaltites and oppression associated with 'capitalism' or 'the state', and what may often be at root a general critique of industrial culture *per se*, based on a presumption of simple authenticity for pre-industrial culture.

A further influence derives from the experience of conducting fieldwork which concentrated upon the social symbolism of the material world. This is the observation that an abiding concern with the precise status and social implications of the object world, which we tend to marginalize as existing only among 'yuppies', may in fact be manifested in an equally extreme form under the very different conditions of poverty, where lack of access to material goods may almost result in an involution of concern with those which are available.

I appreciate that the result of my research is a book which advocates a perilous course of investigation. Both writer and reader may so easily fall prey to either fetishism of the object or else Romanticization of the subject; indeed, the attempt to avoid both of these has determined the very structure of this work. My overall intention has been to excavate certain areas of investigation formerly branded as 'trivial' or 'inauthentic', and to show why it is crucial for these to be reclaimed as pivotal aspects of any present or feasible future industrialized society.

I gratefully acknowledge the assistance given by the often critical readers of sections of this book, including Barbara Bender, Janet Coleman, Adrian Forty, Bruce Kapferer, Alison Kelly of Basil Blackwell and especially Allen Abramson, Stephen Frosh and Mike Rowlands who have provided stimulating debate throughout the period of writing. I am also grateful to Rickie Burman, who has shared many tasks which may not have seemed relevant to this book, but were actually essential to its production.

PART I

Objectification

1

Introduction

This book sets out to investigate the relationship between society and material culture, and to assess the consequences of the enormous increase in industrial production over the last century. It will be argued that academic study of the specific nature of the material artefact produced in society has been remarkably neglected, and that compared, for example, to the discipline of linguistics, our understanding of material culture is rudimentary in the extreme. This lack of concern with the nature of the artefact appears to have emerged simultaneously with the quantitative rise in the production and mass distribution of material goods. The average inhabitant of a country such as Britain uses, and is associated with, a range of clothing, furnishing, technology, buildings, and other objects which is vast in extent, complexity and diversity compared to any previous era. In short, our culture has become to an increasing degree a material culture based on an object form. It will be suggested in the course of this volume that the very physicality of the object which makes it appear so immediate, sensual and assimilable belies its actual nature, and that material culture is one of the most resistant forms of cultural expression in terms of our attempts to comprehend it.

The physicality of the material world is, however, only one of the reasons for this neglect. Equally important is a series of academic trends which have led to an overwhelming concentration on the area of production as the key generative arena for the emergence of the dominant social relations in contemporary societies, and a comparative neglect of consumption, together with a concomitant failure to observe the actual changes which have taken place over the last century in the balance of influence between these two forms of interactions with goods. A further major cause of neglect has been the tendency on all sides of the political spectrum to subscribe to certain blanket assumptions concerning the negative consequences of the growth of material culture. This culture has been associated with an increasingly 'materialistic' or 'fetishistic' attitude, which is held to have arisen through a focusing on relations to goods *per se* at the expense of genuine social interaction. These assumptions are responsible for the emergence of a variety of generally nihilistic and global critiques of 'modern' life, which have tended to detract from the intensive analysis at the micro-level of the actual relationship between people and goods in industrial societies, and a remarkable paucity of positive suggestions of a feasible nature as to how industrial society might appropriate its own culture.

I have approached these questions by starting from a discussion of the subject–object relationship at the most abstract philosophical level and progressing by stages to an analysis of certain highly specific aspects of everyday life. A further understanding of the place of goods in society requires a general perspective on the relationship between people and things. Such a perspective belongs, however, to a larger set of ideas about the nature of society and the processes generally falling into the category of 'culture', and therefore entails wider philosophical questions. In view of this, I have begun by considering a key moment in the development of Western philosophy and its constant struggle with the problem of the subject–object duality: that is, the publication of Hegel's *Phenomenology of Spirit*. I have abstracted from this work a set of processes which are then extended and compared to parallel ideas in a number of other academic disciplines; together, these ideas lead to a general grounding of the original set of arguments in the mundane world. From philosophical studies of the subject–object duality and its resolution in a dynamic process of becoming is derived a tentative theory of culture concerned with the relationship between the human subject and the external world. As a sub-set of this theory of culture, is derived an approach to material culture as a particular form of such externalization. From such abstractions the approach moves on to consider the specific material culture of contemporary Britain, and finally to propose a tentative theory of the nature of modern mass consumption as the dominant context through which we relate to goods.

This sequence results in some unusual juxtapositions. The tendency in modern, highly specialized academic research is for philosophical discussions to take place within the relatively abstract terms set by that discipline, while micro-ethnographic studies of specific aspects of social organization tend to be bound by the relativism of the particular, and lend themselves to philosophical analysis mainly as critiques of philosophy's pretensions to generality. In the present volume, by contrast, the intention is to attempt a better understanding of philosophical concepts by grounding them in the everyday world of the high-street shopping centres, and in turn to understand better the relationship of people to their three-piece suites by reference to theorists such as Simmel or Piaget.

Such a strategy involves the rather perilous activity of taking objects which are generally regarded as trivial, and holding them up for academic scrutiny. Unless one is a Duchamp working within the confines of high art, or has the literary brilliance of Barthes, this breaking of disciplinary 'frames' and the treatment of bay windows and melamine boards as linchpins of modern culture may rapidly lay the author open to charges of affectation. It is evident, however, that those same people who shy away from considered discussion of such objects readily part with a large proportion of their income to acquire them. Indeed, the relative ascription of 'importance' and 'triviality', and the fixedness of these categories, is itself a matter whose explicit discussion may provide major clues as to the nature of material culture, and help to account for its comparative neglect in academic studies.

A further general aim of this work is to concentrate on the positive elements of the model being constructed. Unlike many of the writers who have followed Hegel, I do not intend to strike a tragic pose, bewailing an oppressive fate which we cannot control, in the name of a utopia we have either just left or are about to create. First, because I believe, with the modernists, and in the tradition of some post-Enlightenment theorists, that many of the changes that have taken place during recent centuries are themselves extremely positive, providing the basis for new kinds of equality, knowledge and social development which were previously unimaginable, let alone achievable, for anything but a tiny minority of the population. But secondly because, unlike many modernists, I do not regard these as the exclusive achievement of planners, leaders, artists and individuals, but rather as the result of large-scale social movements which have enabled ever expanding sectors of the mass population to appropriate these advantages. Furthermore, I believe that there are reasons for thinking that this trend may be sustained, though only through continual struggle, in the future. The material surveyed in the latter stages of this book provides evidence for giving credit for such developments back where it is due – to the mass populace – and for claiming a perspicacity and subtlety in mass behaviour which is a far cry from the passivity, illusion and denigration implied in many self-proclaimed radical perspectives.

The development of such a positive stance regarding the possibilities for mass consumption is intended as a critical perspective; that is, one that condemns the status quo by developing a model of society which could be attained and yet is rarely even aimed for at present. As such, this view contrasts with the perspective currently predominant in the academically oriented social sciences. For example, the movements and authors loosely grouped under the 'meta-label' of post-structuralism, the various strands of which claim to be radical on the basis of a similar condemnatory attitude, may actually be found to provide only conservative and nihilistic assessments of the ubiquity and thus the inevitability of oppression. This, along with the massive impact on the social sciences over the last two decades of Marxist theory concentrating on a wide variety of exploitative and oppressive institutions, may suggest that in the late 1980s the principal critical challenge is to produce alternative perspectives directly relevant to the recent transformations and developments in both socialist and non-socialist societies.

My present aim is to examine any such tendencies already evident in industrial societies, and to indicate in what way they offer a model for feasible social change. More specifically with respect to material culture, the book concludes with the argument that these positive possibilities are clearly immanent within the consumption activities of mass populations today.

The Shape of Things to Come

A large proportion of the classic texts on social theory, including, in different ways, those by Marx, Freud, Durkheim, Weber and the Frankfurt School writers, focus on the possibilities for resolving the contradictions of modernity. Over the last century, however, there has been a radical change in our perception of what it is that constitutes the 'modern', and any fresh consideration of these familiar themes must involve some degree of detachment from the trajectories of social theory, and a re-immersion in, and a re-examination of, the nature of the problem itself.

Many of the concerns of this work are based on observations of trends in contemporary British society. At the time of writing I am undertaking fieldwork in London which differs from my previous experience in ethnographic research in a South Asian village or the South Pacific in that most of the discussions and observations have to take place outside the public domain, in the context of people's homes. This experience of entering a series of very private domains, selected not because the occupants share common interests as 'friends' or a common origin as 'relatives', but solely because of their residence on a particular housing estate, gives me the impression that there is an increasing disparity between the subjects of public concern, political rhetoric or academic debate, and the experiences of everyday life. There seems to be a particular discrepancy between an enormous public interest in the levels of people's wages, the dole, and public services, and the lack of any comparable interest, outside the commercial sector, in exactly what people do with the money or services received; that is, how they transfer them back into the construction of worlds. This suggests that we respect in analysis the same public/private duality that we ourselves practise. It is worth noting that the market researcher has shown much less trepidation than the academic in crossing this boundary.

Some of the interests which appear to dominate people's private lives have been reflected in a new literature. For example, the widespread fascination for television soap operas, exploited by large numbers of newspaper articles about the private lives of the actors and actresses involved, is reflected in the rise of 'media studies' (e.g. Collins et al. 1986). There is, as yet, however, no comparable concern with similarly important domains, such as home furnishing and supermarket shopping. In particular, outside of the specific interest in gender roles and domesticity found in feminist studies, there is a comparative lack of literature on the increase in home-centred activities, developing local institutions such as babysitting circles or hobbies from which new social networks are emerging (see, however, Young and Willmott 1973; Gershuny 1978; Pahl 1984; Wallman 1982). While television provides the illusion of a hitherto unrivalled voyeurism, leaving nightly the impression of having witnessed the very private affairs of a wide range of households, its impact on the behaviour of actual neighbourhoods is much less understood.

As an example, imagine walking along one of the streets or corridors on a London council estate. The variety of attitudes people may have to the estate itself has only occasionally been documented (Andrews 1979; Parker 1983). It soon becomes clear that any attempt to use normative models to describe the individual household is ideologically charged. Whether one refers to the traditional 'norm' of the nuclear family or to some alternative, all such models appear to hide the actual experience, which seems to be perversely opposed to any ordered characterization. This contradiction is most evident in the radical difference between the modernist façade of the high-rise flats, with doors painted identical colours by the council, and what lies behind, where each householder has played bricoleur with the facilities provided, supplemented by goods purchased on the market.

Moving along the corridor, if flat one may be imagined to hold a single Cypriot divorcee with her children, then flat two may house a married couple who have moved from Blackpool with the kids and grandparents, flat three a nuclear family born in the area, flat four an elderly retired single male born in Ireland, and flat five a locally born teenager whose parents emigrated from the West Indies. Ethnic and family type are, however, only the most evident dimensions of this diversity, the full extent of which becomes apparent as one begins to examine degrees of affluence, self-esteem, political viewpoint, holidays taken, social networks, allocation of leisure time, or a hundred other variables. This diversity is echoed in the furnishing and style of the interior: in one flat, the facilities provided by the council may hardly have been changed; in the next, a mass of jumbled gifts, redundant furnishings which could not quite be thrown away, and items retained for possible future use may be stored without apparent order and filling the space to its limits; in the third, a striking and dominant style may have been imposed: a series of coordinated colours, textures and shapes creating a systematic and deliberate impression of 'modernity'. One flat seems focused on the television, the next on the dining table, the third on the children's toys. The symbolism of the objects runs the gamut from futuristic hi-tech modernity through to pastiches of Victorian or even medieval styles, often within the same household and even within the same room.

An extraordinary feature of modern British life is the number and diversity of interests held behind these doors: a fanatic supporter of a football club lives next to a family that keeps an exotic range of pets; a follower of a pop group lives next to a political radical. Any one of these different cultural foci may become a central point of concern and identity. Television and the media continue to uncover the world champion hairdresser and the fancy-pigeon breeder, the bibliophile and the expert on coalholes. In this respect, the division of labour from civil servant to store detective, secretary, windowdresser, unemployed person, teacher or machine operator becomes only another dimension of difference.

An inescapable conclusion from such observation is that the culture of most people is of a very particular kind. The average person's relatively passive and infrequent interaction with the performed arts or entertainments appears largely inconsequential, while for those who live on a council estate or suburb in London, social activities based on the neighbourhood or community may be extraordinarily sparse. More striking are the very active, fluid and diverse strategies by means of which people transform resources both purchased through the market and allocated by the council into expressive environments, daily routines and often cosmological ideals: that is, ideas about order, morality and family, and their relationships with the wider society. The bricolage of the streets is no longer aided by the structured conventions of a mythology; as amongst the classic 'peoples' of social anthropology, its foundations are comparatively weak in this respect. Even images of stability, such as nostalgia, are continually restructured and reinvented according to individual domestic situations and expectations. While not denying the impact of the larger social and economic forces which help to construct such relationships, what has been neglected in the analysis of such forces is the mass response which may often be echoed in these micro and home-centered activities. Despite the high degree of our actual involvement in these cultural activities, they tend barely to be acknowledged, and their pivotal position in modern culture certainly remains quite unappreciated.

The trend towards diversity as such is hardly new. Many of the major theorists who have examined the nature of modern society have also attempted to represent the aura evoked by the scale and diversity of the goods on the marketplace. Those who were in a position to observe the birth of mass consumption, such as Simmel, Veblen and later Benjamin, have provided perhaps the most acute accounts. The interest in consumption as the key to the problem of social development, current at the time of Durkheim (Williams 1982) has since markedly declined. In recent years, only one sustained attempt has been made to encompass this diversity within a totalizing perspective which might provide an order for its elucidation, while simultaneously confronting it in its particularity (Bourdieu 1984). Bourdieu's emphasis is on artefacts as a consumer aid in the major struggle for social positioning, this relational activity taking precedence as a practice over the abstraction of class (Bourdieu 1985). Judgements are made according to the brand names used, the up-to-dateness of goods, and their arrangement. Increasingly, however, other activities are placed within the same framework. Political opinions or views on controversial issues may be canvassed less because of concern with the apparent subject of debate than as a means of placing the individual socially; that is of relating their attitude to CND or immigration to our own. Social positioning is, however, only one element in the construction of identity, and Bourdieu's account is usefully complemented by the study of goods as categories (Douglas and Isherwood 1979), the impact of a single object form in a variety of cultural settings (King 1984) or the analysis of a given domain within the mass market, such as fashion (Wilson 1985).

At one level, these features must be connected to the nature of capitalist production. It is clear that branding policies, design, targeting of goods, and company competition are all part of the process of developing close links between social and commodity difference (Forty 1986; Haug 1986), but the relationship is not simple. The predictions of academics such as Galbraith (1979) and several varieties of Marxist critic (e.g. Ewen and Ewen 1982), who emphasized the corporate control of capitalism, may not have been fulfilled. From the 1920s through to the 1960s, commerce, influenced by factors such as economies of scale, attempted to construct a highly predictable, homogenized and consistent market, which would allow for longer factory runs and high profitability. This is clearly reflected in the advertising of the period which was designed to break down local, ethnic and other customary sub-divisions in the population (Leiss 1983: 19). Commerce was thereby attempting to create a world mirrored in modernist imagery of science-fiction, a future in which all forms of ethnic or regional particularity have been suppressed and replaced by a homogeneous, 'designed' population. Observers who lived through the fifties may have seen it as representing the triumph of the logic of technocracy.

In recent years, however, the expected continuity of this trajectory has been called into question. The rise of a new diversity in the market has produced a curious shift in production. Factories have had to move from long runs of identical goods to much shorter runs providing specific forms for increasingly fluid target populations. Given the new ethnicity (e.g. Smith 1981), and the dissolution of the major accepted gender-based models, this diversity seems set to increase. This has led to a less predictable, and for advertising often less 'addressable', population. Naturally, commerce has adapted to such changes. The microchip embedded in industrial machinery now allows for much smaller runs and maintains profits (Murray 1985), but this ability to adapt does not reduce the degree to which industrial production appears to have had to follow rather than dictate these elements of social change.

Academic approaches to modern diversity are almost always condemnatory. Diversity is taken to represent a new superficiality and an alienated form of existence, lacking both authenticity and depth. A number of versions of this critique have recently come together through the development of the term 'post-modernism', which has become a means of both defining and condemning this feature of modernity (e.g. Jameson 1984). The history of academic analysis suggests that such approaches, evident, for example, in many of the Frankfurt School writings, seem destined to end in nihilism and elitism. Most common among them is an evaluative or aesthetic stance based on a view of authenticity found in some narrower definitions of culture which assign the label 'authentic' to the fine arts, opera and literature on the one hand, and to the music hall or a particular form of labour on the other.

Although on the surface such definitions appear to be evaluations of taste and style, they are always in effect denigrations of those people who are associated with the 'other' material and expressive forms. One social group condemns kitsch and soap opera, along with the mass interest in Benidorm or supermarkets; the other is appalled by the mass middle-class culture devoid of any true sense of 'history' or even of the present. In effect, only small minorities may be equated with the 'genuine' cultures of leisure or poverty. This antipathy to middle-class or inauthentic working-class culture may, however, extend to around three-quarters of Britons today. The alternative is to concentrate upon precisely this 'unpopular' culture: the do-it-yourself warehouses, the bingo halls, the fitted kitchens and the 'inauthentic' rag-bag and plurality of identities which make up most people's lives. A similar set of problems would arise if these were treated as positive and authentic simply because they represent mass or popular culture; but it is nevertheless essential to recognize that, however we perceive them, they constitute the major forms taken by contemporary industrial culture. As such, they need to be analysed as specific forms, and not merely dismissed as a fragmented descent from some primitive authenticity of the 'subjects' of classic anthropology, nor as merely the symbol of capitalist oppression, nor yet as the mere surface of a superficial era.

Perhaps the major shortcoming of many theories of the concept of culture is that they identify culture with a set of objects, such as the arts in themselves, rather than seeing it as an evaluation of the relationship through which objects are constituted as social forms. For such theories mass populations may be regarded as themselves inauthentic because of the supposed status of their associated environment as, for example, a capitalist or post-modernist culture. Culture, as this book will attempt to demonstrate, is always a process and is never reducible to either its object or its subject form. For this reason, evaluation should always be of a dynamic relationship, never of mere things.

The mirror image of an analysis of objects in themselves is the assumption that society and social relations exist in themselves. The foundation of this defence of the 'seriousness' of modern mass culture is, then, the refusal to isolate it as a symbol or a derivative of some prior set of social relations. Most critics of mass culture tend to assume that the relation of persons to objects is in some way vicarious, fetishistic or wrong; that primary concern should lie with direct social relations and 'real' people. The belief underlying this attitude is often that members of pre-industrial societies, free of the burden of artefacts, lived in more immediate natural relationship with each other. This kind of academic criticism extends the distaste evident in colloquial discourse for materialism as an apparent devaluation of people against commodities. I shall question the implication that separable real selves and authentic classes are to be found. I shall argue that people cannot be reified under the concept of 'society' outside of their own cultural milieu. Indeed, much of the first half of this book will be devoted to an attempt to transcend the dualism implied in the very concept of 'society'.

Summary of the Argument

This book is divided into three sections: the first, comprising chapters two to five, sets out the general approach through an examination of the concept of 'objectification'; the second, comprising chapters six and seven, is devoted to the specific nature of the object as artefact; and the third, comprising chapters eight to ten, develops an approach to modern mass consumption. Each section utilizes a particular style and methodology, which it may be helpful to have introduced here, together with a summary of the contents.

The key term in the first section is 'objectification', which will be developed as an initial model to which a series of analyses will be compared. The term is used to describe a series of processes consisting of externalization (self-alienation) and sublation (reabsorption) through which the subject of such a process is created and developed. These processes are first abstracted from Hegel's *Phenomenology of Spirit*, and are then used as the basis for a theory of culture. Since this abstraction proceeds by isolating certain elements of Hegel's work while ignoring the surrounding context within which these ideas were developed, the approach, although taken from a specific source, could not be termed Hegelian. As with all of the authors subsequently discussed, the abstraction of a set of particular ideas will be a somewhat violent one, which may involve the rejection of much of the author's contextual argument, terminology and exemplification. This procedure is justified by the contention that both Hegel and the later authorities have captured something in their use of these central ideas which is not dependent upon the particular manner in which they have developed them, but which may be used to construct another meaning through the accretative insights of diverse usages in various domains.

The third chapter is devoted to what might otherwise be a severe problem for any contemporary attempt to use the term objectification as a tool of analysis. This arises because of the strong association in modern parlance of that term with a specific form of Marxist analysis emphasizing the rupture in social relations through which people are effectively reduced to objects, and objects in turn interpose themselves in relationships between people. This interpretation of Hegel's work will be rejected, and the processes which are described under the term objectification will be retained as a positive model of the subject's potential development, rather than as a negative critique of a rupture in any such development. However, while rejecting this particular form of Marxist analysis as an approach to these questions, many other aspects of Marx's grounding of the philosphical abstractions of Hegel in the actual practices of ordinary peoples will be adopted.

Chapter four moves on to consider the discipline of social anthropology, and establishes the concept of objectification as culture in a non-industrial context. It examines Munn's work on the iconography of a group of Australian aborigines and on the Melanesian kula exchange system. Once again, certain striking parallels may be found: not only is the concept of cultural form developed by the anthropologist reflected in the model of culture as objectification, but there is also evidence that a similar model of such processes is held by the peoples amongst whom the anthropologist has lived and worked. The material is important not only for identifying these parallels at an abstract level, but also because it can be applied to the analysis of the construction and use of the external world of objects, and because it asserts the absolute necessity of culture for the establishment of all human relations, and discredits the idea that the relationship between people and the things they construct in the physical world is separable from some prior form of social relation.

The final chapter in the first section moves back to a more direct encounter with Hegel's ideas since the *Phenomenology of Spirit* is the model behind the core text for discussion within this chapter: *The Philosophy of Money* by the sociologist Georg Simmel. Since Simmel remains one of the very few authors who have specifically addressed the question of the quantitative rise of material culture and its consequences, he provides an important bridge between the first section of the present work and the remainder of the book. Furthermore, his ideas have influenced one of my main arguments: that is, an assertion of the intrinsically contradictory nature of industrial society and the impossibility of resolving the conflict inherent in that culture. This will, however, be used to construct a positive, rather than, as with Simmel, a tragic, reading of the possibilities of social development.

The idea of intrinsic and irresolvable contradiction will be used to legitimize a consistent rejection of that Romanticism which stems from a belief that the goal of academic study is the development of a model of society as a coherent totality. In different ways this Romanticism underlies Hegel's absolute knowledge, Marx's Communism, and Simmel's appeal to aesthetics, as well as many later developments in European social theory (Jay 1984). Rather than attempting to propose some utopian end to history, the emphasis will be on the means of living with an inevitable contradiction.

The rather unusual style of analysis of the first section may be accounted for by the dearth of writings sharing a similar perspective to the present study. The method employed is to examine a series of texts by authors who saw themselves as working on quite different issues, but whose ideas are here reinterpreted in order to consider their implications for the concerns outlined above. It is suggested that, although the authors were working in different disciplines on a variety of topics, a series of parallels underlies their texts (as with Piaget and Klein, discussed in chapter 6), which suggests that they were drawn towards a common perspective which may be argued through abstraction to be addressed to the nature of culture.

This attempt to show that texts on one topic may offer insights into a quite different subject results in what may be considered an extremely cavalier treatment of the authors concerned. Such a view is justified in so far as my intention is not to present a balanced representation of the authors' position which would satisfy both themselves and the field within which they worked, but rather to abstract very particular elements of their arguments, distributing emphasis quite differently than is usual, and in a sense rewriting the argument in the light of another goal. I am not concerned, then, to consider or assess the authors in the light of their own history, or the development of their discipline at the time. My overall aim is to gain a better understanding of material culture, not of Hegel or Munn themselves. What all these texts have in common, however, is a very great profundity in their analysis of their respective problems, with which little can compare in the specific area of material culture studies. As a result of this profundity, these texts offer ideas and models which transcend their specific dilemmas and may be employed in discussion of questions the authors themselves may never directly have considered.

The second section, consisting of two chapters, turns from analysis of such academic texts to consideration of the more specific consequences of the materiality of the object as artefact. The approach to culture in general developed in the first section is thereby narrowed to the problem of the artefact as a single example of cultural form. In chapter 6, an attempt is made to address directly the implications of the materiality of the artefact. First, psychological and psychoanalytic studies are examined which suggest a particular place for the object in the development of the subject, underlining certain implications of the discussions of play in order to suggest affinities between language and consciousness as against the artefact and the unconscious.

There follows a more general discussion of the differences between words and things, and an examination of the close relationship between the object, its context and its place in social reproduction as represented by the arguments of the French social anthropologist Pierre Bourdieu. A number of the points raised suggest reasons for the comparative neglect of artefactual studies in academia, providing the background to chapter 7 in which, following a general survey of material culture studies, a somewhat elliptical approach is taken to the artefact in its context. The importance of considering the artefact as such is argued mainly, not in the abstract, but through examination of a number of more familiar fields of enquiry such as function, exchange, space and style. Case studies are shown to offer illustrations of the specific consequences of the physicality of material culture for investigations which would otherwise have tended to ignore this particular aspect of their own evidence.

The view of the object as embedded in specific cultural contexts is fundamental to the third section, which is concerned with mass consumption as the major constitutive arena in which the relationship of people to artefacts is determined in contemporary industrial societies. It is argued that consumption has suffered a neglect in our assessment of history (for example that of Britain over the last three centuries) comparable in some ways to the neglect of the artefact itself, and not unrelated in cause. Disciplines such as marketing which are concerned with present-day consumption are found to provide for very specific interests mainly devoted to the point of sale; by contrast, there has recently developed in social anthropology a degree of concern with consumption as a larger and less transient social process, a dominant influence within which has been a form of analysis in which differences in artefacts become grounded in social distinctions. Particular consideration is given to the book *Distinction* (Bourdieu 1984).

Chapter 9 continues the trend towards particularity of analysis by summarizing a series of studies of the objects of modern consumption ranging from children's sweets to semi-detached houses. Such micro-studies are contrasted to a trend in modern social theory arising in particular from post-structuralism and from the critique of post-modernism, both of which tend towards a global critique of 'modern' society, usually under a general term such as 'capitalism' or the 'sign'. It is argued that these global approaches almost always move from an attack on contemporary material culture as trivial or inauthentic to an implied (though rarely explicit) denigration of the mass of the population whose culture this is. By contrast, the analysis of particular domains of consumption provided in this chapter allows for a more sensitive discrimination between those elements of consumption which appear to generate close social relations and social groupings (such as those among children or neighbourhoods) and those which, by analogy with the critique of ideology, appear to act to prevent sections of the population from representing their interests, and to suppress any expression of those perspectives which might help to develop such interests.

It will be clear that the overall argument progresses through highly diverse material and foci. The justification for such an eclectic approach is provided in chapter ten, in which the original theoretical and philosophical model is reanalysed in terms of the artefact as the object of mass consumption. It is argued that contemporary society consists of a series of extremely abstract arenas of social and material order, including commerce, academia, the state and other major institutions. These have arisen in part as the means of producing vast quantities of artefacts, which are in turn distributed through mechanisms such as the market or government services. The scale of contemporary productive and distributive institutions is such that they are commonly the target of that general analysis of modernity which defines the growth of social complexity in terms of 'fragmentation', 'abstraction' or 'inauthenticity', all of which are posed as major dilemmas and threats to modern life. Here, however, it is asserted that such institutions are essential to a number of developments which are the foundation for all progressive tendencies in modern society, and that although they are never assimilable in themselves they must be preserved. Propositions for a future society involving the elimination or fading away of massive and abstracted institutions such as industrial production or the state are rejected. Since, however, these remain by definition abstract, and since they all include tendencies towards an autonomy in which as separate interests (for example, as capitalism or state power) they may emerge as forces almost entirely deleterious to the interests of the mass population, the argument highlights a central contradiction intrinsic to modern society: namely, how to retain the advantages offered by the existence of such institutions while avoiding their potential dangers.

It is suggested that this contradiction may be partially resolved through the use of these very products, that is the vast quantity of goods and services created by industrial culture. There may be mechanisms which permit the positive appropriation of these goods by, and at the level of, the inevitably pluralistic, small-scale communities which make up the population. This appropriation takes place through an expanded process of consumption by means of which goods and services are distanced from the abstracted and alien, but necessary, institutions in which they originate, and are recast as inalienable cultural material. It is argued that this process of consumption is equivalent to the Hegelian concept of sublation as the movement by which society reappropriates its own external form – that is, assimilates its own culture and uses it to develop itself as a social subject. So, far from being merely an extension of those social conditions and relations generated by the organization of production, consumption is, at least potentially, their negation. I also show to be unfounded the assumption that an increasing orientation towards goods is itself inevitably inimical to the development of communal and egalitarian social relations of a positive nature. Such a perspective must complement the proper concerns with macro-political forces if large-scale political changes are to be understood in relation to their effect on social practices, and not just as academic abstractions. It is not argued that this is a description of all contemporary consumption practices, many of which are very far from expressing any such goals, but rather that these are immanent in the nature of mass consumption, and that, depending upon the outcome of particular social strategies, they may be identified and learnt from even within existing society.

This depends, however, upon a view of consumption quite different from that which is current and colloquial. Consumption is considered here as a process having the potential to produce an inalienable culture. This assumes a recognition that our culture is increasingly a material culture which must in some way be made an instrument of social progression. It is further argued that, while consumption is generally considered to be of greatest consequence and at the same time most oppressive under the conditions of capitalism, it is also the single major means of living with the societal contradictions which would pertain under the conditions of either existing or possible socialism (given that this is taken to be a social order associated with the equitable distribution of goods and services and dominated by a socially concerned planning system, as opposed to the relatively unconstrained operation of the market). Under such conditions of socialism, the role of consumption as outlined above would become even more crucial to possibilities for positive social reproduction.

This argument contains within itself certain limits as a theoretical analysis. Theory itself is identified with those series of abstractions associated with the modern institution, while consumption by contrast is identified with a series of practices which are by their very nature embedded and particularistic. The conclusion therefore points towards an anthropology of consumption. Even under contemporary political and economic conditions, the ideal of consumption outlined here may be found to be practised by at least certain sections of the population in particular contexts, although this ideal coexists with a form of consumption expressive only of individual greed, class oppression and mass alienation. An anthropology would therefore seek to identify those conditions which appear to promote, as opposed to those which appear to prevent, the development of the positive forms of consumption as a process. Yet although research may be instrumental in identifying and encouraging these conditions, they must always in the final instance depend upon the development of mass movements.

In conclusion, an approach to modern society which focuses on the material object always invites the risk of appearing fetishistic, that is of ignoring or masking actual social relations through its concern with the object *per se*. In this book, an attempt is made to develop a non-dualistic model of the relations between people and things. This is achieved by approaching objectification as a process of development in which neither society nor cultural form is privileged as prior, but rather seen as mutually constitutive. When cast in terms of the contemporary political economy, such an approach sheds new light on the place of the artefact within the process of mass consumption as an essential element in the construction of both present and possible societies. By uncovering a model for consumption as a progressive possibility, a critical understanding of society may be achieved, founded upon an image based less upon what industrial culture has forced us to become than upon what it might allow us to be.

2

Hegel and Objectification

Hegel's *Phenomenology of Spirit*

The sources for the ideas used in this volume to construct a theory of material culture are various. Several of them are, however, united in that although they appear to relate to quite discrete bodies of material and to provide different theoretical emphases and conclusions, they derive at least in part from a common inspiration. This is the *Phenomenology of Spirit* (or 'Mind' in some translations) by G. W. Hegel, first published in 1807 (here 1977). This is perhaps the single most influential work in modern philosophy and social theory, and a large number of major studies including works by the early Marx, Simmel, Lukács and Sartre, have been modelled more or less directly upon it. Some of these texts will be discussed below. Many of Hegel's ideas have been further elaborated in the phenomenological tradition within philosophy, while a larger number of studies may have taken over the basic structure of Hegel's work without perhaps realizing this, or without being acquainted with their source, so pervasive have Hegel's ideas become.

Defining Hegel as a starting point is in one sense false. Hegel was not himself the orginator of many of the ideas commonly ascribed to him. Many were developed in their modern form by earlier and contemporary philosophers such as Fichte. The work of many of these philosophers in turn may be more easily understood when analysed in the light of ideas which had previously been developed in theological seminaries. In fact, Hegel's work forms part of an important movement which effectively secularized theological arguments concerning the relationship between God and humankind. Religious ideals and methods are strongly present in Hegel and, through him, in many of those who were deeply influenced by the *Phenomenology* (Kolakowski 1978: 11–39).

The intention of the present discussion is to abstract relatively few elements from the *Phenomenology*, rather than to follow previous attempts to translate the whole structure into some other context. As a result, the majority of Hegel's ideas and the form in which they were expressed will be either ignored or abandoned. The argument will be that one particular concept – to be denoted by the term 'objectification' – represents one of Hegel's most significant achievements in terms of its contemporary relevance. To use this concept for some alternative purpose, however, it must first be abstracted from the philosophical project for which it was created. The method will be to introduce objectification in its original Hegelian context as part of a very brief account of the contents of the *Phenomenology*, and then to examine how, through a process of abstraction, it may be used as the foundation for a theory of culture, and more specifically for a theory of modernity. It will be argued that the popularity and use made of Hegel's work lies in a kind of resonance, a feeling that he had captured the essence of something he may never himself have fully acknowledged, and which is only partially addressed in the manifest content of the *Phenomenology*, about the nature of the world around him.

It is difficult to establish the position of certain of Hegel's ideas within the general context of this work, since that context may be defined in a variety of ways, focusing either upon the philosophical trajectory which led up to it or upon the social conditions which prevailed at the time. Hegel's immediate point of departure was the vast philosophical tradition he inherited, and his work was intended to address directly the questions which had for so long permeated philosophical discussion. These questions centred upon the so called 'subject–object' dualism which had been a pivotal problem in western philosophy since the period of Classical Greece. The particular forms of this dualism addressed by Hegel were those posed by the traditions of Kant and Descartes, traditions which asserted reason against the world, providing two radically different ways in which the world may be apprehended. A similarly immediate concern was the particular use Fichte had made of the Romantic tradition, through which he posited an idealized history of human self-realization as a judgement upon the actual history of mankind.

This dualism was by no means the only philosophical conundrum addressed in the *Phenomenology*. There was also, amidst more general discussions of epistemology, the question of how we can know anything outside ourselves. Hegel was concerned to affirm his idea of an objective science against both the extreme subjectivism and metaphysics of some of the Romantics and the extreme distancing of man from nature, evident in the empiricist tradition which developed from the Enlightenment. There was also an underlying theme, developed more fully in other works, relating to the nature of political and juridical order and, in particular, the place of the state. Study of the *Phenomenology* only partly reveals its relationship to these issues, which might become more apparent in the context of Hegel's other writings. However, since the present concern is not with the place of Hegel or the trajectory of his own philosophy, his contribution to these questions and the place of major works such as the *Logic* will be ignored.

The *Phenomenology* takes the form not of an argument, but of a story: it is a narrative – sequential, accretative and essentially linear. It has been called the 'autobiography of the spirit (or mind)'. One of the many problems of analysing this narrative lies in identifying the subject, because the very essence of this story concerns the transformations taking place in the subject itself as a result of its experiences, so that what at one point may be termed mind can elsewhere be identified with spirit, reason and religion. In short, the definition of the subject is inseparable form the stage of development it has reached.

Fortunately, the process itself is largely repetitive; the Hegelian subject at each stage is carried forward by a sequence of processes in which it first extends itself through creation, and then becomes aware of that created 'something' which appears as outside of itself. This continues until the consciousness of the external becomes a dissatisfaction with the state of separation from that which is properly part of the subject. This dissatisfaction, however, is the motor force which allows for the recognition and then the reincorporation of the external into the subject; now at one with that part of itself which it had externalized as its creation, and the subject is transformed by virtue of this incorporation into itself.

Two quotations illustrate how Hegel presents this process. In the first, where he is talking about the externalization of the world in culture, he notes:

the existence of this world, as also the actuality of self-consciousness, rests on the process in which the latter divests itself of its personality, thereby creating its world. This world it looks on as something alien, a world, therefore, of which it must now take possession. (1977: 297).

The second quotation is an attempt to summarize the process near its end:

Self-consciousness knows the nothingness of the object, on the one hand, because it externalizes its own self – for in this externalization it posits itself as an object, or the object as itself, in virtue of the indivisible unity of being-for-self. On the other hand, this positing at the same time contains the other moment, viz. that self-consciousness has equally superseded this externalization and objectivity too, and taken it back into itself so that it is in communion with itself in its otherness as such (ibid. 479).

The basis of this process is Hegel's conception of the rationality of the actual. Unlike Kant, for whom order arises out of the mechanisms by which we apprehend the world, Hegel posits a universal rationality, intrinsic to the objective world, which we can come to know. This is, however, a highly sophisticated form of knowledge which may be achieved only as the culmination of all history and philosophy. The sequence begins with an unreflective humanity at home in an immediate subject-object relation. From this state, it gradually achieves a distance from nature, moving towards an increasingly self-conscious and differentiated concretization of being. This separation is the prerequisite for the development of an explicit understanding of the ultimate order in the world, mainly through a progressive philosophy. It is this assertion of a prior order towards which humanity strives which allows Hegel to claim that he is describing a necessary and logical movement.

In the very first instance of this process, the subject is hard to describe, since it is entirely unconscious and undifferentiated. In the first stage (1977: 58–103) the subject must struggle towards an awarenesss that it actually is; but this can only be achieved by its becoming aware that there is something it actually is not. Awareness of the self is predicted on awareness of the 'other', and it is the process of creation and acknowledgement of the other which is the key to the achievement of self-awareness. What is required is not merely the process of separation and incorporation but also a knowledge that this process is taking place, and, finally, an understanding of the nature of this process. In short, we start with an undifferentiated substance, which achieves a separation into subject and object. The subject thereby comes to know of itself as non-other, and thus acquires self-consciousness. It is crucial to observe that, from the beginning, development is predicated upon differentiation, as the originally abstract and generalized humanity becomes increasingly concretized into particular being.

This sequence is repeated at a number of levels. At each stage the subject posits an increasingly complex and particular other, becoming aware of this other as a distance from itself. It then realizes that this apparently alien other is in fact a product of itself, created as a mirror by means of which it might further its own self-awareness. This process of understanding permits the subject to reincorporate the increasingly complex external world it has created, and by so doing to emerge as an increasingly complex subject. Having progressed from 'other-awareness' to self-awareness, the subject comes to realize that it is not the only subject to perceive these relationships; it becomes aware of other subjects and thus of social relations and the foundations of morality. At first, the subject is more easily identified as a kind of 'mind' seeking awareness, and indeed Hegel's early examples are of individuals in relationship with each other, for example the famous master and slave relationship (Hegel 1977: 111–18; Arthur 1983). As the subject develops in sophistication, however, its awareness of social relations expands. As humanity comes increasingly to posit nature as its other, and to develop itself by incorporating the knowledge thereby gained, it gradually reaches a level of sophistication which may be identified with reason. Reason confers upon the Hegelian subject an increasing awareness of much wider transcendent and collective forces. This awareness emerges as a new sense of totalizing or universal phenomena, providing the subject with the basis for itself being recognized as a more ambitious and encompassing phenomenon, which Hegel terms 'spirit' (Hegel 1977: 263).

The concept of spirit (*Geist*) expresses Hegel's sense of the universal order which is to be indentified with God's will embodied in the world. As reason develops it is externalized through a series of ever more sophisticated forms which approach this same universality. Since these forms, which are identified, for example, with morality and law, express a relationship which would normally characterize that between the individual and the state or a wider collectivity, Hegel's exemplifications of his argument also take on this more collective form. Later still, the Hegelian subject gains an increasing awareness that even these collectivities rest upon something which transcends them, at first relating this to further levels of externalization such as art and religion. The significance of these last two forms is that they contain within themselves evidence for a still higher unity, but one which will only be achieved when they in turn are appropriated back into the subject.

Each of these phases continues the process first described. For example, there are periods in which the subject is extremely distant from its own externalization (see Taylor 1975: 77), such as the state of absolute reason, in which, with all the detachment of scientific observation, the world is confronted as a totally separate object. Particular forms of estrangement are exemplified as the distance between master and slave, or humanity and God. A period of tyranny or bondage may lead to a sense of detachment which is purely the negative of the impact of the all-powerful ruler: the attitude of the stoic, who achieves inner calm through withdrawal, may be followed by the increasing doubt of the sceptic, which may in turn lead to the extreme sense of distance termed the state of the unhappy conscious-ness. Such extreme externalizations lead to important changes in the subject when the external is finally reappropriated and reconciled. For example, the state of the unhappy consciousness is necessary for the achievement of reason, and the state of extreme objectivity is necessary for the transformation from mind into spirit with its new ethical concerns. Thus, the greater the distance between the subject and its object, the more profound the consequences of the subject's final realization of the truth that the external object, whether in the form of nature, morality or religion is in fact the result of the subject's own projections onto history according to whatever level of intellectual understanding it has reached at that stage, and is therefore an integral part of itself. It is the understanding of this truth which allows the subject to incorporate that which had hitherto been external, since the realization that something is in fact one's own creation is an essential part of one's ability to reincorporate it. Overall, a simple generality which is merely abstract has become a set of complex concepts which subsumes the particularity and individua-lity of things.

This story might be considered infinite, but Hegel in fact draws it to a dramatic and very final conclusion when that transcendence which is developed in the forms of art and religion is itself appropriated, and the subject becomes unified with these images to develop the final state of absolute knowledge. This concept can be understood only when the story is related to its grounding in history and philosophy.

Although at first identified with generic individuals the sequence by which the Hegelian subject transforms itself in the creation of the world is quickly subsumed under the development of society, since individuality can only arise in explicit opposition to the generic mind of the other. For similar reasons, history as the overall development of humanity is plotted as a dialectic in which humanity externalizes itself in a series of increasingly sophisticated and differentiated institutions which are still, however, only partial embodiments of *Geist*. This suggests less that Hegel intended the *Phenomenology* to be read as a history of the world than that history provides the main exemplifi-cation for the trajectory of this subject. Thus, particular periods of history are used to represent specific stages in the sequence he describes. The Englightenment is developed as an example of the extreme distancing of reason from the world; while the Greek *polis* is cited earlier on as a case of extreme, if relatively unconscious, identification – one in which the realization of the individual was to be identified with the realization of the state, a principle which is most familiar from Socrates' reaction to his own forthcoming execution (Plato 1984; Taylor 1979: 90). In a sense, then, human history can be understood not only as the basic metaphor for, but also as evidence for the actuality of, the sequence being described. The French Revolution, understood as an historically pre-emptive attempt at immediate absolute liberty, which then brought about the terror, followed by Napoleon's reimposition of a strong state, was a key historical source of Hegel's ideas (Hyppolite 1969: 35–69). Many of Hegel's examples of possible states and governments are also taken from developments taking place in Prussia at that time.

Another equally important factor which always mediates in the incorporation of history, is that of philosophy. The *Phenomenology* may therefore also be associated with the history of that discipline. The Hegelian subject must be provided with a mechanism which will allow the externality of history to be appropriated into its own development towards universal rationality. An integral part of that movement is the subject's ability increasingly to comprehend the process in which it is engaged. The means by which the subject attains self-understanding is identified with the practice of philosophy; at different stages, forms of philosophy such as scepticism and stoicism may exemplify a 'distancing' which is necessary prior to some advancement in understanding (Hegel 1977: 199–26). At each stage, the understanding the subject needs in order to appropriate increasingly complex externalized forms must itself be increasingly sophisticated. Thus, the history of philosophy is one in which an ever more profound grasp is achieved not only of the relationship between subject and object, but also of the nature of the subject and the extent to which the subject itself is actually constituted by these relationships and these processes.

This leads back to the concept of absolute knowledge, a culmination of the whole trajectory which derives not from any new externalization, any new content as it were, but from a new stage of awareness, a final move that permits a total realization and understanding of the process. Once the Hegelian subject understands not only the manner in which it externalizes itself and reappropriates this externalization, but also the trajectory of its own increasing understanding of this process, it comes to the final realization that it is itself the product of this process, an understanding it can achieve only by going through every stage of this developing awareness culminating in a profound comprehension of the rational nature of the world.

This final stage, which is a kind of meta-philosophy comprehending the very existence and purpose of philosophy as an equally constitutive part of the process of the subjects self-realization, is signified, of course, in the very act of writing the *Phenomenology*, in which for the first time the entire process is described, delineated and presented for further comprehension. This act of writing, then, represents the final bringing together of all experience, (that is, all history up to that point) and simultaneously all understanding (that is, all philosophy up to that point) in the now totally developed Hegelian subject. Hegel understood the sequence of the *Phenomenology* itself to have solved various philosophical conundrums.

At this stage, any latent differentiation between the subject and its object is eliminated; while, by the example of this elaborate sequence of processes, Hegel has demonstrated the enormous gulf between knowledge understood as an immediate relationship with the sensual, and what he saw as the true nature of human appropriation of the world. In Hegel's view, real knowledge of the object is possible only when we come to understand that it is the result of our own activity, and when we become aware of the ultimate rationality of the world which provides for the possibility of objects of knowledge. Hegel thus believed that he had solved the fundamental problems of ontology and epistemology.

This concept of absolute knowledge must also be understood against a background of another kind, whereby philosophy is seen as a guide to social pathologies identified as peculiar to the modern age. From his earliest writings onwards, Hegel had been working on the problem of how society, which appeared so fragmented, might achieve the kind of coherent totality which had been the goal of the whole Romantic tradition in philosophy and the arts. Through absolute knowledge, Hegel hoped that he had uncovered a means by which humanity might come to feel at home in a world whose order it could both understand and become identified with.

For present purposes, the most important aspect of the *Phenonemology* is the nature of the trajectory itself, which possesses several significant attributes. A first characteristic is that the process works from a universal which is first externalized into the particular and then reincorporated, eschewing all immediate relationships between subject and object. Hegel therefore rejects 'natural' humanity and knowledge as static, and insists that humanity only achieves self-realization through the long and painful trajectory he describes. As Hyppolite noted, 'To cultivate oneself is not to develop harmoniously, as in organic growth, but to oppose oneself and rediscover oneself through a rending and a separation' (1974: 385).

This brings us to another major feature of the trajectory, which is its intrinsically dynamic quality. The externalized object is always treated by Hegel as being one stage beyond the subject, and the subject is always dissatisfied with the stage it has reached. In a sense, the subject is defined in such a way that it is never complete, prior to the stage of absolute knowledge, and it is this feeling of unfulfilment which provides the motive force for further development. This dynamism is important not only because it dispenses with any need to find an external causation for its own trajectory, but also because of what it implies about the relationship between subject, object and process. In the Hegelian system these are inseparable; the subject, the object and their variable relationship are products of the process itself. There is never a prior subject, because the subject is always constituted by the process of absorbing its own object. Similarly, the object, if understood as human cultural development, must reflect the capacity of humanity at any given stage of history. Hegel has thereby resolved the central problem of subject–object relations not merely in the utopian state of absolute knowledge, but in the much more important refusal to allow for the existence of either subject or object except in a mutually constitutive relationship which itself exists only as part of the process of its own realization. In effect, the structure of the work is itself responsible for one of its crucial attainments, that of a genuine non-reductionism.

Objectification

It is from this trajectory and its structure that the concept of objectification will be abstracted. There is a severe problem here, in that the German term now translated as objectification (*Vergegen-standlichung*) is not used in any of the 765 pages of the *Phenomenology* (Arthur 1982: 19). The term Hegel uses (*Entäußerung*) today tends to be translated as alienation. According to Arthur, this confusion arises because the connotations of the term alienation have sedimented further since the time of Marx, making it impossible to understand the term in the way Hegel orginally intended. Indeed, the English word alienation would today, outside of academic philoso-phy, have negative connotations quite contrary to the positive meaning of self-alienation, as an essential moment of estrangement necessary for historical development, intended by Hegel. This was a problem for Marx, who clearly felt that the word objectification would have been a more appropriate term for Hegel to have used (see next chapter and Arthur 1982).

In this volume, the term objectification will be used to describe a dual process by means of which a subject externalizes itself in a creative act of differentation, and in turn reappropriates this externalization through an act which Hegel terms sublation (*aufhebung*). This act eliminates the separation of the subject from its creation but does not eliminate this creation itself; instead, the creation is used to enrich and develop the subject, which then transcends its earlier state. The use of this term is therefore an attempt to retain the original positive connotations of Hegel's view of moments of self-alienation and sublation as a progressive process. The particular aspect of this process emphasized by the term objectification lies in the act of externalization which may be considered as synonymous with the creation of particular form. It should be noted that this is not quite the same as 'the giving of form to something', since that something could not exist prior to its own form. Equally there is no (cultural) subject prior to the process of objectification through which it is created although the activity must take place in history and through the material and intellectual media given by that historical period. Form may be related to any medium of human externalization, either internal such as dreaming and sensation, or external such as words, institutions, objects and actions. As such, the term also incorporates Hegel's understanding of externalization as creating a movement through particularization towards further generalization.

The main reason for considering the *Phenomenology* in some detail is that it provides a foundation for a non-reductionist and dynamic subject-object relation. In this book, the process of objectification will be used to consider the relationship between on the one hand a subject which is human (and usually collective), and on the other, first, culture as all external form, and later, the artefact as the humanly produced material object. This is obviously a drastic narrowing of Hegel's own perspective. He addresses the specific question of external material form in terms of two areas: the object of art and the concept of property. With respect to the first of these, he claims:

> The universal need for art, that is to say, is man's rational need to lift the inner and outer world into his spiritual consciousness as an object in which he recognizes again his own self. The need for this spiritual freedom he satisfies, on the one hand, within by making what is within him explicit to himself, but correspondingly by giving outward reality to this his explicit self, and thus in the duplication of himself by bringing what is

in him into sight as knowledge for himself and others (Hegel 1975: 31–2).

The problem of the second area, that of property, is addressed most fully in a later work, the *Philosophy of Right*, where it is deeply embedded in larger issues relating to the legitimacy of particular kinds of government (Hegel 1952: 40–57; see also Marx 1975: 166–80). Property is presented as a key element in the anchoring of will in the world. Although analysed within the general framework of the legitimacy of law, Hegel's expressivist conception asserts a relationship to property through work rather than contract (Ryan 1984: 120–34). Underlying this, however, are statements about the general relationship between people and things and the necessary embodiment of will in objects, as is evident in the following quotations:

> A person must translate his freedom into an external sphere in order to exist as Idea . . . What is immediately different from free mind is that which, both for mind and in itself, is the external pure and simple, a thing, something not free, not personal, without rights (1952: 40).

> One aspect of property is that it is an existent as an external thing, and in this respect property exists for other external things and is connected with their necessity and contingency. But it is also an existent as an embodiment of the will, and from this point of view the 'other' for which it exists can only be the will of another person (ibid: 57).

There are parallels between the discussions of these otherwise disparate topics of art and property which make clear the implications of the overall scheme for this particular aspect of culture, indicating both the relevance of material form as a media for externalization and the dependence of this relationship upon its social and economic context. Hegel is not, however, concerned, as this present book will be primarily concerned, with the nature of the cultural artefact as by definition already engaged in a reciprocal relation with some particular humanity. Furthermore, apart from in the *Aesthetics*, Hegel does not give much prominence to the particular form which is the vehicle for the objectification process (Rosen 1982: chapter 5).

If the term objectification is used to describe this relationship within which the subject and object are created, it establishes first that this relationship is always a process, and secondly that the process is always progressive. Objectification is the very essence of the development of the subject, and without it there can be no progression; as Hegel says, 'The negative of the object, or its self-supersession, has a positive meaning for self-consciousness' (Hegel 1977: 479). This is because, for Hegel, all such stages are steps towards an understanding of the rationality of the actual. It follows that, within the process of objectification, the act of externalization and separation is also understood as a wholly positive moment, because without it we cannot have the reciprocal moment of sublation. It may be noted, however, that if objectification is truncated, so that we have an act of externalization without subsequent sublation, then that act of externalization would have to be seen as negative, a situation of rupture, representing a loss to the subject, rather than a gain.

This term objectification will be the central tenet of the theory of material culture to be developed here. The source of the concept is properly Hegel, since although similar ideas preceded him and were his source, and although aspects such as the nature of subjectivity have been elaborated since, there are elements of the *Phenomenology*, including its dynamism and its refusal of reductionism, which have perhaps never been developed as fully either previously or since. Hegel's ideas have their roots in theological discussions in which God was considered to be objectifying himself in Jesus or humanity, a process which is reversed in the secularization of theology found in Fichte and Hegel. Fichte, however, retained something of the philosophical tradition of dualism, since his objectification is an ideal used as a model for judging history, rather than as a means of characterizing the relationship between people and history itself. In Hegel, this dualism is eliminated through the experience represented by history and its comprehension in philosophy, which are themselves the actual evidence for, and forms taken by, the process of objectification.

Abstracting from Hegel

Having described the concept of objectification both in terms of the general scheme of the *Phenomenology* and in itself, the remainder of this chapter is an attempt to abstract the notion from this Hegelian context, since the further use of the term will not be intended to connote the philosophical premises held by Hegel. At the same time, however, certain characteristics of the process, namely its dynamic, positive and non-reductionist implications, are to be retained.

The potential for such a separation is evident from the writings of Marx, who clearly believed that, through the translation of some features and the rejection of others, he would be able to retain those

elements of Hegel's project which he saw as positive, but ground them
in a quite different set of terms oriented towards an alternative set of
goals. Marx, however, used many aspects of Hegel's ideas, such as the
logical nature of the dialectic, the force of historical necessity, and the
final Romantic goal of society as a coherent totality, which will not be
utilized here.

To take on board only one aspect of Hegel's work, that is
objectification, as a model attempt to resolve the subject–object
dualism, while ignoring other major elements such as the dialectic as a
form of logic and absolute knowledge is, in a sense, to reduce Hegel
from an idealist to a positivist. Nevertheless, there are clearly good
precedents for such an extraction. In addition to Marx, a variety of
later writers have been influenced by, and have in turn privileged,
particular aspects of Hegel's work. For example, French writers such
as Merleau-Ponty and Sartre were inspired by the section on the
master-slave relationship (curiously ignored by Marx, see Arthur
1983; Schmidt 1985: 63–72) to refine both the concept of the 'other'
and the content of subjectivity. Some philosophers have concentrated
on the logic and system of the *Phenomenology* (e.g. Inwood 1983:
259–348); others have stressed its contemporary relevance (e.g. Plant
1973; Taylor 1979). Many other aspects of the work, ranging from the
discussions of phrenology (Hegel 1977: 185–210) to its primitivism
(Inwood 1983: 43), now appear dated.

An alternative grounding for this abstracted concept of objectification lies firstly in the relationship between human subjects and
material objects, and secondly in the specific instance of objects in the
modern world of mass consumption. In relation to material objects,
with which, as has already been shown, Hegel was only tangentially
concerned, there are several ways in which these ideas might be
utilized. It is generally agreed that for Hegel the form of progressive
knowledge necessary for the process of objectification is not some
private introspection, but a public social activity or intersubjective
pursuit such as philosophy (Plant 1973: 88). Scruton (1979: 244–50),
attempting to apply this observation to a particular form of
self-consciousness, derived from its externalization into object form
through creative work. Many other writers, such as Schutz and Mead,
also use this tradition of thought to examine the nature of such
consciousness – that is, of subjectivity and intersubjectivity – and to a
lesser degree the implications of the physicality of objects (e.g.
McCarthy 1984). Here, however, it will not be assumed that
externality necessarily implies individual consciousness or self-
consciousness (see chapter 6), in the sense of a language-based,
potentially explicit and reflexive process of thought. Even, however, if

it never impinges upon consciousness, the creation of cultural form always acts as a transformation in the environment through which society as subject becomes itself, and must always be understood as a socially reflexive praxis.

It is clear that the concept of objectification as derived from Hegel implies that there is no prior subject or object, but rather a process of mutual construction which always takes place in history. This can be expressed within the larger framework of the *Phenomenology*:

> The idea goes out into nature and at first is lost there. That is, it has not yet an adequate expression, and hence there is a division and separation within this world, and between the world and Spirit which cannot recognize itself. The development of an adequate embodiment, and hence the return of Spirit to itself is the work of history (Taylor 1979: 143).

The *Phenomenology*, however, adds more than simply this degree of historical relativism to an intended analysis. One of the properties which distinguishes Hegel from the Romantics is his emphasis upon a sequence of increasing differentiation and sophistication. For the Romantics, whether they looked to art, or to a mythical past or future, the drive was towards a sense of holism, of homogeneity, simplicity and source. That is, they were seeking something to counter that sense of differentiation, complexity and fragmentation which was the historical basis for their unease. By contrast, Hegel, although influenced by the contemporary Romantics and evoking a sense of totality which is quite magnificent, never does so at the expense of variety. Kolakowski notes that 'his purpose was to interpret the universe as entirely meaningful without sacrificing its diversity' (1978: 57). The process of objectification, as initially always a process of externalization, is then always also a process of differentiation, and at each phase this differentiation becomes more complex, since the process is accretative, developing on the basis of what precedes it. It is almost the first fully developed epigenetic structure; that is, each stage depends upon and retains elements of, but always supersedes, those which have led up to it, so that there is an overall process of growing complexity.

In modern parlance, such a characterization would render Hegel, if not a modernist, then someone who has captured the most peculiar and most important single element of modern culture, the ever increasing drive towards structural differentiation. Although Hegel himself is much more concerned with the struggle towards a more rational and explicit relationship with nature than with the rise of complexity *per se*, he directly confronts many classic features of modern society, such as the growth of individual subjectivity tied to an increasingly objective stance taken to the external world. From his earliest writings onwards (Plant 1973: 76–123), he sought to reconcile the progressive tendencies evident in the new fulfilment of human potential rendered possible by contemporary developments with the fact that these same changes appeared to lead to a greater fragmentation of both society and the individual. A number of these themes as they are taken up by Simmel are discussed in chapter 5 in such a way as to connect Hegel's main interests to a specific concern with the increasingly material and concrete form taken by cultural expression ever since the time of Hegel. They provide the basis for the application in chapter 10 of the concept of objectification to the problem of mass consumption.

Primarily then, objectification is intended as the foundation for a theory of culture. Indeed, if culture is defined as the externalization of society in history, through which it is enabled to embody and thus reproduce itself, objectification and culture may be defined with respect to one another. The use of the term objectification then asserts the necessity for a particular kind of relationship between human development and external form. This relationship is never static, but always a process of becoming which cannot be reduced to either of its two component parts: subject and object. The action of externalization and sublation is always constitutive, never merely reflective, and is therefore not a process of signification.

This means that a theory of culture can have no independent subject, as neither individuals nor societies can be considered as its originators, since both are inseparable from culture itself and are as much constituted by culture as constituting it. This process is inherently dynamic; the relation between subject and object is never static. Objectification is therefore an assertion of the non-reductionist nature of culture as process. In so far as the subject is society (usually in a collective sense), the term objectification asserts the necessarily positive nature of this process, which must in turn imply some stance concerning the progressive potential of social being, and the possibilities of this being realized in the concrete determinacy of being. Finally, the term objectification may be used to assert that the process of culture, which must always include self-alienation as a stage in its accomplishment, is thereby inherently contradictory. Since this contradiction is embodied in the particular vehicle or form taken by culture, and since modern culture has become increasingly a material culture, this materiality may play an ever more important part in the constitution of this contradiction.

3

Marx: Objectification as Rupture

Marx's Economic and Philosophical Manuscripts

The development of Marx's thought and the manner in which it grew out of his critique of Hegel became much clearer to scholars when an early study, written at the age of twenty-six and variously called the '1844', 'Paris' or 'Economic and Philosophical' manuscripts, was published in 1932. Most of this chapter will be concerned with exploring how the concept of objectification has been affected by the particular way in which Marx translated the *Phenomenology* into his own terms, as revealed in these manuscripts. It will be suggested, however, that this is of concern not because of the central importance of the manuscripts themselves, but because, with respect to the notion of objectification, the transformation revealed there provides the basis for a set of ideas which continue in an equally strong vein, if not so explicitly, throughout Marx's work and in many of the writings of later Marxists. Since the term objectification is today used mainly within Marxist discussion, and since it is almost always used with respect to Marx's rather than Hegel's position, this transformation, its advantages and its problems must be considered in any contemporary attempt to utilize the concept of objectification.

The chapter will begin with a summary of the argument set out in the manuscripts and a discussion of the relationship between Marx's terms and those used by Hegel. A brief account will be given of the degree of continuity between these early ideas and those found in *Capital*. This will be followed by a critical account of two aspects of Marx's work: first the transformation which took place in the concept of objectification itself, and secondly the problematic relationship between production and consumption apparent in his writings.

The final section of the manuscripts (Marx 1975: 379–400) consists of an explicit critique of Hegel's work, but even in the absence of this, it would be clear from the manner in which Marx develops his terms that Hegel is the direct source for the structure within which his ideas are first expressed, and that concepts such as communism, the proletariat and Marx's particular view of labour emerge as much from his translation of Hegel as from an abstraction from the social world around him.

In a sense, many of Marx's concepts and ideas are generated from one simple act of transformation. For Hegel, the subject develops through a process of objectification in which the external is first created through an act of positing, then reincorporated in an act of sublation. For Marx also, the subject creates an external world, in the mirror of which the human species is realized; but for him this is an act of physical creation by flesh-and-blood people utilizing the material world of nature, and not merely what he derides as mere intellectual positing in Hegel. Marx's transformation of Hegel's concept arose from his conviction, derived in particular from the work of Feuerbach, that Hegel's analysis was an abstracted metaphysic which could not address directly those real issues of society and history to which Marx was committed. For Marx, theory should not relate to the world merely at the level of abstract philosophy, but should be engaged in its transformation. As a result of this view, he developed the concept of praxis, which sought to locate resolutions of philosophical problems in the material world of social relations. Thus, philosophical conundrums concerning the nature of ontology could be solved, but only through the physical transformation of the social world. For this reason, Marx was to abandon the kind of abstracted discussion found in the manuscripts, and thereafter to consider these issues in a more concrete and embedded form.

The translation of the act of positing by the subject into an act of physical transformation is quite explicit in the manuscripts, and Marx's arguments may therefore be presented through direct quotation. The inconsistent use made of the term objectification in these quotations should be noted; this will be discussed in a later section. The order of the manuscripts reflects the major sources of Marx's ideas. The first section is a critique of the logic of the political economy, and the problems of wages, prices, labour and capital – a critique which was to achieve a much greater level of sophistication and detail in later writings. In the next section, concerning estranged labour, Marx explores those ideas which he will use to break open the traditional debates on the political economy. Here we find Marx's first translation of Hegel into his own terms. The third section provides a more direct confrontation with Hegel, and analysis of Hegel's terminology as used in the *Phenomenology*.

Marx begins with the relationship between humanity and the external world of nature, without which nothing can be created. The working of nature is therefore an appropriation of that world through labour. His argument is that

> It is therefore in his fashioning of the objective that man really proves himself to be a *species-being*. Such production is his active species-life. Through it nature appears as *his* work and his reality. The object of labour is therefore the *objectification of the species-life of man:* for man reproduces himself not only intellectually, in his consciousness, but actively and actually, and he can therefore contemplate himself in a world he has created (Marx 1975: 329).

Like Hegel, Marx believes that the creation of this objective external world is necessary for the species to come to understand itself as human, but Marx stresses the physical aspects of this creative process. As he states succinctly, 'The practical creation of an *objective* world, the *fashioning* of inorganic nature, is proof that man is a conscious species-being' (ibid: 328–9).

It is clear from these quotations that culture has a central place in Marx's ontology, but that it is culture seen from the perspective of the act of production. The second major transformation of Hegel is Marx's argument that the process of objectification as outlined by Hegel cannot take place in present circumstances, because production does not occur freely, but under conditions of estrangement. This possibly is clear in Hegel, who argued that at certain periods the subject does not recognize the 'other' as the result of its own creation, and feels distant from it. Marx makes a direct translation: 'Just like Hegel's spirit in the period of unhappy consciousness, generic man does not recognise himself in his own objectification' (Taylor 1979: 144).

Under conditions of estrangement, people cannot develop through objectification, because the process itself is ruptured. The external is created under conditions which ensure that the producer is unable to utilize culture as an instrument for self-realization:

> The object that labour produces, its product, stands opposed to to it as *something alien*, as a *power independent* of the producer. The product of labour is labour embodied and made material in an object, it is an objectifiction of labour (Marx 1975: 324)

There are three main constituents of this condition of estrangement. The first is this separation of the producer from the products of labour, most evident in the factory-and-market distribution system. The second is estrangement at the location of the work process, which should be the site of self-creation, but is often a place of intolerable conditions with which the producer is unable to have any positive association. The third are the legal and political forces which rest upon the notions of private property, through which nature itself, the proper object of productive investment, becomes rather an alienated and foreign domain for the worker. In this sequence, the condition of alienated labour is the prior force from which structures such as private property arise (Arthur 1980).

By applying to this argument the logic of the *Phenomenology*, the roots of many of the familiar terms of Marx's writings may be uncovered. Although Hegel's concepts are translated into a new field, many of the relationships between the terms are retained (Freenberg 1981: 48). Capitalism is here portrayed not simply as an example of estrangement, but as the most pronounced cleavage between people and their work ever encountered in the history of the species. Following Hegel, Marx presents such extreme separation as an index of the extreme nature of the resolution which must follow. This suggests that we are on the threshold of Hegel's concept of the final resolution embodied in absolute knowledge, an idea enshrined in the concept of communism. Thus in Marx's words,

> *Communism* is the *positive* suppression of *private property as human self-estrangement*, and hence the true *appropriation* of the *human* essence through and for man; it is the complete restoration of man to himself as a *social*, i.e. human being (Marx 1975: 348).

As with absolute knowledge, communism must know what it is in order to achieve self-realization: 'The entire movement of history is therefore both the *actual* act of creation of communism – the birth of its empirical existence – and, for its thinking consciousness, the *comprehended* and *known* movement of its *becoming*' (Marx 1975: 348). It must also resolve all those dualisms which absolute knowledge addressed:

> It is the *genuine* resolution of the conflict between man and nature, and between man and man, the true resolution of the conflict between existence and being, between objectification and self-affirmation, between freedom and necessity, between individual and species. It is the solution of the riddle of history and knows itself to be that solution (Marx 1975: 348).

It is clear from these quotations just how much of Hegel's conception of the process of development underlies the origins of Marx's ideas.

Although more developed in Marx's later writings, the notion of class has already begun to emerge as the social force whose tensions have always been responsible for the dynamic movement. Hegel's process of externalization, and the dialectic of his *Logic*, become in turn the dialectic embodied in emerging contradictions between social forces (created by their very relationship to each other as classes), and a series of historical, always partial, resolutions. These resolutions give rise, under new conditions of production, to ever greater contradictions which are, in turn, precursors of the contradiction of modern capitalism. Hegel's sequence is never seen in terms of a process of individual socialization or development, but rather as social history with generic humanity as its subject. The dynamic quality of Hegel's tensions between the subject and its other becomes dependent upon the struggle of different social groups at each phase of human existence to seize their own products for the purposes of their realization as a class. Hegel's idea that the subject exists only in terms of the stage it has reached in the process itself is translated into the belief that the possibilities immanent in the forces of production vary with each historical phase. Overall, Marx perceives the same basic totality, in which the meaning of each part of social life or each social group derives essentially from its position in this historic and historical progression.

Marx's debt to Hegel is more or less acknowledged in the effort spent upon explicit critique, both in the latter part of these manuscripts and in other early writings (e.g. Marx 1975: 57–198, 243–57). This implies that Marx perceived Hegel in ambivalent terms, crediting his brilliant ability to foresee the structure of history and ontology, but criticizing his inability to grasp the actual nature of his own subject. The point is discussed in more detail by Lukács, who argued in a somewhat unlikely vein that Hegel was only able to envisage the finality of the ultimate resolution because he lived in conditions of nascent capitalism, and had sufficient perspicacity to 'see' in mythic form the fall of capitalism even before it had properly arisen (Lukács: 1975). Marx's concern to differentiate himself from Hegel has at times been overemphasized, and it is worth noting that, for example, discussion of the nature and implications of labour as physical and not just intellectual production is central to a number of Hegel's social and political writings (Plant 1977: 103–5).

Before proceeding to the key question of the fate of Hegel's concept of objectification, it is important to examine briefly the significance of the manuscripts themselves. These are early works whose main interest today lies in their contribution to the much more developed later writings of Marx. Indeed, the influential writings of Althusser and his followers argued for a radical break between these 'humanist' beginnings and the true science of the later Marx. Much depends upon how particular 'lines of descent' are constructed for tracing the development of Marx's ideas. For example, the argument that estrangement should be understood as a radical separation of producer and product, involving the inability of the producer to comprehend the nature of that process to which they are subject may be held to be an element within the critique of ideology, resurfacing in *Capital* as the 'fetishism of commodities', in which again social groups are held to be unable to comprehend that commodities which they see as alien are actually of their own production (Althusser 1969: 230). This would, however, represent an extreme narrowing of the initial concerns. There are many alternative links, including, for example, those with the later writings on exploitation and property (Torrance: 1977).

It is also possible to argue that the central foundation of Marx's later work is none other than a grounding of these early concerns in particular issues. The concept of fetishism, and of the expropriation of surplus value in *Capital*, both ultimately derive from the labour theory of value which when used as the foundation for a critique of exchange value, provides the core of that work as a social theory (Rubin 1972). This theory also represents a convenient position from which to measure the degree of continuity between Marx's early and later writings. The central argument in the manuscripts is that the critical power of Hegel's work may be realized only in terms of an ontology based upon the physical creation, through labour, of culture as the constitutive mirror of humanity. That is to say, it is an argument whose central feature is the privileging of the act of production. This is precisely the aim of the labour theory of value as employed in *Capital*. Here, Hegel's self-constitutive activity has been incorporated within a model of the political economy for which labour is the sole source of value. Given the difference in the time of composition of the two works, the central idea is remarkably consistent. It is this assertion of the category 'value', held to be synonymous with the product of human labour, which, when embedded within the complex workings of the political economy, provides the foundation for virtually all the central arguments in *Capital*. Although *Capital* is far more developed in its economic analysis, the relationship between the basic terms used, the notions of class, communism and estrangement, are carried through from the manuscripts to the end of Marx's life.

Marx's Transformation of Objectification

Examination of the different uses made of the term objectification in the quotations from Marx's manuscripts given above reveals that, even at an early stage, there was a clear distinction between his understanding of the concept, and Hegel's idea of self-alienation.

The first example (Marx 1975: 329, p. 36 above) is the closest to Hegel's own conception, in that production is to be understood as the site for the objectification of the species-life of humanity, and for its self-creation as a social force. In the other examples, however, (ibid: 324, p. 36 above, and 348, p. 37 above) it appears that, by means of a process of recontextualization, the term comes to mean something quite different. In these quotations, Marx has separated off the moments of externalization from the promise of sublation, such that objectification tends to obstruct, rather than to promote, the subjects development. Here, objectification is held to be in conflict with self-affirmation: it is the process of the product's becoming alien to its maker. In these latter quotations, the term objectification becomes understood as the production of an object form, which by the very fact of its objectivity appears to lend itself to the process of estrangement; that is, to appear as strange. The objectification of labour here becomes the making of an object which is distanced from the subject's act of self-creation, and through which elements of the subject, by being in a sense petrified, come to appear in an object form that is opposed to humanity as a social formation. In its estrangement from its own product, the subject loses an element of its humanity and itself becomes more of an object. These ideas were to become more explicit in Marx's later writings on the nature of the commodity.

Hegel's brilliance lies in the way he turned concepts such as self-alienation, which might have appeared as negative and threatening processes, into assertions about the positive, though contradictory, nature of those forces necessary to social development. For Hegel, an objective existence of increasingly concrete, explicit, differentiated and particular form, which is nevertheless subsumable in more complex abstractions and totalities, is precisely what the subject gains through self-alienation. Marx retains something of this possibility, which is the source of his continued faith in the significance of the act of production itself as the site of self-realization. As production comes to stand for the process of externalization, however, the term objectification appears to lose the sense in which it is an embodiment of this very process, and its meaning becomes overshadowed by the prevailing sense of estrangement specific to the conditions of the time. Under these conditions, all the negative connotations of alienation and objectification come back with a vengeance. Objectification is turned to as a more literal, in some ways less profound, rendering, in which the implied connotation of giving concrete form to something, of creating an object, is seen as preventing rather than enabling the development of human social and material relations; it has now been transformed into a theory of rupture.

The essential difference between the two writers is that Hegel demands the unity of all processes of objectification, incorporating realization and alienation; he denies that they can be separated into positive and negative connotations. This also means that Hegel's notion of totalities is tempered by its constant tension with processes of fragmentation and abstraction. Marx, by contrast, has a mission to detail, as never before, the intensity of the negative forces enshrined in modern life. For him, therefore the possibilities of positive development have to be completely separated from the actuality of these negative conditions, and this means that he must return to the older dichotomy of a Romanticized positive and a highly empirical negative, and also to the idea of a pre-cultural 'authentic' social relation. Although this was done for the very good reason that immediate involvement was essential to Marx's thesis, the manner in which it was carried out creates severe problems. The difference, then, is that Hegel posits the necessity of contradiction to his understanding of ontology, while Marx increasingly renders objectification as alienation resulting from a particular and contemporary historical condition.

Was Marx correct in implying that Hegel should have separated off a notion of objectification from that of alienation, and that he failed sufficiently to recognize that this alienation was the dominant feature of a specific historical period which had begun during his lifetime? I do not wish to defend, in general, Hegel's idealist and philosophical system against Marx's brilliant social critique, but with respect to this particular issue there is some confusion. In asserting that alienation is a consequence of that objectification characteristic of capitalism, Marx inverts Hegel's idea that objectification as a process is only made possible through self-alienation. Giddens endorses this inversion, suggesting that 'Many secondary writers have failed to grasp this essential distinction between objectification and alienation' (1971: 11n).

A more sustained analysis is provided by Arthur (1982), who illustrates the complexity of the issues involved, a complexity increased by the absence of the term objectification in Hegel's *Phenomenology*. Arthur provides a detailed, balanced and illuminating account of the use of the relevant terms by both authors (see also Torrance: 1977). He shows that Marx was quite aware of the positive nature of Hegel's conception of objectification (which in some respects he adopted in the idea of the unrealized potentiality in both production and communism). Marx also makes quite reasonable criticisms of Hegel's idealism and abstraction, setting them against the urgent demands of praxis. He finds fault with Hegel's inability to perceive objectification except as linked to alienation, which Marx (unlike Hegel) sees as tantamount to estrangement. His central criticism, however, is that Hegel failed to acknowledge the true historical nature of alienation, which is to be identified with the particular nature of capitalism. At the end of this analysis, Arthur follows and confirms the logic of Marx's critique of Hegel, asserting that 'Hegel's tragedy is that, though objectification and alienation are conceptually distinct and are so distinguished brilliantly by Marx, Hegel cannot grasp this possibility, for it depends upon an historical potential beyond the limits of his bourgeois standpoint' (1982: 22). One of the implications of these comments is that Marx did indeed make a clear distinction between alienation and objectification. In his writings, however, as illustrated above, Marx often uses the term objectification to provide precisely the same feeling of estrangement as that implied by the term alienation; both become elements of his theory of rupture, and they are therefore not so much differentiated as equally transformed into expressions of the negative situation under capitalism.

In effect, Marx criticized Hegel on the grounds that he unduly conflated the concepts of obectification and alienation, and proposed a mystificatory rendition of historical processes. In opposition to this criticism, I wish to argue that Hegel's terms imply a deeper contradiction, one that is lost in the writings of Marx. Hegel's concept of objectification implies the necessity of certain processes which may be identified with the creation of culture in general. He describes externalization as the process of objective form arising both through fragmentation into the particular, and resolution through abstraction, both of which are essential to modernity. These processes are simultaneously positive and negative, and this very simultaneity is an intrinsic part of the process. This seems deliberate and clear in Hegel, a profound assertion of a 'tragic' but intrinsic feature of all human culture. That it represents a contradiction which is inescapable and must be lived will be further argued in chapter 5, through an examination of the writings of Simmel.

The problem with Marx's critique is summarized most clearly by Hyppolite:

> By objectifying himself in culture, the State and human labour in general, man at the same time alienates himself, becomes other than himself, and discovers in this objectification an insurmountable degeneration which he must nevertheless try to overcome. This is a tension *inseparable from existence*, and it is Hegel's

merit to have drawn attention to it and to have preserved it in the very centre of human self-consciousness. On the other hand, one of the great difficulties of Marxism is its claim to overcome this tension in the more or less near future and hastily to attribute it to a particular phase of history. It is surely an oversimplification to imagine that this tension can be reduced to a super-structure of the economic world. It is undeniable that the capitalist system represents a form of human alienation, but it can hardly be the only one (Hyppolite 1969: 87).

This point applies equally to the notion of objectification as cultural process. It allows us to retain the original Hegelian proposition that self-alienation is an inescapable part of a positive process, but one which has an intrinsically contradictory nature. One unfortunate result of Marx's transformation of objectification is that the positive 'other' tends increasingly to be absorbed into the abstraction of communism, which is asserted as the antithesis of capitalism. The concept of communism retains the most Romantic aspect of Hegel's belief in totalities, in the unmediated form of absolute knowledge, instead of being grounded in the immediate problems of living through modernity, a problem which has become even more significant with the development of socialism.

The term objectification is used and understood today mainly in the tradition of Western Marxism, a tradition which incorporates the work not only of Marx himself, but also of the various influential writers who have developed Marx's ideas since his death. In general, these writers have extended Marx's treatment of the term along the same trajectory so that objectification has become increasingly divorced from its original positive context, and is now understood as a negative expression of 'petrification' as the major instrument of estrangement. In relation to later Marxism, however, the term cannot be considered in isolation, since, depending upon the particular form of Marxist theory concerned, it has become firmly enmeshed in the use of three further terms: alienation, fetishism and reification. Each of these three terms has different connotations, and these in turn vary from writer to writer. The examples of their use given here represent only the briefest summary of their extremely complex and diverse semantic trajectories.

The notion of alienation is closest to the concept of estrangement, since estrangement represents the conditions under which alienation takes place. Alienation may then follow the model developed by the early Marx as the distance between the workers' potential relationship with their products and their actual circumstances. Since the time of

Marx, this term has developed its own complex literature within the wider tradition of Marxism (e.g. Dupré 1983: 15–57; Joachim 1979; Ollman 1971; Schmidt 1971); but it is also connected to a more general discussion, in which it has come increasingly to stand for a kind of 'modern human condition' characterized by a sense of loss of authentic or proper identity. As such, it provides links with general concepts of anomie, as used by Durkheim, and the writings of existentialists, especially the later work of Sartre (Chiodi 1976; Sartre 1976).

The concept of fetishism is the only one of these three terms which is still used today to refer back to Marx's original argument in *Capital*, although it may be bracketed as the final recasting of Marx's early writings about the separation of the workers from their products (though see Rubin 1972, for an argument as to its greater prominence). The idea is that such are the conditions of the modern world that the vast array of the products of labour cannot be understood as such by the worker, who confronts them in a different sphere, where they appear to be the result of other forces. This is in part a consequence of contemporary representations of the political economy, which portray commodities as a result of the abstract working of capital itself, and dispense with the social relations which created them. In a sense, fetishism allows for a critical analysis of the field of consumption, but one in which the entire sphere tends to be treated as merely a mode of 'false' representation, consequent upon other spheres.

The third term, reification, is the most problematic, since it is best identified with certain Marxists rather than Marx himself. It can, however, be related to Marx's understanding of Feuerbach's critique of religion. The central tenet of reification is that human beings create objects in order to understand themselves, but become separated from this positing and perceive the object as having an external reality and an origin separate from themselves. Such products thereby develop an autonomy, deflecting society's attention from critical self-awareness to this mysterious other. Feuerbach saw the notion of 'God' as an instance of such an inversion. In Marx's later critique, the language of economics in which 'capital' is given a life of its own may again serve as an example of reification.

This term has, however, become closely bound to the trajectory of thought which develops through the work of Lukács, whose influential essay 'Reification and the Consciousness of the Proletariat' (1971) is itself modelled on the argument of Hegel's *Phenomenology*. Lukács argued that the proletariat, as the most estranged social fraction, was thereby best positioned to become the instrument of the

ultimate resolution of societal contradiction in communism. Following Lukács, the term is further developed by several members of the
Frankfurt School, particularly Adorno (Rose 1978: 27–51). The
writers of this tradition effectively expanded their analysis into a more
general cultural critique, examining those forms of knowledge and
authority which pertain to things as rational, technical and positivis-
tic. Because of its relevance to contemporary anti-welfare politics, this
critique of technocratic control and efficiency continues to exert
considerable influence today, through the works, for example, of
Marcuse (1964) and Habermas (1970). From such writings has
developed the modern Marxist concept of objectification which views
as equally problematic the epistemological notion of objectivity and
the representational problem of object form.

These ideas will be referred back to, throughout the present work,
since they are still the major means of identifying the process of
rupture as they exist in modern society. The writings on ideology and
reification help us to understand how and why certain groups retain
control over the very means of objectification, while others are forced
to attempt to objectify themselves through forms which are produced
in the image of other people's interests. Through this argument, the
term objectification will be used in chapter 9 to refine the concept of
ideology as a form of contemporary social critique. In so far as the
degree of control over the media of objectification is an outcome of
conflicts generated by the social relations of production, the original
Marxist structure within which these ideas have been developed
continues to be relevant today.

One casualty of these trends, however, has been the original
Hegelian conception of objectification. The positive side of Hegel's
process is absorbed into the Romantic notion of communism, where
all is resolved and where objectification is possible. Meanwhile, all
social analysis takes place under conditions of such extreme rupture
that this is all that can be concentrated upon, and objectification and
rupture gradually come to be seen as identical. An interpretation of
the term objectification as meaning the creation of an object form is
compatible with many of the major and familiar elements of the
modern critique of capitalism. These include the idea that social
relations have been reduced to the appearance of object relations, with
the human subject becoming increasingly debased as merely the object
of extreme bureaucratic and institutionalized forces. This is closely
related to the positivist idea of an objectified epistemology which
eliminates any consideration of subjective elements from the criteria
of knowledge; and finally, through reification, to the idea that modern
concepts are themselves an array of false objects with false attributes

and false subjects which have to be, in modern parlance, 'deconstructed'.

Production and Consumption

A final element of this brief critique is most relevant to the third section of the present work, which will attempt to provide an approach to modern consumption. The specific point that Marx privileged the area of production and largely ignored the contribution of consumption has been most forcibly argued by the French social theorist Baudrillard in *The Mirror of Production* (1975) and further developed in *For a Critique of the Political Economy of the Sign* (1981).

Baudrillard takes as the major point of contention the central pillar of Marx's work, the emphasis on labour as the site of self-creation whether as an ontological definition of humanity in the early work or as the true source of value in the later work. Baudrillard places Marx in the context of other Victorian British thinkers faced with the trauma of the contemporary industrial revolution, arguing that, in effect, Marx was establishing one version of a theme common to conservatives, liberals and radicals alike, an ideological commitment beneath the level of overt political confrontation. This was the idea of work as the only true means of human self-creation, with the corollary that the factories of the day were producing every kind of product but were reducing their workers to the level of machines. Such ideas, which have only recently been conclusively challenged by theories resulting from the rise of feminist studies and the decline of manufacturing, were central to the beliefs of influential writers such as Ruskin. One of their consequences was the comparative devaluing of all forms of human action and social relation outside the workplace (with the exception of art).

It is this which allows Baudrillard to recast Marx as a conservative Victorian true to his time, and to suggest that Marx 'made a radical critique of political economy, but still in the form of political economy' (1975: 50). Baudrillard's technique is to examine the processes of signification employed by Marx, which remain unquestioned in his writings (for an argument that Baudrillard thereby misrepresents Marx in several respects see Preteceille and Terrail 1985: 29–34). In common with a number of recent theorists, Baudrillard argues that the process of signification may result in the emergence of an apparently unproblematic and natural signified which is actually no more than the product of this process. For Marx, then, the transformation of nature is the occasion of its objectification as a productive force under the sign of utility (the same is true simultaneously of human labour). Even before the stage of exchange value and the equivalence through time of abstract social labour, labour and production constitute an abstraction, a reduction, and an extraordinary rationalization in relation to the richness of symbolic exchange' (1975: 45).

The concept of production, then, is one which stresses the utilitarian value of work; that is to say, we create our identity through socially useful labour, which is the transformation of nature to fulfil our needs. This notion of utility expresses another central Victorian value, which Marx extends through an additional symbolic process represented by the term 'use value'; that is, an assertion of that value pertaining to goods by virtue of the genuine human needs to which they relate. The products of labour are assumed to be aimed at the fulfilment of fundamental, often biological, needs, which lie at the basis of the materiality of humanity. In this respect, Marx proposes an essentialist notion of humanity in opposition to which Baudrillard, using the results of social anthropology, asserts the cultural and historical source of perceived needs (see also Sahlins 1976a: 126–65, 205–21; Steadman 1979).

Baudrillard models his critique of use value on Marx's own analysis of exchange value (1981: 130–42). Just as the latter had become a 'given' of economic theory which mystified its actual basis in social relations, so also use value is mystified by this assumption of basic biological needs. Baudrillard claims that Marx developed his own 'Robinson Crusoe myth' of the type he challenged in other economists, seeing utility as a place of direct, isolated relations between person and nature. For Marx, there is no social relation which corresponds to use value. Just as Marx reduces exchange from fetished form to a signifier of social relations, he fails to recognize that utility has precisely the same mystificatory quality. Marx thereby, in effect, reproduces and extends the fetishistic character of utility. Even more than exchange, the notion of function lends itself to an underscoring of the essentialist view of human nature which prevents its exposure as a cultural construction (see also chapter 7 pp. 115–18 below).

The reason for employing Baudrillard's work as the basis for this critique is that he is a key figure in pointing out, not only these limitations of Marx, but also their consequences for aspects of modern society which have thereby escaped the kind of radical analysis to which they might otherwise have been exposed. Marx is often accused of devaluing cultural relations at the expense of economics as the source of social relations. But Baudrillard more specifically focuses on the devaluing of consumption as opposed to production. His argument is that these privileged signifieds of use value and productive labour have blinded us to the oppressive nature of the play of commodities as signs; and he implies that the belief that commodities ought to signify 'real' values prevents us from appreciating the oppressive mechanisms by which commodities actually fail to operate in any conventional significatory role, referring only to themselves and appropriating all other aspects of social relations to themselves through consumption. This last, complex, (and dubious) point will be returned to in the third section of this book, which deals directly with the nature of modern consumption.

The accusation that Marx devalued consumption seems to be supported by his own work, since the only place where he provides an explicit analysis of consumption is in the introduction to the *Grundrisse* (Marx 1973: 83–111). In terms of the present perspective, however, this is a highly unsatisfactory section, in which Marx asserts the totality of the relations of consumption, distribution and production. Although this represents the content of the section, in essence it is an attempt to deal with aspects of Hegel's logic and the very concept of totality. These relations and terms are used to exemplify the workings of this logic, rather than in a serious attempt to deal with consumption as an actual human practice. Although Marx appears to assert the mutuality of production and consumption, through which production demands consumption of its subject, and consumption demands production of its object, Sahlins demonstrates that what starts as reciprocity quickly develops into hierarchy. Because there is no independent consideration of the cultural construction of consumption, this area becomes merely the logical outcome of the sphere of production, that moment which completes the production cycle, reducing practices back to practical reason (Sahlins 1976a: 153–57). This suggests, then, that the labour theory of value and the concept of use value are jointly responsible for a conservative attitude to the place of work and utilitarian practices as the 'proper' sites of human self-creation, and a concomitant failure to examine cultural and consumption activities as creative of social relations.

The charge that Marx de-emphasized consumption is closely connected to the earlier criticism of his general account of objectification. Marx's intention was clearly oriented towards a holistic understanding of history. Observing the degree to which Hegel appeared to permit ideas of both consciousness and culture as form to become independent of their social and economic base, Marx attempted the task of regrounding these ideas within their larger historical context, through the development of a concept of social relations which spoke of a larger totality in which the two elements could not be separated. It has been argued in this chapter that, despite protestations to the contrary (e.g. Dupré 1983: 17), Marx unfortunately submerged elements of culture he had intended merely to integrate. When taken as a redressing of a balance, the emphasis on material culture and mass consumption in the present work need not therefore contribute to a new autonomy or fetishism, but may serve the continued aim of this tradition in academic analysis which attempts to refuse the tendency towards autonomy of both subject and object.

To conclude, the writings of Marx and the later Marxists are so firmly entrenched in our cultural and academic structures that they provide part of the common backdrop to any analysis proposed. The intention of the criticisms made in this chapter is not to reduce their achievements, but to draw attention to those emphases which were lost, and to examine the consequences of that loss. This provides for both an analysis of consumption which is no longer merely relegated to an outcome of conflicts centered elsewhere, and a use of the concept of objectification to understand the nature of contradictions and strategies which cannot entirely be reduced to the nature of capitalism as the conditions of rupture.

4

Munn: Objectification as Culture

Introduction

This and the following chapter are intended as complementary expositions of an approach to culture as objectification. An attempt to assess the implications of the concept of modernity will be begun in chapter 5, but if the concept of objectification is not to be reduced solely to a critique of capitalism, as has been the tendency since Marx, anthropology may provide a context for its elucidation which is relatively free from considerations of industrialization and modernity.

Social anthropology has commonly been employed as a kind of ruse, by means of which, through the exploration of different 'non-modern' societies, a degree of relativism is introduced which permits a more sophisticated analysis of complex societies. For this purpose, societies such as the Australian aboriginals, who produce and use a minimum of material artefacts, have often been invoked in contrast to industrial cultures. Such a procedure has rightly come into question because the original basis for the development of such polarities, the idea that the simpler the technology of the society the more it represents some pristine or primitive condition, as implied by various evolutionary perspectives, is unacceptable. It is, however, possible to accept the fundamental equality between societies, and acknowledge their contemporaneity, while continuing to recognize the significance of the distinction with respect to industrialization and material produce, in which case the original project of social comparison accomplished by anthropological investigation retains its validity and interest.

Even in anthropology, however, the analysis of objectification cannot be easily divorced from the tendency to construct simple dichotomies of capitalist as against pre-capitalist society, rather than to engage in a more general comparative discussion. This is clear if one considers the foundations for anthropological discussion of the subject–object relation. The statement which continues to dominate debates on this within the discipline was written by Mauss in 1925 in his book *The Gift*: 'it is clear that in Maori custom this bond created by things is in fact a bond between persons, since the thing itself is a person or pertains to persons. Hence it follows that to give something is to give a part of oneself' (1954: 10).

In this statement, Mauss attempts an interpretation of the Maori concept of *hau*, which he sees as referring to the inalienable essence of an object which is retained throughout the exchanges to which it is subject. This concept partly explains why the giving of a thing always, in effect, obligates the recipient to provide a reciprocal gift. Mauss further claims that such exchanges not only implicate the persons who participate in them, and the labour by which the artefact is created, but also all those moral, religious, economic and juridical norms which in 'gift' societies are inseparable, making the gift what Mauss terms a 'total' social phenomenon (1954: 76).

Within the book, Mauss makes clear that the concept of the gift, though replete with empirical ethnographic examples, is also conceived of in direct contrast to the market, in which the exchange of things is entirely separable from the attributes of the persons who participate in that exchange. The sale of the commodity is a completed action with no further implications, while the gift is part of an infinite cycle of exchange. The gift thereby provides a focus for a whole series of dichotomies between the segmentary, holistic, communal tribal society, and the fragmented, hierarchical, individualistic societies of capitalism. Thus, although Mauss's prime positive models were drawn from friendly or mutual societies, rather than communism, the irreducible link between object and person is still conceived within the Romantic vein of a world lost and therefore re-established only as critique (1954: 63–81).

These arguments have spawned a large literature and a core tradition within later social anthroplogy. Some have chosen to dispute the fidelity of Mauss's interpretation of the *hau* to the original Maori text, variously suggesting that it refers rather to the profit or increase gained by the object which must be repaid, to several different concepts which Mauss conflated, or to an aspect of witchcraft (e.g. Firth 1957; Gathercole 1978; Hanson and Hanson 1983: 65–6, 417–21; Sahlins 1974: 149–62). The link between object and person has also been more directly related to questions of inalienability (especially with respect to the concept of *kitomu* in the Kula, see Damon 1980; 1983: 323–7; Gregory 1983: 108–9; Weiner 1983: 148–9; 1985). Most importantly, Sahlins recognized that *The Gift* in effect makes the claim that exchange constitutes a 'social contract' approximating to the formation of a society, but without necessitating the establishment of a state (1972: 165–83). In a sense, this abstraction is taken to its extreme by Lévi-Strauss, who in his key work on kinship, *The Elementary Structures of Kinship*, dismisses the native text as mere rationalization and interprets exchange as an initial constituting of society in terms of abstract structural relationships (Lévi-Strauss 1969; also 1982 for direct commentary on Mauss).

The dichotomous tendencies in *The Gift* are contradicted by other aspects of research in this area. Mauss recognized that gift-exchange may develop extremely aggressive and competitive features, as in the Potlatch of the North-West American Indians, and cannot be separated from personal interest. Another prime example of the gift is the kula ring, which will be discussed further below; this is practised alongside *gimwali*, which is classic market exchange abstracted from the participants and characterized by haggling and business acumen. Bourdieu (1977: 3–9) has criticized those who interpreted gift reciprocity as a series of abstract rules, noting that given the lapse of time between gift and counter-gift, there enter various considerations of strategy; in view of this, he follows Mauss in refusing to confuse the appearance of disinterestedness with its actuality. If the gift has commodity-like aspects, Appadurai, following a series of anthropological critiques of overly economistic representations of capitalist societies, has recently argued that the commodity also has gift-like aspects, which have been neglected as disciplines such as economics remove the commodity from the cultural context within which it operates (1986: 12–13).

These discussions may lead us to address the nature of objectification. In a recent article, Weiner returned to the original Maussian interpretation of the *hau* and re-emphasized the question of inalienability, noting how the object in its own history may encapsulate the ancestral links which define a person's social being. She argues that 'the primary value of inalienability, however, is expressed through the power these objects have to define who one is in an historical sense. The object acts as a vehicle for bringing past time into the present' (1985: 210). In the anthropological discussion of gift and commodity in general, however, the degree to which the person is implicated in the thing, and the thing has qualities of the person, is subordinated to the question of how society is constituted in and through exchange. The work of Nancy Munn, to which the remainder of this chapter is devoted, is therefore unusual in that she has sought to incorporate the analysis of exchange within a more general understanding of the nature of culture as practice (e.g. Munn 1986: 268).

Although Munn is not among the dozen or so anthropologists normally used by academics in other fields to represent the discipline, with respect to the nature of objectification her studies are of major significance. In her most recent work, Munn has become involved with one of the core examples of this tradition, that is the kula, but having come to the study of exchange following previous work in the analysis of visual representation, it will become evident that she understands exchange in relation to objectification and not entirely the other way around.

In this case it is the corpus of studies rather than a single article which will be used, since these reveal certain significant trends. Her earlier writings are concerned with the nature of culture mainly within a single social group, and show the influence of structuralism and symbolic studies; while in some of her latest work these concerns are supplemented by ideas from the writings of Mauss and Marx, phenomenology, and a concern with the relationships between different societies.

Objectification Within One Society

The particular group studied in Munn's major early work (1973a), which focused upon the nature of iconography, are called the Walbiri and live in the desert region of central Australia north-west of the tourist landmark of Ayers Rock. Today, the Australian aboriginal, as known from anthropological studies, is almost entirely associated with such small nomadic bands adapted to extreme desertic conditions. It should be noted, however, that the native peoples of Australia appear to have been no more inclined to such extreme natural deprivation than peoples elsewhere, and the major concentration of the population had always been along the rich coasts and tropical areas, until the decimation of aboriginals by Europeans forced them into the most inhospitable regions.

The Walbiri appear to have most of the commonly found attributes of extant aboriginal desert society. There is a strong sexual division of labour: women gather and men hunt. The largely nomadic existence is centered on the water holes, or dry creeks where water can be found by digging temporary wells. At such places, camps are set up consisting of little more than hearths and wind breaks made of bark or corrugated iron sheets. The patterns of kinship are complex, but in brief there are shallow genealogies with lines usually represented by only seven to twelve males, based upon patrilineal 'lodges'. These male-based divisions are cross-cut by other social divisions, some of which are female-centered. Men are often polygamous and control junior males. There is no evidence, however, of the hierarchy of segmentary lineages familiar from African ethnography.

The pattern of social relations is only comprehensible when it is related to the land. Without many portable artefacts, the Walbiri have developed a detailed and profound relationship with their environment. Groups are defined in terms of territories with specific rights to areas and sometimes to foods. This relationship is not an immediate one, however, but always represented as a relationship between people and the ancestral figures of the dreamtime (the period during which the world was created). It is these ancestral figures who are held to have created the landscape with all the features visible today; each is accredited with a track across the landscape showing, for example, where an ancestral marsupial mouse raised up hills, dug the water holes with a digging stick or its penis, and created depressions in the ground with its footprints.

Claims of relations to land are always made in terms of knowledge of the ancestors who created it; and the recognized rights of a social group are always rights to the representation of a particular ancestor. Thus, it may be granted that a certain patrilineal lodge possesses the rights to represent a wallaby ancestor, while another group has the rights to oversee the first group in carrying out any such representations, which usually take place during a number of life-cycle ceremonies such as the initiation of young males, or funerals. These rights mark the groups' relationship to each other and their exclusive rights to part of the track of a given ancestor, and thereby to territory. Since rights derive from knowledge about ancestors, the major ceremonies for initiating a young male into maturity consist largely of the enactment of these representations, thereby revealing to the initiate that knowledge, often of an otherwise secret nature, which marks the authority of the group over the land. The possession of this knowledge is seen as essential for formal inclusion of the individual into the controlling group.

Most of Munn's book (1973a) is a detailed account of the iconography involved in a number of systems of representation, the main emphasis being on the nature of symbolism and iconicity, topics which became especially prominent with the rise of structuralism and semiotic analysis. Although there remains a significant degree of interest within anthropology in the nature of symbolic systems, the precise details are less relevant to the present work, and will only be briefly summarized. One contrast which emerges strongly from the study of the Walbiri is between the forms of representation carried out by women, and those carried out, usually in the absence of women, by men. A typical woman's system of representation are the sand stories, simple patterns made in the sand by women who may be recounting some everyday event in the camp, or telling a generalized story about the ancestors. The designs are very simple and can be reduced to some thirteen basic elements, such as circles, lines, U-shapes, wavy lines etc. Since many of these elements may relate to more than one potential referent, they are usually used in combinations which allow the actual meaning to be clarified. For example, a U-shape is likely to be interpreted as a male sitting in a camp if the line next to it appears to represent a spear, which is normally associated with males.

The stories follow a certain pattern. First, the ancestors emerge from a hole in the ground; they then engage in various activities, and the story ends with their disappearance down another hole in the ground. The activities described in the sand stories are simple and familiar, such as gathering foods, dancing or sharing food. Munn notes the origins of the design elements, which may be 'discovered' by individuals in their dreams. The originator may be either the user or her husband, but these designs are not individually owned, and once discovered will be shared. The stories are either set in the ancestral dreamtime, or related to the events of the day, but in the former case the conception is generic, and no single ancestor or particular locality is designated.

There are several contrasts between these and the forms of representation mainly used by men. While the women's stories revolve around the campsite, the men's are usually based on the tracking of animals across the landscape. In this case, it is the specific named ancestors who are being tracked, and with respect to particular localities. The designs are inherited directly from the dreamtime and are individually owned. In a sense, then, the women's forms of representation are displaced by their lack of immediacy and specific referent, and the mediation of the dream. This becomes important when considered in terms of the different rights held by the two sexes. The capacity to represent is itself the mark of one's rights. Although women have their own ritual activities, it is during the secluded male rituals that the identity of the key ancestors is learnt and the more abstracted representations are translated, so that the initiate is aware of which particular ancestor is being referred to.

Munn concentrates on the analysis of one particular ceremony known as the *Banba*, which forms part of male intiation rites. During this ceremony, which consists mainly of preparations, since the actual enactment of the ancestor's movements is a fairly brief dramatization, Munn shows that several transformations are being conducted. The central change represented by the ritual is the transference of the young male from an agnatically related lodge (i.e. a female-centred kinship set) to the male patrilodge of which he will from now on be a full member. The enactment can also be understood from analysis of the symbolism to be the appropriation by the males of the female procreative power, in the sense both of the female-controlled biological power of reproduction being subsumed by the male cultural control over social reproduction, and also of the male dominance of inventive and procreative forms. This appropriation takes place in part through the transformation of an internal personal relationship with the ancestors into an externalized 'institutionalized' relationship (1973a: 216).

Such an appropriation of female reproductive power, which may be related to the wider concept of the relationship of nature to culture, here suggests that the difference in degrees of access to means of representation may itself be efficacious in ensuring the continued dominance of certain groups in a given society. This is a theme which will be returned to. It would only be a valid point, however, if it could be shown that these forms of representation were themselves major elements in social transformations. This is suggested by Munn in one of her earlier articles (on the Murngin people), in which she criticizes the implications of those studies of symbolism which concentrate on the place of symbols as 'units in conceptual systems, or as ritual condensation points for complex social meanings' (Munn 1969: 178), and argues instead that these systems of representation possess a more integral and efficacious quality. What emerges from these works is a sense of how the individual projects out in representation, but in so doing comes to understand personal experience in relation to a set of media, most particularly the landscape, which contrast people as social beings having certain relationships. The internalization of these externalizations thereby creates the individual's 'being' in relation to age, gender, social group and other familiar social categories.

This constitutive quality of Walbiri iconography is further enhanced as a possible model of objectification by the extent to which the Walbiri themselves appear to have developed a parallel concept. This emerges from Munn's analysis of the structure of certain myths known to the Walbiri and the nearby Pitjantjatjara (Munn 1971). These myths reveal that the process by means of which the ancestral beings created the landscape was one of self-alienation and externalization. In the myths, the ancestors undergo several forms of transformation from sentient beings into objects. First, the ancestors may transform the whole of their body into some visual feature such as a rock outcrop (metamorphosis); secondly, they may leave their imprint upon the ground through the impression of a part of their body, such as a footprint (imprinting); and thirdly, they may take out from within their body an object which then is transformed into a natural feature of the land (externalization) (Munn 1971: 142) Although the ancestors are perpetually in motion, they may leave behind a number of such permanent and static signs of their transformations.

Munn notes the ways in which the ancestors may create such object forms: 'In their view, the ancestor first dreams his objectifications while sleeping in the camp. In effect, he visualizes his travels – the country, the songs and everything he makes – inside his head before they are externalised. Objectifications are conceived of as external projections of an interior vision: they come from the inner self of the ancestor into the outer world' (Munn 1971: 145). Munn's article provides detailed material on precisely how the people conceive of these subject–object relations, which, for the Walbiri, may be compared with the experience of the individual in dreaming. This highly subjective experience is in fact linked to a relatively direct experience of the world of the ancestors, and thereby the objective world of history, which is a distanced, generalized place of appraisal with respect to the events of everyday life. This process of externalization and interiorization may be repeated in a more controlled vein through ceremonial and ritual activities (Munn 1973a: 117–18).

From the study of myths it is clear that the Walbiri's view of this process is quite different from that of most psychologists (for examples see chapter 6). The Walbiri can envisage the individual as the creator of a new external form, such as a new design derived from dreaming. But, unlike psychologists, who concentrate on the individual process of self-development through objectification, it is clear to the Walbiri that such processes occur in a world which is already created as a culture by history. This sense of the historical foundation of culture, and therefore of any attempt to comprehend social activities, is a central tenet of most anthropological studies; and it is at least implicit in the discipline that it arises in part because it is closer to the self-conception of most non-industrial small-scale societies with their central concern for 'custom'.

For the Walbiri, the human process of objectification is the mirror image of the process enacted by the ancestors. The ancestral beings did not go about this process of objectification systematically or deliberately; it was merely an integral part of their being to create the world: 'In sum, ancestral transformation involves a free, untrammelled creativity and 'self-objectification' inherent in the nature of the subject' (Munn 1971: 145). This distinguishes ancestors from humans, who are involved in a process of objectification which must always submit to the prior existence of the world. It also distinguishes the conception of a cosmology in which actions are always re-enactments from the concept of history in the Western sense of 'origins'.

Munn makes clear that this is not merely intellectual positing. The ancestral forces have created the details of the landscape which are crucial to the self-identification of the extant social groups. These are in effect land rights, whose proper inheritance is established through the mythic form. Munn relates this process of inheritance to the problems of generation mentioned above. The transformations of the ancestors are linked in a number of images with ideas of birth and fecundity. The appropriation by males of female reproductive power can thereby be represented in the appropriation of a set of objects (boards). The child starts as an objectification of woman (represented by ancestral female spirits), but, through the appropriation of the boards, may be separated from the continued presence of woman which is inherent in it through its origins in birth (1971: 155–6).

In the study of the Walbiri, the particular and privileged medium of objectification is the landscape. In a sense, the surface of the land becomes the surface upon which the process is enacted. The ancestors originally emerge through a hole in the ground, enact their activities and descend into the ground through another hole. The systems of representation always use designs based upon the impression made in the ground: thus, a tree is represented by a circle, a person sitting on the ground by a U-shape, an animal by the tracks of its feet, tail or penis dragging along the ground. As Munn says, 'The country is the fundamental object system external to the conscious subject within which, as we shall see, consciousness and identity are anchored' (1971: 143). The image may also follow for dreaming; in dreams, one goes beyond the surface of the world into the time in which the world was created, the dreamtime, and then emerges from that back into the world of lived experience.

Clearly, this is an example of reification. The moral order and the social order of the society are understood only as they are mapped out onto a cultural landscape which is 'naturalized' by being mapped in turn onto the natural features of the geographical landscape. The immediacy of this medium for a people living by hunting and gathering, and thereby dependent upon the location of water holes and other such natural features, will be evident. As a medium of objectification, the properties of the landscape become of central importance; it provides the permanence, the authority, and the massivity which can legitimate the social world. When seen in relation to the Walbiri, however, the concept of reification need not necessarily have to be understood as suppression or rupture. It is clear that the differential access to modes of objectification is crucial to the relations of hierarchy and power amongst the Walbiri, but this does not mean that these have to be understood as prior causal mechanisms accounting for the process itself. This subtle cosmology should not be reduced to mere functional mystification; rather, the process of objectification which is essential to the creation and reproduction of the group is shown to be always available for manipulation as ideology, so that the means by which the group creates its identity are used to serve particular interests.

The significance of the particular medium of objectification and its potency is also clear in a parallel example used by Lévi-Strauss in his book *The Savage Mind* (1972: 237–44), where he discusses an artefact called the *Churinga* used by some aboriginal groups. The *Churinga* are painted elliptical boards which lie hidden or buried in certain caves or crevices. Their location is known to senior males, and they are revealed to juniors as part of an initiation ceremony. At such a time, the junior males are led to the place where the *Churinga* are kept, and these are excavated or revealed. They are then repaired or repainted if necessary, and returned to the ground or crevice. Lévi-Strauss remarks on our desire to see the authentic and original document even when we have perfectly good copies; in this case, the males are granted the privilege of seeing objects which have actually come from the time of the ancestors. In a world where material objects are scarce, and where those which exist are largely transient, a particular cultural form which is visibly the product of the remote past and is destined for the remote future has a profound implication matched only by the permanence of the landscape itself. Here again, it is the very materiality of the medium of objectification which is important for the process taking place (see also Weiner 1985), a process which reinforces belief in the ancestors as the historical legitimators for the present order of the world. Material forms thus provide a medium for present, transient and particular history to be subsumed under a large experience, in which past and present are absorbed into an infinite dreamtime where cultural order merely re-enacts its own self-creation.

In portraying another society as an image of totality, in which the cultural environment through which the society is created is understood as a continual self-referential and complex whole, this example employs one of the basic devices which account for the emergence of social anthropology as such. Structuralist techniques commonly emphasize the multivalent character of the symbol; thus for the Walbiri, a circle and line motif may stand, individually or all at once, for sexual intercourse and thereby other aspects of sexual relations, for the relationship of past to present, for the movement of people to and from the camp and of ancestors to and from the landscape, and for many other forms of 'coming out' and 'going in' movements (Munn 1973b). Anthropological anaylsis attempts to reveal how this multivalency is not an element of difference, but something which binds culture together as a kind of fabric, establishing connections which reinforce pervasive cultural images, and rendering the individual fragments or elements of both an iconography and a cosmology meaningless except in relation to a cultural totality. The importance of this emphasis is that it portrays an image of an unfragmented consciousness or culture, which is drawn in opposition to the plethora of characterizations of industrial societies as fragmented or suffering from anomie or alienation. The only exceptions to this are some Marxist anthropologists who focus upon contradictions within pre-capitalist societies. In such studies, anthropologists apply the techniques of micro-scale analysis of the particular and relativistic features of the individual cultural practices, indicating how the fragmentation of people into the variety of material and object forms taken by culture is a medium which constructs the unity of the group, rather than its rifts. This provides a strong contrast with the analysis by Simmel of the same set of relationships in industrial societies (see chapter 5). Both the abstraction of the dreamtime and the particularity of the tracks come back to the people in the form of an understanding of those processes by which they are created as a people.

Objectification of a Relationship between Societies

In Munn's more recent work, this interest in the individual in relation to society has been extended to an analysis of the relationship between societies. In common with her earlier work, however, is the emphasis upon the manner in which the use of external relations acts to construct the self-image of a society, as a subject in relation to some 'other'. An article written in 1977 (see also Munn 1983) concerns the construction of canoes on the small island of Gawa to the north-east of New Guinea. Gawa forms part of the kula ring, one of the most extraordinary phenomena for which anthropologists have been called upon to account. The kula ring has traditionally been represented as a rough circle of islands connected by an exchange network around which circulate a series of valuables, with shellbands travelling in one direction and necklaces in the other. The expeditions by which one group of islanders cross the seas to obtain these valuables and thereby enhance their reputation were made famous by Malinowski in his book, *Argonauts of the Western Pacific* (1922). Since then, a large number of books and articles (including Mauss 1954: 19–29) have focused upon the kula from perspectives which emphasize its economic, ritual, political or totalizing implications, in order partly to account for its existence. This work has also clarified the nature of the objects involved (e.g. Campbell 1983; Damon 1980; 1983: 323–7; Firth 1983; Scoditti 1983: 265–72 on the major kula valuables). Most recent work has shown that earlier accounts were too schematic, and the description given above would have to be refined by considering, among other factors, the very different uses made of the valuables in the various island groups within the kula (Leach and Leach eds 1983).

The particular focus of Munn's article is on one small island, Gawa, which provides canoes to be 'launched' out as part of the kula. She describes in some detail the decoration of the canoes and the process of their manufacture, and what emerges most clearly from her account is the sense in which the people 'invest' themselves in the act of creating a cultural object. The process of production and exchange is considered in terms of a series of transformations in spatiotemporal perspectives, through which the canoe moves, symbolically as well as physically, from the island to the outside world. The major factor dominating the production of symbolic form is the eventual fate of the canoe, which will take it far from its actual makers. The symbolism of the decoration is therefore resonant of a whole series of transformations which relate to movements from the society outwards. These include transformations from the heavy, stable tree to the light, seagoing canoe; emphasis on the place of manufacture as a beach which links the territory of the community to the outside; and emphasis on the kinship ties between individuals and between clans and their land (Munn 1977: 41–2). All of these are 'commented upon' through the canoe decoration; the 'investment' of the subject in the creation of this object is made explicit in, for example, the anthropomorphic symbolism applied to the canoe prowboards, which are ornamented and beautified in a manner analogous with that of the human body (Munn 1977: 47–9). These two processes are connected in that the transformation of the canoe from a static to a mobile entity can be related to its anthropomorphic qualities as animate human over inanimate object.

What is being protrayed here is a concern with the creation of an object in which social relations are implicated, but which will ultimately be delivered up for the use of other people, by being launched into the kula ring. This is an example of the problem of alienation: certain conditions serve to separate the creators from the object of their creative processes. The solution to this problem emerges most clearly in terms of the relationship the people have with the objects for which they exchange their canoes. These objects of exchange, known as *kitomu*, gain their significance from the social relations which are objectified by the act of exchange, a signficance which therefore could not result entirely from manufacture itself. The canoe is always sent out from the island in a particular direction which helps 'fix' the island in the circuits of kula exchanges. Through various exchange ceremonies, these external exchange systems are articulated with internal exchange networks. The *kitomu* received in exchange for canoes are closely associated with the self as personal possessions comparable with parts of the body (Munn 1977: 51). These objects are redistributed internally through those same kin networks which were mobilized to produce the canoe.

Munn's conclusions have been taken further by Damon (1980), who sees objects such as these as representative of 'congealed labour', and is thereby able to relate the manipulation of exchange to the appropriation of certain aspects of labour. As with Mauss, the object itself is seen as creative of social relations, through a process by which people self-alienate as an externalization, only to have this aspect of themselves returned in a new form which has accreted to itself the substance of the exchange. Munn suggests that 'the canoe's irreversible journey as an exchange valuable does not alienate it from its producers: all its conversions return to the owning clan' (1977:45). Objectification can here be understood as a process of externalization and sublation which is dependent upon the relationship between two societies, and not merely the internal workings of one. As such, it may assist in the overall problem of accounting for phenomena such as the kula, which appear to place such emphasis upon the movement between societies of objects of no apparent intrinsic worth. In her most recent work Munn incorporates the problem of explaining the kula within a more generalized account of value transformation by means of which the islanders of Gawa, a particular community within the kula, are enabled to act as agents of their own self-production. She argues that

> Gawan society has to be understood in terms of its grounding in this inter-island world. On the one hand, the community asserts its own internal viability through the concept of its positive evaluation by these external others, expressed in the Gawan emphasis on fame (butu-), the renown or good name of Gawa in this world. On the other hand, fame itself (like kula shells) can

be produced for Gawans only through an initial externalization process involving the separation of internal elements of Gawa (especially garden crops and canoes, which are the produce of its land and trees) and their transaction into the inter-island world (Munn 1986: 6).

Munn begins her account with a quotation from the early Marx, from whom such a perspective is clearly derived (Munn 1977: 39). The relationship to Mauss, and also to phenomenological traditions, is further developed in her latest work (1983, 1986). Here, Munn stresses the dynamic nature of kula activity, in which the participants, in attempting to gain strategic control over the 'roads' by which the valuables pass around the Kula, thereby construct their own place in this spatiotemporal order. As with Mauss, she argues that people and valuables are 'reciprocally agents of each other's value definition' (1983: 283). This is exemplified in the manner in which both men and valuables gradually attract fame and name through their activity in the Kula, and their ability to persuade or 'move' the mind of other participants (1983: 284).

As with the Walbiri, these modes of development through social self-alienation may be controlled by certain groups to the detriment of others, and indeed recent surveys suggest that the internal impact of the kula is often quite different from that of egalitarian reciprocity. It is rather the means of creating social hierarchy through the display of differential ability in the manipulation of its potential, though these differences take various forms according to their common articulation with internal exchange networks within the particular society. That exchange as a process of objectification may be used for production of hierarchy does not mean, however, that only power relations can account for it.

Subjectivism and Objectivism in Objectification

Munn's work has here been somewhat artifically separated into two sections, one dealing with intra-societal and the other with inter-societal relations. In practice, the two are obviously closely connected. Malinowski's account of Trobriand men's participation in exchanges with other islands is matched by Weiner's account of the relationship between this, and women's exchanges of valuables within the Trobiands (Weiner 1976; Weiner 1983). Munn, Weiner and other recent writers on the kula (Leach and Leach eds 1983; Munn 1986) have made it very clear that the articulation between these external and internal exchange systems is the key to the construction of individual reputation. The individual–social dichotomy is closely tied to another even stronger dualism in anthropology between subjectivism and objectivism. Munn's work may be used to illustrate how the concept of objectification may aid in the resolution of such artificial extremes.

The core traditions of social anthropology have always shown a prime concern with the collective and historical creation of culture, as opposed to the individual's self-creation. Although the critique of the individual as the privileged subject of analysis has come to prominence in post-structuralist writings in recent years, this is hardly an innovation within social anthropology. All the major traditions of evolutionary studies, functionalism and structuralism eschew the individual subject; indeed, with the work of Lévi-Strauss (1969) and Leach (1954), the individual society has also become suspect as the unit of analysis, with social structure and culture being understood as sets of transformations occurring over a continent, reducing individual social groupings to mere vehicles for their expression. The abiding influence of Durkheim and Marx has created a tendency towards a highly objectivist emphasis in much contemporary anthropology.

A characteristic feature of much of this tradition is that society is always prior to culture; it is social relations and categories which are given form in cultural classifications (Durkheim 1965: 10; Durkheim and Mauss 1963; 87), an emphasis which continues through the work of many contemporary anthropologists (Sahlins 1976a: 106–20). What these authors are describing, then, is not properly a process of objectification, since society as subject appears as independent of, and ultimately of a higher ontological status than, the media through which it is expressed. For these writers also, the individual is not considered as either author or recipient of these processes, a legacy of the original stress on the differentiation of anthropology from psychology, and of another of Mauss's influential papers which argues for the relatively unique and recent conception of individualism and the moral and juridicial self in capitalist society (Mauss 1979).

In direct contrast to this tradition is the concern with the subject–object relation as expressed by some versions of the incorporation of phenomenological questions into anthropology. The influential book by Berger and Luckmann (1967) may serve as an example. These authors take on the one hand the work of Schutz, which focused on the manner in which concepts were given a sense of concreteness as everyday reality, and on the ontological implications of this activity. On the other hand, they consider the Durkheimian tradition, which attempts systematically to relate these processes to the nature of the social world. At first glance, the process of externalization, objectivation and internalization (1967: 149), which is clearly modelled on Hegel, would appear to be the same as that being analysed here. But there are some major differences. The term objectivation, which is central to their work, refers to the process by which the subjective idea is externalized in order to be made available both for intersubjective meaning, and also for institutionalization and other processes which fix it in the external world (1967: 49). These in turn may be seen as available for being retrojected back into consciousness in the course of socialization (1967: 78).

For Berger and Luckmann, the crucial relationship is that between objectivity and subjectivity. For them, a dream would be an extreme example of subjective activity, rather than, as here, a mode of objectification. A further distinction would be in the significance of history to the two approaches. Berger and Luckmann tend to start with the creative subjectivity of the agent, which they recognize as always social in form but with society understood as a constraint, determining the process of externalization through the necessity of intersubjective order; there is much less emphasis upon the historical nature of culture. The question of conscious perception of these processes is also far more important for their definitions than within the mainstream anthropological tradition (Thomason 1982: 130). In contrast, the approach developed here allows for no subject prior to the process of objectification, although it does allow for the historical nature of the media of objectification. Despite the similarity of terminology, then, Berger and Luckmann often appear to affirm the kind of dualism of subject–object relations which the Hegelian tradition is intended to eliminate, although it should be noted that they would make no claim to be faithful to any such tradition.

These opposing traditions share a common difficulty, in that one preserves society as prior, the other subjectivity. Munn's early work commences with a process much like objectivation, where the objective world appears as a kind of constraint upon the free range of subjective creativity (Munn 1969). Although she retains the language of a more phenomenological approach throughout her work, by the time of writing the article on myth, the concern with the individual subject has become part of a study much closer to the notion of objectification as used here (a term which Berger and Luckmann restrict to a still narrower connotation; see 1967: 84). In part, this may be a result of her extensive use of representations by the people she is studying. Concepts such as the dreamtime and practices such as the Kula are not reducible to questions about the relationship between subjectivity and the objective world, but demand a deeper analysis of the representation of culture as history, and the dependence of any concept of the subject upon an understanding of the process of its becoming. This emerges as a gradual change in the emphases to be found in Munn's own writings, though it is not necessarily recognized as such.

At the same time, Munn is able to employ a process of objectification to explore the relationship between individual and society, while rejecting both psychology and subjectivist analysis. She can consider the contribution of the individual agent, while showing how, by this same contributive act, the individual is constructed in culture (contrary to the critique of her work by Dubinskas and Traweek 1984). To quote from the article on myth: 'As a result of this projective process, the material world comes to provide the individual with images or 'fragments' of himself. In the normal personality these 'images' are recognized as being outside the person and separate from him, and yet are experienced as inextricably bound up with him' (1971: 158). The linkage is again manifested in the practices of Gawa where metaphor is used to illustrate the anthropomorphic nature of the externalization of the canoes as a part of the 'body politic' (1977). In both cases we see the externalization of aspects of the subject in acts of self-alienation through which the subject develops further. Since these elements have no independent meaning, they are not really fragments; they are always firmly embedded in the larger totality, which, however, has to be realized in the dynamics of the process of identification itself.

Although strong parallels have been noted between the concept of objectification as abstracted from Hegel's and Munn's writings, clear differences also emerge. Munn as ethnographer separates herself from the philosophical notion of positing, and may thereby more effectively portray an idea of culture which is effectively lived through and experienced as being-in-the-world. The concepts of the Walbiri or Gawa are therefore a praxis rather than a philosophy, and Munn is critical of those anthropologists who study symbolism as an autonomous conceptual sphere. The strongest difference, however, is in the directionality of the process of objectification. Unlike all the models analysed so far, Munn does not provide a developmental sequence; there is no reason to expect that the culture will grow of its own accord towards greater levels of duality between abstraction and particularization .

This has led some to criticize social anthropologists such as Munn for having an essentially synchronic view of a relatively passive and unchanging society. This may be a reasonable charge in some cases, especially where the present incorporation of the peoples concerned, by colonialism and the pressures of modernity, has been screened off in an effort to preserve some anthropological subject as pristine and 'traditional' (e.g. Asad 1973). There is a danger, however, in thinking that social change can only be understood as being of one, developmental, kind. The subjects of Munn's analysis, the cultures of Melanesia and Australasia, have undoubtedly changed continually during their long period of existence, but there is no reason to assume that they need ever have changed in the direction of greater material complexity without such external pressures. The problem lies more with the current tendency to envisage only a single model of social change, that of modernity.

This does, however, represent a clear contrast with Hegel. It was suggested in chapter 2 that Hegel's model appears so resonant because it captures the articulation between different processes of development. One of these is clearly that which we term modernity. In this respect, a distinction may be made between societies which have not followed this particular developmental line of their own accord, and those which have. As will be suggested in the next chapter, it is quite possible to understand this difference without implying that one culture is more advanced than, and therefore superior to, another. The Walbiri as presented by Munn are not more primitive than we are, and they are our contemporaries, but they are clearly a lot less modern.

5

Simmel: Objectification as Modernity

Introduction

The work to be considered in this chapter provides for a temporary completion of the argument concerning the nature of objectification to which the first part of this book has been devoted. It also introduces a brief discussion of material culture, which is the subject of the next section, and provides a bridge with the major subject of the third section, the nature of mass consumption. Simmel's work has been selected on the grounds that I consider it to be the most convincing analysis of modernity consistent with the concept of objectification as outlined here. This is not at first apparent, mainly because of the particular uses to which his work has been put. At one time, he was taken as a founding figure for American sociology of a quite different complexion; while, more recently, interest in his work had developed from an assessment of his considerable influence on Lukács and, through him, to a certain tradition of Western Marxism. Within this tradition, the argument has been that Simmel's *The Philosophy of Money* provides an important critique of alienation, which, unfortunately, the author perceived as a condition of modernity itself instead of a specific attribute of capitalism; but, once his philosophy is directed back to its proper object, there is much to be learnt from his examples.

In a sense then, the fate of Simmel's work is at present parallel to that of Hegel's, in as much as later authorities have appropriated his ideas and aligned them with a theory of rupture seen as specific to capitalism. In this chapter, I shall argue that Simmel's assertion that his analysis is one of modernity rather than solely of capitalism should be taken seriously, and that the contradictions in modernity which he analysed are not resolvable through Marxist conceptions of a future society, but are dilemmas which have to be investigated as integral aspects of modern life. Indeed, to see them as representing a kind of problem to which some solution might be found is to misunderstand their nature. Simmel's further contribution, which has been largely ignored, is his explicit account of the quantitative increase of material culture and its effects upon society, concentrating on the area of consumption. In some respects, he is the last major social theorist directly to have confronted this issue in its own terms, despite the fact that this same quantitative rise in material culture has continued, and appears set to continue, at a most extraordinary rate.

It is not, however, the work of Simmel in general which is the subject of this chapter. Much of this work, such as his theory of social forms, which has been seen as one of the foundations of the discipline of sociology, will be ignored. The particular text to be examined is *The Philosophy of Money*, first published in 1900 (here 1978). It is this work which most clearly follows the Hegelian model, and which is most explicitly concerned with the nature of material culture and modern society. In addition, use will be made of a series of articles concerning the nature of modern culture.

For Simmel, modernity is defined by societies which are highly monetarized, and therefore strongly permeated by high levels of abstraction and quantitative forms, which may also be related to the rise of industrialization. For the purposes of the present work, there will be an emphasis on structural differentiation and the availability of industrial products to the mass population, providing a material rather than an evolutionary legitimation for the exclusion, with respect to issues thought to be specific to modernity, of countries without monetary wealth or the necessary degree of equitable distribution. Such a definition also excludes approaches to modernity and modernism which focus upon an outlook or attitude usually restricted to elite sections of the population such as artists and planners (for example Berman 1983).

The Philosophy of Money

As Simmel and every subsequent commentator on this work has stressed, *The Philosophy of Money* is not intended primarily as a treatise on money as an economic form, but as an examination of the increasingly abstract nature of human relations, for which money provides a symbol and an instrument. The construction of the book follows a pattern which appears to be closely modelled upon Hegel's *Phenomenology of Spirit*, though not explicitly so. Simmel starts with the original separation which engenders the subject as consciousness, and traces the stages of increasing distance between subject and object. Each stage is characterized by a simultaneous increase in abstraction and particularization, which are held in tension with one another, and each is taken to present greater difficulties for the subject attempting to resolve these into its own development. Simmel implies specific stages of historical or philosophical forms to equate with his material rather less than Hegel, but his text is much richer than that of his predecessor in the wealth of sociological models based upon such a sequence.

The work begins in classic Hegelian style: 'Mental life begins with an undifferentiated state in which the Ego and its objects are not yet distinguished; consciousness is filled with impressions and perceptions while the bearer of these contents has still not detached himself from them' (1978: 63). It is only through the development of subject–object relations that the subject as such comes to be constituted. Subjectivity is not prior to, but is contingent upon, objectivity. The object emphasized by Simmel in grounding these ideas is, significantly, very different from that of Marx. Whereas the subject of Marx's early work should develop through the productive construction of the world, Simmel's examples most often related to the potential provided by the exchange and consumption of goods not of one's own production. The simplest relationship is the sheer pleasure of immediate consumption of an object which offers no resistance. As Simmel notes, in such circumstances we merely 'lose ourselves' in the object, and no consciousness is generated by the relationship. It is only through the creation of a distance between subject and object that consciousness may arise, as the awareness of being a subject, which 'is already of objectification' (1978: 63).

This distance between the subject and object is considered by Simmel to represent desire. The influence of Kant's aesthetic theory on the forgoing of immediate pleasure is clear and explicit; Simmel states that 'We desire objects only if they are not immediately given to us for our use and enjoyment; that is, to the extent that they resist our desire' (1978: 66). This first step towards abstraction is complemented by the initial stages of differentiation. Simmel echoes later structuralism in his conception of a nature undifferentiated except through the imposition of human order, which here takes the form of desire as selective preference. The book starts with a statement about the natural equality of all entities (1978: 61), which Simmel, writing in the Romantic mould, perceives as the first primitive imposition of subjective value upon nature. From a generalized application, the subject moves towards greater differentiation of surrounding objects, and an increasing specificity of desire.

As with Hegel, following the initial creation of subject–object relations in consciousness, there arises an increasing awareness of the existence of other subjects, and therefore also the possibility of other values and social relations in the world. Any comparison between these is dependent upon the further externalization of these values as objective forms. Exchange therefore appears as the means by which subjective values are overcome, and it thus the essential condition of all human relationships (1978: 82). Here, we move to a further degree of abstraction, since things are no longer of interest for some essence they may possess but for their exchangeable aspects. For Simmel, objectification is the precondition for culture and thus society; but it is mediated by exchange, which, as the expression of the relationship between things and desires, is the source of value. Simmel places exchange at the point at which Hegel constructs society, and this articulates well with a major tradition in anthropological theory, where it is exchange, often viewed in terms of the polarity of gift and commodity, which is seen as constitutive of society itself (e.g. Appadurai 1986; Lévi-Strauss 1969; Sahlins 1974: 165–183).

At this stage, the sequence has developed towards what Simmel calls the relativistic world view, which he understands as contributing to certain attitudes to the world which comprehend processes rather than just entities (1978: 101–8). Throughout the work, Simmel is concerned with the relationship between the degree of abstraction here found in human relations, and that found in the emergence of modern scientific enterprise and modes of thought. This represents a clear overlap with the concerns of Weber, although this later aspect of the approach is much more poorly developed by Simmel.

The stage is now set for the introduction of money as the relational element between goods: 'Money is the reification of the general form of existence according to which things derive their significance from their relationship to each other' (1978: 128). Money is not just the result of an increasing capacity for abstraction, but becomes instrumental in supporting this relational view of things. Again, paradoxically, objects are seen as increasingly exchangeable with one another, but also increasingly specific in terms of the particular values assigned to them in the form of prices. In the second chapter of his work, Simmel traces the manner in which coinage as the medium used for money gradually loses any intrinsic value, and becomes exclusively a symbol for all other relationships. This stage is seen as characteristic of other elements of abstraction, such as the growth of intellectual abilities.

Having established the presence of money as pure symbol and medium of abstract and relational thought, Simmel goes on to address several major features of such a state and to show how money may stand as the quintessence of each. He looks first at purpose, which he takes as the basic means by which the subject abstracts itself from, and imposes itself upon, nature. Money acts as pure directed purpose, since there is no other reason for its existence except as a medium through which ends may be accomplished. It is therefore the purest example of a tool: 'The tremendous importance of money for the understanding of the basic motives of life lies in the fact that money embodies and sublimates the practical relation of man to the objects of his will' (1978: 211). Simmel recognizes, however, that this particular variety of means has a tendency to become an end, as with the accumulation of money for its own sake. He investigates some of the resulting attitudes to money, such as that of the miser, for whom, instead of acting as a tool, money becomes a barrier between means and ends; this is also the case with excessive extravagance, where the overcoming of price as a constraint becomes the source and end of action. As money in itself becomes more important, so too does the strategy of asceticism which rejects wealth as its prime mode of expression. Simmel concludes this section of his *Philosophy* with an argument that money represents the end point of that cultural process which may be described as the reduction of quality to quantity, a line of argument which was to prove particularly influential in later traditions of Western Marxism.

Simmel asserts that many of the attitudes which surround, and were created through the impact of, money as abstraction are most evident when it has not completely achieved its role in transforming its own social context, and where there are still structures which resist this transformation and hark back to a non-monetarized era. Here in history (but also in many anthropological examples, see Taussig 1977; Worsley 1957), the nature of money and its role in the transformation of social relations is made explicit.

These arguments provide the foundation for Simmel's account of the contradictory nature of modern life. Having pursued a pseudo-Hegelian sequence with an emphasis on the ever increasing abstraction, which leads to an ever more radical separation of subject and object, we are faced with the question of the nature of subject–object relations in this new era. This may be divided into two sections: first, the problem of the nature of the subject, and secondly, the problem of the nature of the object in relation to that subject. These may be roughly equated with chapters 4 and 6 of Simmel's text respectively.

One of the most common clichés of everyday life is the equation of money and evil. Money itself is commonly blamed for unpleasantness in human character, attitudes and behaviour. It is this which makes the next section of Simmel's work so difficult to accept, in that it appears to work so deeply against the grain of modern consciousness.

Simmel's essential argument is that money is the prerequisite for, and major instrument in, the accomplishment of freedom and potential equality. The strength of his argument is such that it cannot be dismissed as merely a distortion of the formula by which 'capitalism' is understood as the guarantor of 'bourgeois freedom'.

The argument is easier to appreciate when set against a non-monetarized society. As represented by anthropologists, such societies often appear to embody the Romantic conception of close social relations within highly communal environments; but what is less often underlined are certain more difficult aspects of the actual experience of living within such conditions. In a close knit society, the sense of personal obligation is overwhelming. Such obligations, usually based upon kinship relations, are highly specific as regards both the actions demanded and the identity of the individual subject to them. That is to say that every individual lives according to a highly structured set of personal obligations which he or she must continually fulfil. This condition is characteristic of societies dominated not only by kinship but also by feudalism or slavery; it is also characteristic of the peasant village. All actions seem to be controlled by a sense of propriety or tradition. The constancy of personal obligations may appear, to the outsider, unremitting and intensely claustraphobic. This may also be the case for the participant, either because the cosmologies themselves, which are often contradictory, admit of an alternative, mythical, more individualistic model of freedom, or because that alternative is evident in the nearby cities, where its attractions outweigh the possible negative features.

Money as abstraction is understood by Simmel to be the root of impersonal relations between people. In a monetarized regime, the individual may be under obligation to a far larger range of people than was hitherto possible, through mortages, tax systems and so on; but these obligations are almost entirely anonymous. The personal figure of coercion, such as the bailiff, may be held at bay through the provision of money, which allows for exchange outside of the nexus of personal social relations. The amount of money received for a service rendered is not dependent upon who you are, but upon the abstract relations within which the service is performed, for example as wage labour. Money therefore tends to extend a concept of equality, in so far as the perception of inequality becomes based upon differences in the possession of money, rather than on an essentialist notion of intrinsic differences in persons. The same condition which favours the emergence of equality as an ideal may provide the means for the further refinement and exactitude of inequality. Non-financial reward for services is likely to be of a highly specific, immediate and implicated form; financial recompense, however, may be translated at any time into a large range of goods and alternative services, according to the desire of the recipient. Under these conditions, lack of money becomes equated with lack of freedom.

It must be recalled that money stands here as the symbol of abstraction in human relations. That same abstraction allows for quantitatively based technological rationality, and for science. Monetarization is thereby tied to the rise of industrialization and bureaucracy. It is this whole series of changes which effect the transformation we recognize as modernity. Although these changes are usually the subject of fulminations against wage labour and the evils of rural or urban proletarianization, the conditions of wage labour may prove attractive to villagers and town dwellers, not necessarily because they are duped by promises or pressurized by taxes, but because of the very real specific constraints of non-monetarized social orders. What commentators often forget in their Romantic imagery of 'traditional' society is the very heavy burden of strong personal and specific obligations. Indeed, one may imagine that in their private lives these same authors may well feel that the visit of the in-laws or attendance at some social function of a distant relative, two of the few reminders of the once overwhelming burden of personal social relations, are curbs upon their own 'freedom'.

In the non-monetarized society, the individual is likely to be tied to activities which are far more tightly constrained by the necessities of daily life. The exception are aristocrats, who are served by a sufficient number of other people to be freed of this daily burden. However, with money, and all the abstractions associated with it, it is not only those who can directly command the labour of others who are free to indulge, if they so wish, in areas outside of productive work, such as education, but also those who wish to use the money from their labour to secure such opportunities. Money, paradoxically, provides the major means of detachment from direct economic involvement, and is the basis of the professions and pure research.

In relation to the politics of his time, Simmel's more detailed arguments often appear confusing. He clearly favours a state which involves itself essentially through monetary transaction rather than direct intervention in other more qualitative spheres of life. He appears progressive in advocating an income tax as the basis of an arrangement by which people might give according to their means and take according to their need, and sees this in terms of the possibilities of socialism, but at the same time he lends himself to a strong laissez-faire interpretation highly restrictive of the involvement of the state (1978: 315–18). Money is held to provide the basis for that level of abstraction at which people are regarded as fundamentally equal to one another, bereft for purposes of social construction of their personal characteristics. Money is thus the foundation for ideas such as socialism and equality between the sexes, which, as abstractions, would be literally inconceivable outside of a highly monetarized society. Simmel is, however, highly sceptical of claim that liberalism has achieved equality in education and other such institutions (1978: 439). Much of this is surprisingly consistent with the writings of Marx. Translated as the historical purpose of the bourgeois, Marx saw money as the necessary stripping away of every vestment of the ancien régime, every personal relation of family and society, which would provide the essential foundation for the possibility of communism. In this respect, Marx was a committed a modernist as Simmel (Marx and Engels 1967).

The process which has been described in the development of abstract social relations is also accomplished in the relationship between persons and things. As has been argued throughout this work, the concept of culture is one which assumes the indivisibility of person and forms (that is, with respect to material objects), and of being and having. According to Simmel, possession is not a static state but an activity (1978: 304). Following the same Kantian argument referred to earlier, possession is held to indicate a profound relationship, since its durability goes beyond the pleasure of immediate gratification. Private property, as an institution, effects not a closer relationship between people and objects, as is often thought, but a greater separation than was hitherto possible. It is a means by which a relationship may be maintained with objects which are at the same time always potentially alienable.

Property is central to the relationship of people and things, and, whether this is experienced individually or as a member of a group, it is one of the foundations of modern culture. In the absence of money, property will tend to be highly specific, and the group it may be related to relatively small. Money as abstraction furnishes opportunities for possession, but mediates in this relationship to give rise to some separation between the specificity of being and the specificity of having, since money alone does not determine its further use by its presence, and is entirely ahistorical. Money is thus an extreme expression of the possibilities inherent in property. Once again, it accomplishes the flexibility of abstraction while potentially being translated into the most specific of things and individual demands: 'Money's remarkable achievement is to make possible the most adequate realization and effectiveness of every individual complication through the equalization of the greatest diversity' (1978: 319).

Money as property is therefore most attuned to serving our particular and independent will. In Simmel's view, then, freedom consists, in part, in the articulation of the self in the medium of things.

Marx's own celebration of capitalism is an ironic one, demonstrating its historical necessity, but always presenting it as an instrument of a doomed social formation permeated by the image of proletarian suffering. We find a more genuine reconciliation of the two authors when we turn to Simmel's analysis of exploitation and alienation. The reduction of individual people to a quantitative mass of wage labourers, who are appraised only in terms of their contribution to capital, is clearly dependent upon the abstraction represented by money. The rise of science, and of technological rationality with which it is closely asociated, provides the basis for this reduction of human relations from qualitative to quantitative forms, of which money is the dominant model. Simmel's eloquent rendition of this process led in the work of Lukács and more generally in Western Marxism, to the condemnation of mechanisms such as reification and alienation. As such, Simmel understands the place of abstraction as a process of rupture. The difference, however, between *The Philosophy of Money* and most of the later works is that in the early book the rupture created through the rise of money is seen to be inseparable as a historical moment from its positive aspects; that is, it is seen as representing freedom and potential equality. What is stressed rather is that the same phenomenon provides the foundation for both historical tendencies.

The Quantitative Rise in Goods

Simmel differs markedly from Marx – and almost all other commentators on modern society – in that he stresses the relationship between people, the products of industrialization and the monetary economy in terms not only of production, but also of consumption. It is this which he takes as the key to an understanding of contemporary society, and of culture itself. It wil be clear by now that Simmel recognized the necessity of culture for the development of society, and saw the massive increase in material culture as constructive of new developments in the very possibilities of societies. Whether the objects are books, furniture, or cars, individuals are seen by Simmel as increasingly coming into relationship with them, not as producers who fail to recognize their products, but as consumers who have to determine their own development in this world of goods. Simmel's definition of culture is premised upon objectification; he states that 'one of the basic capacities of the spirit is to separate itself from itself – to create forms, ideas, values that oppose it, and only in this form to gain consciousness of itself. This capacity has reached its widest extent in the process of culture' (1968: 45).

Simmel effectively extends Marx's concept of rupture to account for the inability of modern individuals to recognize themselves in the world of goods. The problem is that the massive increase in objective culture has not been appropriated by the subject in such a way that material goods become the instrument of the subject's self-development through the sublation of its own projections; instead, the subject confronts the world of material goods as an alien sphere. In short, the spread of objective culture has outstripped the capacity of the subject to absorb it. This is a result of that historical process by which, through new media such as printing, material goods have been created with cumulative effect; as a result of this powerful force for cultural production, the present generation has inherited a vast accretative mass of products in terms of which it is expected to know itself. Simmel uses Marx's writings about fetishism as the basis for a general theory of the negative aspects of modern culture (1968: 42). He notes the self-perpetuating nature of modern mass production: 'Thus vast supplies of products come into existence which call forth an artificial demand that is senseless from the perspective of the subject's culture' (1968: 43), and argues that just as academic pursuits such as philology and archaeology, which start with certain aims, may develop as methods creating infinite classificatory refinements for their own sake, so people may become the mere instrument of that which they originally developed: 'The infinitely growing supply of objectified spirit places demands upon the subject, creates desires in him, hits him with feelings of individual inadequacy and helplessness, throws him into total relationships from whose impact he cannot withdraw, although he cannot master their particular contents' (1968: 44).

The division of labour facilitated by money leads to extreme differentiation of its products. The subject is now surrounded by a multitude of objects from which only a few can be selected and invested with a sense of self, but Simmel argues that: 'our freedom is crippled if we deal with objects that our ego cannot assimilate' (1978: 462). There are parallels with Durkheim on anomie, who was also much concerned with consumption (Williams 1982: 322–342), and with other writers of the period. The subject continues to invest itself in cultural forms, identifying, for example, with sports, cinema, clothing, a political line, or certain relationships; but such is the scale of modern society that the same individual may become absurdly overextended into essentially superficial relationships, none of which augments his or her being, and yet simultaneously, may have nothing at all in common with another overextended individual who has selected entirely different areas of the surrounding culture. Hence the two highly 'cultured' individuals who meet at a party and find they have nothing in common to talk about. Material objects provide immense specificity, but potentially also extreme fragmentation. Having extended the narrow problem posed by Marx, of the separation of the worker and product, to that of the separation of the subject from culture, Simmel does, however, begin with the premise that the subject might develop in relation to forms which are not his or her individual or class product, a proposition which will be explored further in chapter 10.

Thus the two end products of the development of modern culture, its degree of abstraction and its degree of specificity, are the component parts of the sense of alienation in the modern world. Like Hegel, Simmel exemplifies the result with a characterization of certain attitudes to the world. For example, he suggests that cynicism, which starts with philosophical distance and becomes a refusal of all values, is caused by the observation of values being universally reduced to their money equivalance (1978: 225–6.) If money as abstraction engenders this cynical attitude, so the plethora of products and pleasures creates the blasé attitude in which all objects are perceived as dull and unexciting, and only a new stimulation which rises above the others can produce some, usually temporary, interest (1978: 256–7).

This argument was later extended with respect to the experience of living in the modern metropolis, which Simmel suggests provides for a massive intensification of stimulation and experience, but which threatens to overwhelm us as objective culture (1950: 409–24). This is the key domain of the calculating, rationalist attitude, obsessed with time, which sees other individuals as merely partners in a transaction, rather than individuals in their own right. Even those who do not exemplify the cynical or the blasé attitude tend towards a certain reservation in their social relations which barely conceals an aversion to direct personal contact (1978: 331).

It is this critique of alienation which has been seized upon by some as Simmel's major contribution to modern critical analysis (e.g. Bottomore and Frisby 1978: 1–49; Frisby 1984: Schmidt 1975). It would, however, be just as unfortunate for our understanding of Simmel to be confined to this aspect of his work as it was for his philosophy to be reduced to the simple model of freedom enshrined in an earlier tradition of American sociology. The significance of Simmel's work is that he breaks away from one of the most predominant tendencies in the grounding of Hegel in social analysis:

that is, the suggestion that we can separate off the positive side of sublation from the negative side of externalization as rupture.

What Simmel accomplishes is a realization of the inseparability of the positive and negative consequences of these social transformations. For Simmel, contradiction is not merely an instrument for, but an intrinsic condition of, the dynamic force of history. In short, his argument is that it is the very abstraction which confers the material advantages of modern science, and the social advantages of both modern freedom and equality, which is also responsible for the dilemmas of exploitation and alienation. the central conflict is not, therefore, one between liberalism and equality, which come from the same root, but one emerging from a recognition that both of these entail consequences which may turn against the interests of the subject. It is an integral part of modern culture that it is simply not possible to envisage a model of freedom, including that abstraction needed for the achievement of equality, which would not have as one of its component parts the tendency towards alienation. The prospect of providing variety cannot be dissociated from a sense of swamping the subject in its alternatives. It follows that a society which had removed capitalism, but which nevertheless sought to retain the benefits of science and the flexibility of money, would still be faced with the problems of these intrinsic contradictions of modern life. Capitalism is thus to be opposed for its exploitative practices, rather than its non-utopian form. Equally, a socialism which restricted itself solely to solving the problem of exploitation in the social relations of production, and failed to respond to these contradictions in culture, might find itself far less attractive – to an electorate, for example – than it envisaged. This is not an affirmation of the status quo; there is nothing in Simmel to reduce antipathy to class conflict or economic exploitation. There is, however, a refusal of the Romantic notion of an ultimate resolution of culture. Hegel's use of this Romantic tradition to develop his idealism with respect to the rationality of the actual and his striving for the transcendence of duality do, however, find their parallel in Simmel's highly positive attitude to art, affirming its ability to express and overcome fragmentation.

Simmel emphasizes the paradoxical nature of culture, recognizing the esentially positive process of modernity which has allowed for hitherto unimaginable possibilities; but he is wary of the forces which lead towards reification and autonomy, both of which are inimical to human interests. This inherent contradiction is what Simmel calls the 'tragedy' of culture. As he describes it,

It is the paradox of culture that subjective life which we feel in its continuous stream and which drives itself towards inner perfection cannot by itself reach the perfection of culture. It can become truly cultivated only through forms which have become completely alien and crystallized into self-sufficient independence. The most decisive way of making this point is to say that culture comes into being by a meeting of two elements, neither of which contain culture by itself: the subjective soul and the objective spiritual product (1968: 30).

This is an important point in considering non-modern culture. Culture for Simmel is not constituted by the material world in itself, but exists only as a process of the subject's becoming. To that extent, modernization represents only a potential for development, not necessarily an actual development; inded, form itself, in its stability, may challenge the continuum of lived experience (Arato 1974: 158; compare Giddens on routinization 1984: 61). It was suggested in the last chapter that analysis which tends to deal with the nature of modernity itself is always in danger of leading to assumptions concerning the superiority of certain 'advanced' peoples over others, which are in effect a version of primitivism. This does not follow, however, from Simmel's approach; for him, the Walbiri's intimate relation to the objective forms taken by their social products, and their classifications of the landscape, might well have appeared more 'cultured' than the attitudes of his German contemporaries, who, in spite of having at their disposal the enormous possibilities of mass culture, did not possess the means for assimilating these into the development of person or group. A social group may be deprived by missionaries or a new education system of access to their own historically inherited forms, and a mere glimpse of the possibilities of industrial culture, without the means for appropriating that culture, is hardly an adequate substitute for such a loss. These observations follow from a recognition that objectication is a process, not an entity.

There are many limitations to Simmel's analysis, the most frustrating being his style and his level of generality. In many respects, Weber provides an alternative source for a study of the rise of abstraction, the attitudes which relate to it, and the institutions it produced. One of the major weaknesses in Simmel's analysis is a possible interiorization of the radical subject–object dichotomy he is describing, in particular a leaning, on occasion, towards an essentialist given self. Simmel tends towards a Romantic style of analysis which takes for granted a primitive undifferentiated nature, and various latent versions of totality, for example in art and aesthetics as models of utopian, if transient, resolutions. He also tends to construct spurious histories of the world bases on his sequence. On the other hand, Simmel provides an excellent example of the grounding of Hegelian ideas as a model of culture, and specifically modern culture, and clearly demonstartes how these ideas may be used in the exploration of the everyday goods of the mass market (e.g. 1957).

Conclusion

Simmel's work provides a focus for a review of the metamorphosis of the concept of objectification. It may be defined as a constitutive process for the development of some subject in and through the medium of culture, which is the form taken by all social productions. Since this includes all those forms which are conventially termed subjective, it is clear that the distinction between individual and society is only one of the selection of an analytical level, since the two are inseparable. Culture, then, is not to be understood, by the concept of objectivation formulated by Berger and Luckmann, as the necessary externalization of subjective processes onto intersubjective domains where they become institutionalized. Culture is derived as a historical force prior to the extistence of any individual subject, but is only realizable through agency. It is therefore the means by which the individual is socialized as a member of a given society, and is, in turn the form of all individual and social creativity.

Objectification describes the inevitable process by which all expression, conscious or unconscious, social or individual, takes specific form. It is only through the giving of form that something can be conceived of. The term objectification, however, always implies that form is part of a larger process of becoming. When using the term to describe a developmental process, one starts with a relatively undifferentiated and unselfconscious subject such as a baby, or with a society which preserves a relatively high degree of cultural inalienabi-lity. Through several stages, the subject moves to an increasing degree of separation which allows on the one hand for the development of greater variability and specificity, and on the other hand for the development of abstraction. These two are always concurrent aspects of the same process, and are always united in a subject's mode of becoming.

These processes are viewed as essentially positive, but as possessing intrinsic dangers, in as much as either specificity or abstraction may develop in such a manner as to be no longer assimilable by the subject through sublation, in which case they become both alien and oppressive. In particular, the subject has to be able to recognize these externalities as intrinsic aspects of itself. Ideology, defined as the control over certain potential media of objectification in society by interest groups such that those who externalize themselves on to those media are unable to recognize that section of themselves, is a common historical phenomenon. Even without a conflict in interests, the attempt to encompass a vast specificity of goods, or the abstractions of academia, have their dangers to the group involved.

These problems arise from the intrinsic contradiction in objectification by which the very form necessary for the subject's development is always an exercise in self-alienation and is therefore a potential source of estrangement. This is one of a number of aspects of the model which originally stem from Hegel, but the model itself is not Hegelian. It accepts the priority of the process of objectification over either subject or object and recognizes that it is only the process itself which accounts for their appearance as discrete. On the other hand, it does not involve the complex Hegelian construction of the world as ultimately rational; it allows for no philosophical or transcendental resolution, no expressive totality or teleology, no absolute knowledge or ideal communism. The contradictory nature of the process allows for no ultimate resolution.

Different elements of the term objectification may be emphasized, depending upon whether it is applied to the process of ontogenesis, culture or modernity. Analogies between these are themselves important, though their dangers have been pointed out. Habermas, for example, recently attempted to equate ontogenetic and phylogenetic growth using the work of Piaget (Habermas 1979: 130–77). In as much as these are, however, different groundings, the term objectification preserves a fluidity, its meaning always dependent upon its particular use. Such relativity is an inevitable consequence of the shift away from philosophy towards anthropology. Objectification as an approach is only useful in so far as it is an aid to understanding a given process in the world. This summary is only a temporary closure in the meaning of objectification. In the third section of the book a far more detailed grounding of the process will be attempted as a means for understanding mass consumption.

PART II

Material Culture

6

The Humility of Objects

Introduction

Up to this point, the principal focus of analysis has been the concept of objectification, which refers to a process of externalization and sublation essential to the development of a given subject. It will, however, have been evident in the previous chapters that one particular potential medium or vehicle for objectification has been emphasized: the concrete material object. In this chapter, I aim to narrow the area of discussion down from the larger field of objectification as a process to the question of the nature of the object *per se*. More specifically, the subject of the next two chapters is the artefact, that form which is the result of human labour, as opposed to equally concrete natural phenomena.

The reasoning behind the present emphasis is that, as observed in the introduction to this work, there is an extraordinary lack of academic discussion pertaining to artefacts as objects, despite their pervasive presence as the context for modern life. In philosophy, for example, there are numerous discussions of objects which refer to some observed attribute or perceptual property pertaining to things as such, but books with titles such as *Words and Things* (e.g. Brown 1958; Gellner 1959) will be found to have very little to say about the social implications of things as objects, while having plenty to contribute to an understanding of the nature of words. Political philosophy is more concerned with objects as properties than the properties of objects, while phenomenology, as that branch of philosophy which claims more direct concern with everyday objects, considers these mainly as media for addressing the role of agency and the nature of subjectivity (though see McCarthy 1984 for the contribution of Mead). The scale of this discrepancy between theory and practice may ironically itself become important evidence for uncovering the nature of objects in the modern world.

The approach in this chapter will be largely ahistorical and asocial, focusing on the properties of things in themselves, while in chapter 7 the artefact will be returned to its historical context in order to examine how its various potential social attributes are actually realized in diverse circumstances.

The first approach to the object *per se* will follow the structure of previous chapters by investigating the process of ontogenesis (individual development) through the examination of two particular texts. These will be used to illustrate the way the necessary relationship between object and subject in ontogenesis follows the general pattern of objectification already outlined. Although these studies, derived from psychology and psychoanalysis, show little concern with the specific nature of the culture within which socialization occurs, the detailing of the process itself strongly reinforces the argument that the human subject cannot be considered outside of the material world within which and through which it is constructed. The study of the infant's development also throws light on two further matters which will be addressed more fully later on in the chapter: the relationship between the symbolism of the object and that of language, and the use of the artefact in play.

This will be followed by a consideration of the relatively few attempts systematically to distinguish the social properties of the object from those of language as expressive medium. The differences found between them may throw light on certain rarely remarked properties of the object which suggest that it has a major role in the development of cognitive abilities and the ways in which the world is perceived, understood and lived in. Some of these factors may also account for the lack of academic analysis of the object, compared with the extent of linguistic research. These issues in turn relate back to the process of socialization, which, towards the end of the chapter, will be considered from a more general anthropological perspective, providing a bridge with the concerns of chapter 7.

The Object in Ontogenesis

Ontogenesis as a process always results in a socialized subject existing within the objective structures of a particular cultural order. Beginning as it does, however, with birth and the very earliest development of the infant, it may be a useful starting point for an examination of those more general properties of the material artefact which are relevant to the place of objects within the general process of objectification.

Two particular texts, both published in 1946, will form the basis of the analysis: Jean Piaget's book *Play, Dreams and Imitation in Childhood* (1962), and Melanie Klein's article 'Notes on some Schizoid Mechanisms' (1975: 1–24). These works examine infant development from the quite different perspectives of cognitive psychology and psychoanalytic studies respectively, but it is worth noting that, within the context of these separate disciplines, Piaget and Klein are both distinguished by their emphasis upon the early stages of infant development. The selection of these particular texts is on the grounds that they succeed in overcoming a dualistic representation of the relationship between the human subject and culture by avoiding reductionism (either to the external world, as in behaviourism, or to the given subject, as in essentialism). Piaget and Klein also show that it is only through the intrinsically dynamic relationship between the infant and its environment that the subject is able to become itself. While sharing these basic featues with the concept of objectification, both authors also provide a grounding in particular mechanisms which provide exemplification of how such processes may operate.

Play, Dreams and Imitation in Childhood may be related to a whole series of studies of cognitive development by Piaget. In these, he adopts a Kantian constructivist position which proposes certain basic categories through which alone the world may be apprehended, but recasts them as dynamic forms achieved only through a long process of interaction with the environment, in which the infant develops cognitive abilities as a means of dealing with the world. This allows Piaget to argue for a direct congruence between the structures of the mind and those of the environment.

This constructivist approach is opposed to psychological behaviourism. The external world exists for the child only at that level of complexity which is compatible with the stage of development it has reached. As the child's mental processes become more complex, it becomes increasingly able to absorb and construct for itself the complexities of the external world. In this dynamic process, action is at least as important as perception. Through action, the child encounters the world directly, literally feeling its possibilities and constraints.

The developmental process was found by Piaget to work through a series of stages, beginning with what he called sensory-motor actions, which are very simple, and culminating in adult life with formal operations, such as that sense of a mathematical and logical order in relation to space, time and other domains which may be equated with the mature Kantian series of categories. Piaget's is an epigenetic sequence in the sense that each stage is dependent upon the previous developments and to an extent absorbs, rather than replaces, the early stages. The sequence does not develop of necessity, however, but only through a continuance of the process of dynamic interaction which is the basis of its genesis (Piaget 1971a; 1972).

Central to Piagetian psychology is a dynamic relationship between the processes of accommodation and assimilation. Through accommodation, the mental structures at whatever stage they have reached are themselves changed in order to encompass the particular characteristic of the environment they have encountered. In assimilation, by contrast, the environment is incorporated only at the level of comprehension the child has attained at any given stage (Furth 1969: 14). The same environmental phenomena will therefore be perceived differently by a young child and an adult, according to their respective assimilatory capabilities. As a simple example, at the level of concept formation, one might envisage a child encountering an object which looks rather like a table, though slightly different from any tables previously noted. The child would then assimilate this object into its already formed concept of table, with no further consequence. If, however, a whole series of such objects was encountered, the child might be forced to accommodate its basic concept of what a table was in order to take in these experiences. For Piaget, cognitive development consists of a series of stages in which these two processes advance asymmetrically, but with the mature phase of what he called 'operational thought' only becoming possible when a balance or equilibrium has been achieved between them. A consideration of the cultural context of such concept formations is largely absent from his work.

In *Play, Dreams and Imitation in Childhood*, Piaget begins the developmental sequence from the earliest cognitive mechanism, which is a simple stimulus-response form of imitation (Piaget 1962: 81). He suggests that at this stage no object-notion has been formed, and imitation is merely a device for prolonging an interesting event (1962: 85). This process of imitation is an example of pure accommodation, where the child is at the mercy of the environmental events it encounters. Imitation, however, gradually increases in complexity, and becomes more systematic and deferred. Sets of repeated actions may then develop as independent schema, which emerge as play once these sequences achieve sufficient autonomy to be carried out in the absence of any direct stimulant. For example, a child may be observed rubbing its hands together and saying soap, even though there is no water.

There are two elements to this initial use of symbolism: a representational imitation which derives from the early mode of direct imitations, and the new ludic mode which distorts the environment, changing the significance of a given external object, and permitting it to be used as the subject desires (1962: 102). While accommodation was dominant in imitation, it is assimilation which dominates in play, as in the classic example of a stick used as a hobby horse (Gombrich 1963). Play leads to increasingly complex imagined worlds over which the child assumes control.

The development of play leads naturally towards involvement in games, which begin in imitative practice such as tying a shoelace, and develop towards symbolic constructions such as of villages or weddings. At this stage, what began as an expression of pure assimilation, in which anything could provide the basis for the child's construction of images, turns increasingly into games with a much stronger accomodative element, as a genuine resemblance is required between the signifier and the signified, and the actual characteristics of the village or wedding observed must be taken into account. Accommodation then gradually moves towards a higher level, at which the egocentricism of play is confronted with the external rules of the social game. The child's gradual acceptance of rule-based games is an important element in the development of its sense of morality (Piaget 1932).

From this point onwards, Piaget's account progresses towards more complex forms of symbolism through which the adult's conceptual apparatus and capacity for cognitive representation are fully developed. In these later stages, the earlier stress on accommodation and the later stress on assimilation come into equilibrium, attaining the reciprocity and balance of fully operational thought. Assimilation in play has allowed the child greatly to improve its powers of abstraction in space and time; that is, to imagine objects far away in both of these dimensions (see also Vygotsky 1978: 92–104).

In a more limited sense, Piaget, like Hegel, is attempting to transform Kantian ontology into a dialectical movement. It is only through a process of dynamic interaction that consciousness is achieved as a sense of self and other. This 'other' is, however, always understood as a projection equivalent to the stage of development of the subject, which progresses through an epigenetic sequence of increasing sophistication and abstraction. For both Piaget and Hegel, the initial stages are highly egocentric, equivalent to the development of mind, but in the later stages the subject is increasingly confronted by the social world in which rules are imposed from the outside. Piaget's work also exhibits a parallel with Marx's concept of praxis, in his insistence that all development is derived form practical interaction with the material world, in which we live, and with which we are held in tension. There are also parallels with (and differences from) anthropological structuralism (Piaget 1971b; Turner 1973). The final outcome of the stages of development outlined by Piaget is also utopian, in so far as he links formal operational thought with the structure of the 'real' world. Like absolute knowledge, operational thought is conceived of as representing the final balance between the processes of externalization (assimilation as projection) and embodiment (accommodation as introjection), which have been held in asymmetrical relations in all previous stages. There are also parallel assumptions concerning the rationality of the actual, which underlies an essential teleology, providing the context within which this developmental process occurs.

As an alternative perspective on infant development, Melanie Klein's article 'Notes on some Schizoid Mechanisms' (1975: 1–24), provides a rather more sophisticated analysis of actual mechanisms which may be involved in ontogenesis, revealing a more complex cycle of interaction between subject and object, which does not presuppose an entirely positive sequence of development. Klein's work developed through several stages, and the article considered here is representative of her later work (Greenberg and Mitchell 1983: 119–50).

Klein's model may be introduced in her own words:

> I have often expressed my view that object-relations exist from the beginning of life, the first object being the mother's breast which to the child becomes split into a good (gratifying) and bad (frustrating) breast; this splitting results in the severance of love and hate. I have further suggested that the relation to the first object implies its introjection and projection, and thus from the beginning object-relations are moulded by an interaction between introjection and projection, between internal and external objects and situations. These processes participate in the building up of the ego and super-ego and prepare the ground for the onset of the Oedipus complex in the second half of the first year (1975: 2).

The crucial terms for an understanding of the development of the infant's sense of the self and its relationship with the outside world are projection, introjection and projective identification (see also Klein 1975: 141–75). These are not to be understood as a simple cycle of something being externalized as object, recognized as such, and then embodied, but rather as a complex series of strategies which may include splitting and inversion. They are, however, based around a concept of object relations which asserts that the external forms which are the subject of these mechanisms are always to be understood also as projections. The infant's orientation is not towards a 'real' external world, but its own internal projection, through which that world is constructed. This means that the infant's cognitive and emotional response to the object (which is usually a person) is one of interiorization. Both the ideal good and the ideal bad objects are understood, not as a something external to the subject, but as inseparable from an emerging sense of the world in which such a division is as yet unperceived.

The sequence begins (as with Hegel) with the establishment of the first object relation, which is therefore the first stage towards eventual self-consciousnesses. The object concerned, or, as it may be termed in relation to the mother, the part-object, is the breast. The infant is held to be beset by anxiety which is believed to be related both to the notion of the death instinct, and to its confrontation with the complexity and contradictory nature of its environment. This anxiety is primarily associated with the infant's ambivalent perception of the breast, which is the major source of satisfaction and of benign feelings, but, because it is not always available when desired, it is also the major source of frustration. At this stage, the infant cannot cope with the contradiction implied by the fact that two opposing feelings are aroused by the same object. This first object is therefore not a whole, coherent form, but is split between two forces which the infant tends to see as uncomplicated ideals: one wholly good object and one wholly bad object. The wholly good object may become a focal point around which the emergent ego can form, while in reaction to the wholly bad object, the infant develops a set of strong persecutory feelings.

This stage, in which the infant is concerned only with part-objects such as the breast, is called the 'Paranoid-Schizoid Position'. For Klein, it is the defensive mechanisms the child develops in response to its sense of anxiety which form the basic building blocks of ego development. In such circumstances, the infant may feel hatred, love or fear; but it will understand these as feelings assigned to an external form, which may be introjected. This kind of splitting is a mechanism which is actively pursued by the primitive ego. Thus the goodness which is associated with the good breast may be preserved and protected by being introjected, to appear as an attribute of self; but if the infant's anxiety is aroused by its own feelings of frustration and hatred, the same good object may be projected outwards in order to protect it from the overwhelming badness which the infant feels to be within itself.

The complexity of these relations, and the manner in which they might be used as a model of dynamic mechanisms to extend the concept of objectification from a simple dialectical cycle, is evident in Klein's discussion of infantile hallucinatory gratification. One aspect of the infant's early mentality is its belief in its own omnipotence, which may lead towards an attempt simply to deny the existence of the bad object, thus safeguarding the presence of the good object, and projecting both as idealized forms. Since, however, this is an object relation – that is, since that bad object is itself a part of the ego – this denial is to some extent also a denial of a part of the ego. The basic mechanisms which utilize splitting are therefore always to be understood as a division in the subject as well as the object.

Klein suggests that 'The process of splitting off parts of the self and projecting them into objects are thus of vital importance for normal as well as for abnormal object relations. The effect of introjection on object relations is equally important. The introjection of the good object, first of all the mother's breast, is a precondition for normal development' (Klein 1975: 9). The strategies of splitting are essential for the infant's attempt to deal with the genuine contradictions it encounters in struggling to form some image of itself and the part-objects it confronts. The pathological connotations of the term paranoid-schizoid are more appropriate to the reappearance of certain of these strategies later in life, when they become overextended from their normal place, and therefore develop as aspects of rupture, as when an adult attempts to gain power and control over another person as a substitute for the development of self-discipline.

Later, when the infant becomes capable of relating to whole objects, such as the mother instead of just the breast, it develops more integrative mechanisms in terms of what is called the depressive position. In the depressive postion, the infant can no longer rely on seeing the good and bad objects as entirely separate, but has to recognize their simultaneous presence in the form of the mother as whole object. This results in a more integrative ego dealing with a more integrative object. Integrative does not, however, mean cohesive; rather, the new position leads to still more sophisticated forms of internal and external contradiction and relationships, exhibited in part through more developed emotions, such as guilt and mourning, as the infant deals with the contradictory nature of the mother.

For Klein, the equivalent of the central place of symbolism in Piagetian analysis is the concept of phantasy, which is the form taken by all the mechanisms so far described. The initial model for this work may be Freud's concept of the super-ego, which is the interiorized form taken by parental authority. What is implied by the notion of the super-ego is that the child may react less to the actual external forms of its parents, and more to its own projection of them, interiorized as its moral order. Klein's theories of projection and introjection greatly extend this model. The forms taken in projection are often personifications – that is, sensations such as envy, love and hatred understood through an anthropomorphic objectification. This constructivist notion of phantasy is understood by Klein as the primary basis for all symbolic processes, whereas for later object-relations theorists it becomes a kind of false consciousness, or misapprehension of the real world. These processes provide the foundations for the ego, and thus become highly integral and largely intractable. As the sense of self, they provide the basic attitudes and perspectives which are taken for granted in relations with the external world, by virtue of the extent to which they are models into which that world must be assimilated. The parallel with Bourdieu's notion of habitus (see below) may be noted.

Again, there are elements of Klein's work which may be aligned with ideas explored in the previous chapters. Klein provides perhaps the least teleological analysis of the development of a subject, and her examples of adult psychosis may be linked to Hegel's, and especially Marx's, models of rupture, since they appear to result from the subject's belief in the alien nature of some fragmented aspects of the self it has become unable to sublate. Klein's work rests upon a moral and normative order which can either, as in the work of other object-relations theorists, become associated with a particular status quo in terms of family structure and roles, or else, if rechannelled, be used for a radical critique of these same institutions (e.g. Frosh 1987). The most interesting element in this analysis is, however, the complex nature of the mechanisms themselves, whose twists and cycles are able to capture a sense of dynamic interaction in a manner which may escape that vulgarized version of the dialectic which is commonly used to represent processes of this kind.

Play

The implications of these general approaches to ontogenesis for the nature of the artefact become clearer when they are directed at a specific problem, the nature of play. For Piaget, the activity of play represents a major advance in the ability of the child to control its own evironment and engage in a variety of strategies. To illustrate this point, Piaget uses the following examples: the creation of imagined characters to provide a sympathetic audience for a child's actions or speech; catharsis, as when a doll is allowed to ride a machine which a child fears; and compensatory combinations, as when a child goes through the motions of pretend washing up when forbidden access to the real thing by its parent. The manipulation of this internal world may provide a safe basis for trying out combinations and ideas prior to, and sometimes instead of, attempting them in the real world. It is also an essential aspect of the development of the internal world of thought.

Compared with the majority of recent social theorists, Piaget is unusual in de-emphasizing the role of language in the development of symbolism. Indeed, for many other writers the two are seen as virtually synonymous. Piaget, however, asserts in the introduction to his work that 'We shall rather show that the acquisition of language is itself subordinated to the workings of a symbolic function which can be seen in the development of imitation and play as well as in that of verbal mechanisms' (1962: 1–2; see Vygotsky 1978 for a contrary view). One of the first uses of language is merely as a subordinate subject for play. Piaget attempts to map the increasing capacity for abstraction implied by the symbolic function, showing that in this development, language, which depends on an entirely conventional relationship between sign and signified, is bound to come at a relatively late stage. Play with objects, which retain a physical similarity between sign and signified, or where some concrete form may be used to represent the distant other, then becomes an essential prerequisite for the development of the symbolic faculty found in language. It is only after the child has interacted with the external world and its construction at a sufficiently sophisticated level that language as abstract reference becomes feasible. By then, however, the semiotic function of language is already established. Later Piagetian writers, such as Furth, have shown through their work with the deaf how inessential language is to the development of intelligence (Furth 1969: 119–20).

Klein's emphasis on play develops from more pragmatic concerns. The use of toys is central to Klein's major methodological addition to the psychoanalytical tradition of pyschotherapeutic analysis: that is, her 'play technique' (Klein 1975: 122–40; Segal 1979: 35–44). This technique arose from the inability of a child to perform the 'rituals' of the adult psychoanalytical tradition in couch-based sessions of verbal exposition. Instead, Klein supplied the child with a variety of material forms such as human figures of various sizes, plasticine and other malleable substances, and attempted to interpret its actions in relation to them. Some of the interpretations she provides, especially the emphasis on overt sexual imagery, may strike the reader who does not belong to the psychoanalytical tradition as quite unconvincing, but even if the specifics of her analysis are rejected, what emerges clearly is the centrality of play to the infant's projective processes; that is, the use of play as enactment.

Klein is not the only psychoanalyst to have commented upon the place of material objects in play. Freud's example of the *fort-da* game in which the child pretends to lose and find something as an enactment within a domain it can control, of its sense of separation from, and the return of the mother, provides a classic case of the problems of how to interpret vicarious activity. (Freud 1984: 283–7). Of particular significance is the account by Winnicott (1971) of the role of the 'smelly blanket' in the development of the self. The smelly blanket is that particular, usually soiled, object from which the child hates to part. Winnicott observed that such 'transitional objects' were important, precisely because they may appear to the infant as not fully part of the external world, and therefore not entirely separate from the child's own body.

While studies such as those of Klein, Winnicott, Piaget and Vygotsky have resulted in elegant explanations of the place of play with material objects in child development, there is a common inference that this becomes relatively redundant in later life. However, to interpret play as merely a stage towards, for example, the more satisfactory situation of pure verbal expression while lying on a couch, would be unfortunate. If language is seen as increasingly taking the place of explicit negotiation, communication and conscious thought, there is the possibility that, simultaneously, material objects become increasingly important in the formation of the unconscious, a possibility raised by Freud (though only briefly) in relation to repressive mechanisms (e.g. 1984: 206–8). This provides a link with the more general tradition developed from Freud, which emphasizes the unconscious as an alternative site for the study of the contradictory nature of the individual (and social) body, especially in its relations with the external world seen as a 'reality principle'. This ambiguous position of the object, between self and the outside, and its relationship to the unconscious, will be further explored below.

Objects and Language

In contrast to the study of objects, the study of language is surely one of the most flourishing of all academic pursuits, a major success story in the social sciences. One result of this has been the pervasive influence of linguistic methodology upon such studies of objects as have developed in recent decades; and while the rise of semiotics in the 1960s was advantages in that it provided for the extension of linguistic research into other domains, any of which could be treated as a semiotic system (e.g. Eco 1976: 9–14), this extension took place at the expense of subordinating the object qualities of things to their word-like properties. Major influences were the linguistic studies of Saussure (e.g. Humphrey 1971) and Chomsky (e.g. Faris 1972; Krause 1978). In this literature, questions have been raised around a whole host of categories, relating to how far objects signify, symbolize, connote, denote, realize, constitute, reflect, embody and perhaps also objectify. There have been fierce debates over the differences between objects as sign and as symbol, and over degrees of iconicity, most of which can be reduced to levels of abstraction involved in the process by which objects become vehicles of meaning (see Lyons 1977 for survey).

Dominating such studies has been a tendency to perceive objects as being reflective in a relatively passive sense. As noted in chapter 4, social anthropology has tended to privilege society and social structure as prior phenomena which posses a certain profound reality, and in this tradition patterns located in objects might be held to reflect back to some social division or model from which they derive their source and significance. The concept of objectification provides the basis for examining such an assumption, and any critique of the notion of society as the privileged signified over culture may be extended to consider the nature of the sign in general. On these grounds (but not on others), the implications of objectification have much in common with a whole series of critical writings which argue that representation or symbolism, as a relation between signifier and signified, tends to promote the unproblematic assertion of the signified (for example, the modern conception of the self) rather than investigating the mechanisms by which these are constructed in the symbolic process itself (e.g. Coward and Ellis 1977: 122–52). A further example is the critique by Baudrillard of utility as privileged signified, which was noted in chapter 3. Any simple notion of signification as reflection trends towards a subject–object dualism which fails to acknowledge the process underlying their mutual construction.

Two problems emerge from this literature: first, the absence of any consideration of the specificity of the object; and secondly, the relatively simplistic form of reference which tends to be used in object analysis. In order to direct the discussion towards the particularity of the artefact form, rather than the problem of the mainly linguisitc sign, artefacts need to be explicitly distinguished from language. There have been very few attempts systematically to contrast their different properties. The only cases I have encountered come from discussions of aesthetics, although that by Langer (1942) is dominated by the image of the painting, while those by Colquhoun (1981) and Scruton (1979: 158–78) are based on the example of architecture. Langer represents the distinction as one between 'discursive' and 'presentational' forms. Language and thought are discursive processes from which a series of independent component parts derive their overall meaning through sequential articulation. The rules of grammar are intended to anlayse the structure underlying this discursive order. A presentational form such as a picture, on the other hand, has no natural divisions; one could not take, for example, the division between light and shade as independently meaningful. In assimilating a presentational form we have to take it in all at once, rather than sequentially, and there is nothing equivalent to grammatical structure underlying it (1942: 90–3).

Langer discusses in detail some of the implications of these differences, focusing upon their capacity for expression. She sees presentational symbolism as the major vehicle of objectifying feelings, and argues that these are thereby under-represented in our philosophies (1967: 101–2). A limitation of her analysis, deriving from its emphasis on aesthetics, and found also in some of the recent discussions of media and advertising, is a tendency to exaggerate the unique properties of the individual object, as against the type-token nature of words which almost always refer back to some generic category. Art and unique objects are, however, only a minute proportion of the material world, and our ability to discriminate through perception is as pronounced for the everyday observation of fashion and cosmetics as in any appreciation of fine art. In most material culture, the individual object is as much a type-token of the larger group of identical handbags, armchairs, spears or canoes as is the case with words, and, even when held as individual property, may thereby mark the relation of object and owner to the set of items it represents.

Scruton's (1979) critique concentrates on the claims of semiotics. He argues that the structures found in architectural rules should not be credited either with direct semiotic import, or, necessarily, with propositional content. Architecture also differs from language in its strict observation of its own rules and conventions, and in its sense of detail. The analogy with syntax or grammar is therefore rejected. Rustin (1985) notes that Scruton places undue emphasis on the referential approach to language in semiotics, ignoring the equally powerful structuralist component (see Sperber 1975 for a parallel comment on anthropology). Colquhoun (1981: 130) is also concerned to expose the limitations of semiotic studies of objects based on Saussure, but in this case mainly with respect to their synchronicity, attempting to characterize several differences of objects from language in the way in which architectural styles change. For example, in language change occurs only in one part of the system at a time, while in aesthetics whole styles may alter, as in the transition from Gothic to Classical architecture. Colquhoun also notes the impossibility of abstracting some 'arbitrary' meaning outside of the spatial and functional context within which the materials of buildings operate, underlining particular differences such as the realiance of architecture upon self-referential and 'traditional' modes for its meaning; in other words, its historicism.

Less remarked on are the inadequacies and crudity of language when faced with objects in everyday interaction. This point is easily illustrated through a simple reflective exercise. Imagine for a moment attempting to describe in detail the difference in shape between a milk bottle and a sherry bottle, or the taste of cod as against haddock, or the design of some wallpaper. Clearly, compared with our ability to make fine discriminations of perceptual qualities and immediately to recognize and discriminate amidst a profusion of ordinary objects, linguistic description may appear slow and clumsy. This simple observation is crucial to the argument of this chapter, as it allows us to question ingrained assumptions concerning the superiority and greater significance of language over other forms of expression.

Another difficulty arises when trying to assess how far different media may be taken as propositional. That this cannot be assumed of language, which appears to serve just such a purpose, has been illustrated very clearly by the linguist Lehrer in an analysis of the language used in the description of wines. Through her experiments it became evident that, despite the extensive elaboration of wine descriptors and the beliefs of the participants, neither lay persons nor experts were actually communicating knowledge about wines to their fellows in conversation, such that the wine referred to could be recognized from linguistic description alone (Lehrer 1983). By contrast, many studies of objects such as buildings, which discuss the links between architectural form and a set of ideals such as scholasticism or imperialism, indicate the degree to which such objects are significant as propositional forms, even as to the nature of the world (e.g. Panofsky 1957; King ed. 1980). It appears, then, that although the object has different qualities from language it may be equally impressive in the areas of expression and communication in which language is most esteemed. In the next section, however, the emphasis will be on qualities of the object which language cannot share.

The Artefact *Per Se*

An analysis of the artefact must begin with its most obvious characteristic, which is that it exists as a physically concrete form ependent of any individual's mental image of it. This factor may provide the key to understanding its power and significance in cultural construction. The importance of this physicality of the artefact derives from its ability thereby to act as a bridge, not only between the mental and physical worlds, but also, more unexpectedly, between consciousness and the unconscious.

The question of the place of objects in the formation of mental imagery may be referred back to the discussion of play. It is clear that during a certain stage in the child's development, artefacts become its principal means of articulating feelings and desires. The linguistic mechanism is a more sophisticated means of articulation which requires the complete break between sign and signified essential to the development of the arbitrary basis of pure linguistic symbolism. Objects, however, by virtue of their concrete nature, can never possess that entirely arbitrary and abstract capability. While perception of objects may not be prior to those mental apparati which absorb them (a version of the Kantian categories), it does act as a firm physical constraint upon them.

It appears that play begins during the period when the separation between consciousness and unconsciousness is becoming more deeply dichotomized, and that, following the development of language, objects never again have such a prominent place in our articulation or self-expression. This feature of child development has echoes also in social development, where there is an analogy with the role of objects in social reproduction before the acquisition of writing skills; at this stage objects as authentic objectifications of the ancestors were, along with oral tradition, the major means of ensuring the continuity of social reproduction (Weiner 1985).

These accounts may therefore imply that, as language strengthens its hold on consciousness and, through writing, on the explicit world of knowledge, objects may retain their place in the ordering of the unconscious world. Consciousness appears to be almost wholly dominated by language as the medium of thought and expression, so that the entire surface of cognitive processes and voluntary responses appears to be channeled through language. It is to this domain that we conventionally ascribe our image of self and of importance, identifying strongly with our controlled ability to articulate what appears to us to be the content of our own will. Contrary to approaches influenced by Lacan, there seems little reason to suppose that the unconscious is structured largely in relation to language or some other grammatical form, since in the intellectual representation of the external world it is possible to account for symbolic processes through a variety of other cognitive mechanisms (e.g. Sperber 1975; 1979).

Most of the major advances in the social sciences over the last two centuries, including the work of Freud and Marx, should lead us to be suspicious of any equation of importance with surface, suggesting that there are other forces both historical and unconscious which underlie this arena of language and linguistically articulated intent. We have some knowledge of these processes in cases such as proxemics, where our spatial orientation to objects may be observed as both cultural and normative (Hall 1966). In general, however, it is only the massive gulf between perceptual ability and linguistic competence of conscious articulation which provides evidence in day to day experience of the power of an unconscious oriented towards objects rather than language; but this alone implies that the object world holds great significance. This is not to deny the vital role played by language in naturalizing cultural differences such as gender roles, but rather to assert that artefacts may be still more powerful mechanisms in this process.

This relationship between object and unconscious is by no means obvious. Indeed, the very concrete physicality of objects might lead us to expect quite the opposite conclusion, which is that it is language which organizes the deep unconscious, while objects as visible images are a relatively superficial phenomenon. If, however, the social properties of objects are not as 'evident' as they are visible, this very factor may actually be, in part, responsible for our inability to appreciate the significance of the object. This, in turn, might account for our difficulty in dealing with objects through academic studies dominated by language. Rather as with other areas fundamental to the operation of the unconscious, artefacts may resist conscious articulation and in a sense be embarrassed by language.

This argument may be exemplified by considering one of the mechanisms through which we deal with the everyday world. It was suggested earlier that our image of the artefact is constantly dominated, not only by linguistic analogies, but also by the concept of art and the uniqueness of the object of art. One of the very few art historians to have moved away from the unique art object to consider more mundane phenomena is Gombrich, whose book, *The Sense of Order* (1979) attempts to make generalizations about the nature of design, as opposed to art. In distinguishing between these two, Gombrich uses the picture frame as an example of design. This is a felicitous choice, since it serves the dual purpose of examining design at the same time as providing a basis for a definition of art, from which it is distinguished. Following Kant, many aesthetic theories emphasize the particular manner or attitude of regarding the object of art; for example, the way a work of art commands our concentration and consideration, producing an abstracted and contemplative gaze. By contrast, the definition of a good frame is almost exactly the opposite; it should be immediatley absorbed without any period of consideration and, rather than being the focus of attention in itself, should direct our attention to the object within it. In short, the frame enhances, but it is not itself, the subject of attention. What is crucial to this argument, if extended a little beyond Gombrich's own assessment, is that the frame's anonymous and modest presence belies its significance for the appreciation of the work of art. It might be suggested that it is only through the presence of the frame that we recognize the work of art for what it is, perceiving it and responding to it in the appropriate way. In short, it is the frame rather than the picture which establishes the mode of appreciation we know as art. Placed in another context, such as the billboard, the work of art might well fail to attract either attention or interest. Where the conventional wooden frame is inappropriate, as in many forms of modern art, the gallery itself provides the larger frame which is an index of the nature of its contents; or, at a still more abstract though obviously more explicit level this function is performed by the category art itself.

In this intance, by establishing a relationship of immediacy with our unconscious, one object is able to control the nature of our consciousness, making it appropriate to the context within which that object is working. This principle proves to have general validity. There have emerged at different times a number of theories of social pyschology or sociology which provide versions of what Schultz (1970: 245–62) termed multiple realities. Goffman's version, presented in his book *Frame Analysis* (1975), most directly extends the example used by Gombrich (see also Giddens 1984: 73–92 for a parallel case using discursive form). Goffman's emphasis is upon a wide range of cues which tell us what kind of activity or behaviour we are engaged in. Quite often these are object cues, such as the theatre or church, which signify more general catagories such as drama or religion, thereby providing an appropriate setting for particular attitudes and kinds of behaviour. As in these two examples, the frame may occasionally be conspicuous and possibly highly ornate, but, more commonly in everyday living, objects as frames play on inconspicuous and normative cultural role. Even when an object such as a picture frame or set of clothes is highly ornate and may be the topic of conversation, it is usually intended to pall before the glory of that which it encloses: the work of art or the person.

The humility of the common object is especially clear in an area of mass material culture such as furnishing. While it is possible to draw attention to these object frames as forms of display, more commonly they are the appropriate background for living. What is important is that they should not draw our attention towards them by appearing in some way wrong, inappropriate or misconceived. More appropriate terms are warm, friendly, modern or stylish, and if our attention should focus upon the pattern or texture of the wallpaper or upholstery, this should always be in order to comment on the taste of the selector. In modern linguistics, we are often told of our remarkable ability to construct meaningful sentences which we have never previously heard; yet this is surely matched by our ability to absorb the social implications of an array of furnishing consisting of a combination which is not only almost certainly in some degree unique, but some of whose basic elements may also be new to us. It is clear that this impression made upon us is no less significant in determining our conception of the individuals concerned than the articulate self-expression represented by the conversation we may be engaged in within this setting.

This example illustrates one of the many ways in which unconscious, non-linguistic processes may act to control conscious and linguistic articulation. This is not to deny some level of autonomy to the latter, but to reject assertions of its virtual total autonomy. Even in linguistics, the recent rise of pragmatics as opposed to syntax and semantics as the basis for understanding the nature of meaning (e.g. Sperber and Wilson 1985) should suggest that, while the contextual world of objects may be the last and most overlooked component of the mechanisms of social interaction, it may very well prove, when finally excavated from its embedded relationship to the unconscious, to be the most significant factor of all.

Few anthropologists have focused specifically upon the place of the object in social reproduction. Most tend to privilege language and the interview as media of expression. In the crudest forms, the informant is reduced to that which he or she says, and the idea of the anthropologist going beyond or against that particular limited form of expression is considered suspicious, though this attitude is unusual. Exceptions to this bias towards language include a crude behaviourism still strongly asserted in some archaeological theories which reduce the artefact as cultural construction to merely part of the process by which an environment works its determinant force upon the human subject. Other exceptions are the highly objectivist forms of analysis such as structuralism, which tend towards the opposite extreme of a virtually autonomous logic of cultural forms.

One anthropologist who has been noted for attempting to retain a balance between objectivist and subjectivist analysis is Pierre Bourdieu. In his work as in the present study, there has been an attempt to mediate between the physical world of practices as a determinant material structure and constructivist analysis of the material world as inseparable from the cognitive means of its appropriation. A brief account of Bourdieu's notion of 'habitus' provides an example of how we might assimilate the apparent paradox of an external physical world which is nevertheless in a more immediate relationship with the unconscious than the world of articulate symbolism. It also allows us to consider directly the implications of the object as physical form which mediates between the subjective and objective worlds, and to do so within an anthropological mode sensitive to the specificity of culture. This may facilitate a return from the ahistorical concerns of psychology and linguistics, where analysis of the object threatens to remain fetishistic, to the world of social action where such analysis is reintegrated into cultural studies.

In his key work on this subject (1977), Bourdieu begins with a critical account of that anthropological structuralism which provides him with one of his main methodological tools. Structuralism may be employed to excavate the principles of classification and order which unite what on the surface appear as highly disparate domains, so that for a particular society food preparation, kinship and myth may be revealed as transformations of each other. The problem with this 'high' structuralism is that it tends to offer only an extremely objectivist account of social action, in which the human actor is merely a vehicle for the autonomous working of certain ordering principles. When used to account for anthropological observation, it may become a series of mechanical and inflexible models.

Bourdieu wished to retain what we have learnt from structural analysis, and yet to mitigate its objectivist implications by emphasizing that such structures produce not rules but dispositions, and underlie not determinacy but strategy. Structuralism may help us to understand the construction of the subject as cultural being, but must then allow for the action of that self-referential subject upon history. Bourdieu, by virtue of his many anthropological examples, provides one of the most satisfactory resolutions of this age-old conflict between being made in history and creating history. This positive concept of strategy is also very different from the more common nihilistic rendering of the same problem (e.g. by Sartre 1976). The account of habitus given below is, however, greatly traduced by summary.

The 'habitus' is that structured set of classificatory schema which is inculcated in the child as its sense of cultural propriety and normative order. As excavated by structuralism, the underlying order found, for example, in house layout, exchange relations or morality, may be reducible to certain basic patterns or transformations. By absorbing these, the subject is then in turn able to impose them upon some new domain not previously encountered, and thereby immediately to assimilate this into its particular cultural order. These closely woven principles are specific to certain groups – for example, gender or class – and lead also to a sense of identity between those who share habitus. This sense of order is a given, fundamental, rather than negotiated, disposition.

Habitus is learnt through interactive practices, as the acts of living within a world which is composed of this same order are continually reinforced in different domains. In fact, this is a process of familiarity rather than learning. Since these domains are physical, they act to provide the agent with objective probabilities producing subjective (rather than individual, Bourdieu 1977: 86–7) aspirations which are usually restricted to aims the agent has some prospect of accomplishing (Bourdieu 1977: 77). It is these same practical taxonomies which serve to exemplify the principles of cultural order. In certain societies, formal education may attempt to make explicit and controlled some of these processes of learning, and it is no coincidence that Bourdieu is otherwise known as a writer on the French educational system (e.g. Bourdieu and Passeron 1977; 1979). In both cases, he explores the hierarchies within and between these classification systems, and their importance for an understanding of ideology and power. It will be clear that for this approach an artefact which already embodies a categorization process is clearly distinguished from a natural object which does not.

Bourdieu's concept of habitus starts as constructivist rather than behaviourist, with the external environment being differentially absorbed and interpreted from the perspective of the subject as a member of a social group. It thereby links socialization processes, by which a new generation is culturally incorporated, with the longer term movements of history and the process by which culture itself is reproduced, thereby developing as a dynamic praxis, or an objectification which avoids determinism. The habitus is viewed as a structured set of dispositions which provides a basis for the enactment of strategy according to interest, perspective and power. As with language, the generative order does not dictate the result of its use. Our ability to 'read' objects for their social appropriateness and to impose upon any series of new forms that order which would make them culturally acceptable does not in any respect lessen the place of strategy, or the possibility of intent; both, however, are accomplished within objective conditions of which we have an underlying experience, even if we choose to deny them in formulating strategy.

In common with Langer, Bourdieu stresses the relationship of this object world to feelings rather than language; it is those expressions of disgust, distaste and discomfort which best express our sense of something being 'wrong'. It is a world in which the grimace is often more eloquent than the phrase. Although concerned to embed his ideas in practices Bourdieu is not himself especially concerned with defining the role of the artefact, but it is clear how his work contributes to such a task. His examples taken from fieldwork amongst the Kabylia of Algeria, using house form, motor-habit and calenders, provide abundant further evidence for this relationship between the order of artefacts and the unconscious absorption and creation of cultural form. He constantly affirms the effectiveness of order embodied in details such as dress, body movement and manners, and argues that it is a function of the mundane artefact almost always to be regarded as an example of mere 'trivia' unworthy of systematic academic study.

At this point it is possible to return to the most evident implication of the physical nature of the artefact as symbol without appearing to invite a crude behaviourist concept of materialism. Clearly, an object may always signify its own material possibilities and constraints and therby the more general world of material practices. What is of importance is certainly not the idea of physicality as some 'ultimate constraint' or final determining factor, but rather the manner in which everyday objects continually assert their presence as simultaneously material force and symbol. Our images of the house are continually modified by the actual houses we encounter, and our perceptions of their size, shape, order and limitations; and the effect of this is most pronounced when we engage in attempts to alter, extend, or discover pleasure in some physical aspect of this materiality which may resist these constraints. The use of artefact as symbol does not in any way detract from its significance as tool, material worked, or environment experienced. Material culture studies derive their importance from this continual simultaneity between the artefact as the form of natural materials whose nature we continually experience through practices, and also as the form through which we continually experience the very particular nature of our cultural order. This is most especially the case in industrial society; in London, for example, there is no 'natural' environment to be opposed to the socially constructed form. In view of this it is reasonable to conclude that all experience of physical force is mediated by its prior constitution as a cultural category.

Using the example of the work of Bourdieu, it has been argued that, although the object may be closely associated with the most fundamental and hidden aspects of socialization, this does not mean that it must be analysed only by determinant, rule-based objectivist procedures, since as an instrument of social strategy it retains a high degree of flexibility. This flexibility is suggestive of certain properties of the artefact as physical form. Recent social theory has emphasized the variety of interpretations to which texts may be subject, with linguistic texts, as usual, providing the dominant models. Yet, clearly, any account of the death of the author as arbiter of the final 'meaning' of a given text (Barthes 1977; Foucault 1977a), is potentially matched by the important, though much less addressed, question of the transcendence of the industrial designer, who, as Forty (1986) has shown, should never have been ascribed the autonomy often assumed. The problem of interpretation is closely linked to the place of the artefact in intersubjective order. In the examples discussed in the previous chapters, such as the work of Munn, it was clear that the individual is already closely oriented towards a social order by external forms such as the landscape, in which conceptions of the person and of society are literally grounded. This idea can now be refined through Bourdieu's concept of habitus, in which the social group's perspective upon some form is always predicated upon the historical construction of its dispostions, interaction being a conjuncture which cannot be reduced merely to its immediate context (Bourdieu 1977: 81). The artefact plays an important role here, because once again its physical and external presence belies its actual flexibility as symbol.

Symbolism, which is always a relationship of evocation, is held in most studies to be a highly variable process which is dependent upon the social positioning of the interpreter and the context of interpretation. This is fairly obvious with a relatively abstract form such as a moral code. We are used to the idea that a statement of belief or propriety is continually open to challenge, and that debates concerning its correct interpretation are never fully resolvable. The artefact, on the other hand, tends to imply a certain innocence of facticity; it seems to offer the clarity of realism, an assertion of certainty against the buffeting of debate, an end or resting point which resolves the disorder of uncertain perspectives. All this is, of course, quite illusory; the object is just as likely as the word, if not more so, to evoke variable responses and invite a variety of interpretations. In fact, language, through abstraction, is a much more efficient form of communication and possesses much more control over its interpretation, and it is rather that this difference in evocation is less likely to be evident in artefactual symbolism than in linguistic symbolism.

This is of major importance. In so far as differences in social position, such as class and gender, lead to different perspectives, that which is evoked by the objects in society will also be different. This problem, which, where conflicts of interest are involved, becomes one of ideology, need not lead to overt conflict, however, because the groups concerned may be quite unaware of the discrepancy. A male may not be aware of the possibility of a female's alternative reading of what an object constitutes or signifies; similarly, it may never occur to a member of a one social class that some revered object may be subject to a parodied and subversive interpretation by members of another. If two groups acquiesce in the representation of their perspective through the same array of objects, which for one group is acceptable because it is bright and cheerful, while for the other is acceptable because it enshrines a sense of good design, each may project its own perspective onto the other; in this case, the object permits the coexistence of two perspectives, rather than the dominance of either. The fact that objects may become the source of actual struggles over conflicting interests will be discussed in chapter 9 as part of the general problem of ideology.

To conclude, in order to examine an area which is rarely focused upon in itself, it has been necessary in this chapter artificially to abstract the object, considering it in rather universalistic terms, and in relation to a perhaps overdrawn dichotomy with language. In practice, of course, the object is usually a historical phenomenon, which confronts us as evidence for a larger, anterior cultural tradition within which we exist, and is inseparable from the linguistic mechanisms which are central to our knowledge of it. Nevertheless, it seems reasonable to assume that the specific nature of the object, and in particular its physical presence, will result in a tendency for it to act in certain distinctive ways, compared with other media of cultural expression.

It has been argued that the artefact may perhaps best be understood as playing a series of bridging roles. It does not lend itself to the earlier analysis of symbolism which identified distinct abstract signifiers and concrete signifieds, since it simultaneously operates at both levels. Instead, it has been suggested that the object tends towards presentational form, which cannot be broken up as though into grammatical sub-units, and as such it appears to have a particularly close relation to emotions, feelings and basic orientations to the world. The artefact may be used to promote fine distinctions through its relation to extremely sophisticated mechanisms of perceptual discrimination which tend to remain outside of consciousness. finally, its physical presence exemplifies the concept of praxis, in that this materiality is always an element in cultural transformation.

In relation to Bourdieu's concept of habitus, the artefact was noted as playing a pivotal role in social reproduction, where it forms part of a reconciliation of objectivist accounts exposing the mechanisms which create the subject in history with an interpretation of the social subject's role as active agent in the formulation of historical strategy. The artefact's affinity to the unconscious also allows it to play an important role in marking different forms of social reality, and allowing these and the perspectives arising from different social positions to exist concurrently without coming into overt conflict. In objectification, the artefact appears to be instrumental in linking these major processes of abstraction and specificity. Finally, these two characteristics of the artefact – its extreme visibility and its extreme invisibility – may also, through their relationship, in large measure account for our difficulty in appreciating the importance of material culture for social relations.

7

Artefacts in their Contexts

Introduction

Although in chapter 6 an attempt was made to investigate the nature of the artefact *per se*, even a cursory examination of artefacts as actually employed within different societies reveals the extreme diversity of uses and connotations among physically similar forms. Whatever properties are delineated as especially appropriate to material artefacts in general, these cannot be regarded as necessary attributes of an individual artefact when considered in any particular social context. Societies have an extraordinary capacity either to consider objects as having attributes which may not appear as evident to outsiders, or else altogether to ignore attributes which would have appeared to those same outsiders as being inextricably part of that object. In this respect, the study of the properties of objects in the social sciences is quite dissimilar to equivalent studies in physics or chemistry, where statements about these properties take the form of law-like propositions. An attempt to identify those social properties which pertain to objects as artefacts, for example, as opposed to the properties of words as discovered by linguists, or dreams as discovered by psychologists, can only be achieved through a balance between two procedures. On the one hand, it requires the transcendence of cultural relativism in order to discuss objects in terms of their general potential, but on the other hand it demands the recognition that these potential attributes need not necessarily be realized or acknowledged in any particular cultural context.

It was argued in chapter 6 that the physicality of artefacts makes them much harder than language to extricate from the particular social context in which they operate, and that for this reason they pose a particular problem for academic study. My intention in this chapter is not to construct a systematic model of the properties of material culture in society, but rather to investigate through a series of illustrations the interaction between material culture and certain contextual dimensions, emphasizing the implications of the materiality of the object as symbol.

There is at present no academic discipline which sees it as its specific project to examine the nature of artefacts as cultural forms. The physical properties of objects revealed in the natural sciences may well have an important bearing upon discussions of the technological constraints on manufacture and utility, but these studies do not differentiate, as a prime dichotomy, between the artefact and the natural substance, and indeed are largely concerned to reduce the former to the properties of the latter. More surprisingly, this distinction is equally absent in the discipline of psychology. Studies of cognition which seek to elucidate the nature of that cultural order which we might impose upon or recognize in the world may well be concerned with the classification of objects, but they generally fail to acknowledge, let alone address, the difference between artefacts such as cutlery which already incorporate categorization in their manufacturer, and objects such as trees which do not (e.g. Rosch 1978: 30–5). Consumer psychology attempts to relate sets of objects to groups of people as 'target' populations, but, whilst it deals entirely with artefacts, it does not address the question of their particular nature as concrete material culture. A similar failure to analyse the artefact *per se* has already been noted in philosophy.

The only branch of academic analysis which, by virtue of its title, might have been thought to represent a candidate for this specific area of study is that sub-section of anthropology known as material culture studies. Yet although this sub-discipline has from its origins been concerned with the nature of the artefactual world as an element of culture offering insights into that part of social behaviour which is oriented towards the creation and use of objects, the rather particular history of this series of studies has hitherto severely limited its application.

At that period of the nineteenth century when the discipline of anthropology was coming into being, material culture studies represented the very core of this emergent social science (e.g. Haddon 1895; Tylor 1881). Both to armchair academics, and, though museum displays, to the population as a whole, objects were representative of the peoples of distant cultures. They were closely integrated into the emerging central paradigm of social evolution, according to which the level of sophistication of these objects was held to symbolize the place of such peoples as a kind of fossil record of social development from the primitive to the civilized (Steadman 1979; Chapman 1985). This significatory potential of the object was seen as being affirmed by archaeology, which produced a sequence from the early stone age to the iron age and beyond, providing a temporal foundation for these assertions of social evolution (Lowrie 1937: 22). If evolutionary studies provided a vertical dimension within which objects could signify the development of societies, this was complemented by the growth of diffusionary studies in which the horizontal distribution of objects over the globe was thought to be further evidence for the movements of both peoples and ideas, for example, from origins in ancient Eygpt or Germany. These two dimensions provided the basis for the first coherent theories about the connections between the peoples of the world.

In the twentieth century, however, there was a revolt against the dominant paradigms of anthropology, and evolutionary and diffusionary theories were rejected in favour of direct participant observation, in which objects no longer mediated in the relationship between the anthropologist and the informant. The discipline became dominated by two new theoretical models: first a functionalist theory of synchronic adaptation, and later structuralism. Both of these rejected the notion of the primitive as used in the earlier studies, as well as the evolutionary concepts which had legitimized that notion. The very success of material culture studies in having been so firmly integrated into the older paradigm meant that such studies become invalidated by their own historical associations, and were no longer able to play a significant role in the new anthropology. The amount of research in material culture studies declined (e.g. Fenton 1974), and tended to become reduced to two of the peripheral areas of anthropological enquiry. These were either the study of technology integrated within a general study of human adaption to the environment, which presupposed a particularly immediate rela- tionship between society and the environment, or alternatively an anthropology of art which, by contrast, emphasized the greatest possible distance between people and their environment, in order to focus upon exotic and esoteric practices. The middle ground, within which lie most of the current concerns of social anthropology, was increasingly ignored, as far as consideration of the social use of objects is concerned.

The discipline within anthropology which maintained the closest relation to material culture studies was archaeology, which has always been highly dependent upon such studies, since its task of resurrecting ancient societies is based in large measure on the interpretation of the material remains excavated from those societies. During the course of the nineteenth century, archaeology moved in a quite different direction, becoming, like the earlier diffusionary theories, increasingly obsessed with objects as such, and treating them as having an independent behaviour in a manner which separated them from any social context and which amounted to a genuine fetishism of the artefact. A series of archaeological studies in the 1960s (e.g. Clarke 1968) proclaimed a science of the object based on systems theory and patterns of artefact change, or highly detailed examination of the properties of flints, bones and pottery. Only in the sub-discipline within archaeology called ethno-archaeology, where archaeologists worked in contemporary ethnographic situations in order to study the relationship between peoples and their material world, was it usually impossible to ignore the social basis of material culture (e.g. Gould ed. 1978; Gould and Schiffer eds 1981; Hodder 1982a; Kramer ed. 1979). Recently, however, there has been a reversion to analysis of pre-historic artefacts in terms of their contextual social relations, as semiotic and ideological representations, with respect both to users in the past and for us today (e.g. Hodder ed. 1982; Miller and Tilley eds 1984).

To conclude, the fact that there has been to date remarkably little progress towards an independent discipline of material culture is due, at least in part, to the particular history of that field within anthropology. Other reasons for this relative absence were discussed in chapter 6. In order to pursue the implications of the generalized account given there of the artefact as symbol, the following sections examine a set of particular domains. These are chosen somewhat arbitrarily, and, needless to say, others might have been included. In each case the intention will be to emphasize the artefact's constitutive character, rather than treating it as mere reflection of social relations, that is a 'human mirror'. In most cases a single example of the relationships between the object and a given contextual domain has been selected for illustrative purposes, although it will be obvious that there is a vast number of alternative relevant instances.

The Artefact as Manufactured Object

The factor which distinguishes the artefact from the natural object is that it is the product of human labour. Although structuralism, in its extension of the Kantian position, has constantly asserted the cultural nature of those natural phenomena which impinge upon us only through being assimilated by our own categorizing processes, these may still be differentiated from artefacts, within which such a system of categorization is an inherent attribute. In formulating the category 'artefact', some notion of intention is also usually attributed to their creation; for example, a gas cloud may emerge as an unpredicted by-product of a technological process, though this product of human labour is only marginally an artefact.

Since manufacture always has to be practised upon materials, its first implication is that it may show signs of the constraints these materials bring to the technological process (Gombrich 1979: 63–94). Some materials, such as stone or wood, are largely subtractive, in that there is a natural substance from which parts are taken away, through chipping, sawing and other means, to create the finished artefact; while others, such as cast metal or clay, are additive, in that a quantity is utilized in a plastic state which can take the shape of a template or mould. Any such artefact may seek either to proclaim or to hide the material used and the constraints the material has imposed upon the technological process: a mask may be thought to incorporate the spiritual properties of the wood from which it is taken; a group of people may refuse to purchase an item known to be of seal skin; a plastic may seek to copy a more traditional material; the gold from which an object is made may have far greater significance than the actual form into which it has been hammered.

In a society with a relatively unpronounced division of labour, it may be difficult to distinguish manufacture as a separate arena of social relations which are specifically signified by its products. As in the case of the construction of canoes for the Kula (Munn 1977), technology may be thoroughly embedded in cosmology, and even social theorists who would eschew a technological determinism, but wish to characterize societies through more mediated concepts such as 'modes of production', have often had to subordinate the organization of production to a host of other elements of social organization such as kinship and ritual (e.g. Godelier 1972; Hindless and Hirst 1975; Kahn and Llobera eds 1981).

An insight into the relationship which may be found between technology and cultural form in such societies is offered by the argument formulated by Franz Boas (1955) concerning the origins of primitive art (see also Gombrich 1979). Boas identified two major sources for this art: the drive towards representation and the tendency to create pattern. The latter, he suggested, stems from the basic motor-habits involved in simple technological processes which revolve around regular and repetitive movements, such as those of the hand in sewing, basketry, or weaving. These sequences may give rise to a kind of play, in which they are exaggerated, inverted or otherwise re-ordered in such a manner that a regular pattern or rhythm emerges in the finished product. The interplay between these sequences and the tendency either to see representational figures in pattern, or alternatively to repeat representational figures in such a way that they reduce to pattern, was held by Boas to be the foundation of art and design, providing the basic dimensions which united the diverse media of craft production, music, dance and poetry.

Using material from the Kwakiutl peoples of the north-west coast of America, Boas showed how the major stylistic features of their material culture, such as an extensive use of bilateral symmetry and the disintegration of animal representations into pattern, could be understood as emerging from the interplay of technology and constraint. For example, the problem of representing three-dimensional figures in two dimensions lent itself to the splitting of animal forms so that they faced out in both directions, joined by a centre line around the mouth and spine. In turn, these tended to become complex and ambiguous images such that, as anthropomorphized animals, they could represent the transformation of human and animal forms (Vastokas 1978), or through the focus upon the mouth could illustrate the principle of voracity according to which human killing and eating of animals ensured the cyclic reproduction of all life in the world (Walens 1981). Here, then, manufacture as technology involving materials with certain properties becomes an integral part of the emergence of culture incorporating the visual embodiment of the nature and legitimacy of a certain social order, which in turn forms part of an encompassing ontology (Goldman 1975: chapter nine).

With a more developed division of labour, and particularly with industrial production, the separation of the sphere of manufacture, as found, for example, in Marx's privileging of this particular domain, has tended to become more pronounced. An object may then become a conspicuous example of non-industrial production, such as the homespun *Khadi* cloth of India popularized by Gandhi as a symbol of Indian independence, and still a potent emblem for Indian political parties (Bayly 1986). The nineteenth-century arts and crafts movement developed by William Morris and others was also succesful in advertising the hand-crafted status of their products. This kind of 'natural' product gains its meaning entirely from its opposition to industrialization, and is thus always indirectly produced by industrialization. The contradictory nature of this relationship is illustrated by the experiences of a community of potters in Japan, who, through the equivalent of the arts and crafts movement, were held as exemplifying a natural, anonymous and traditional form of production. When publicized as such through a visit by the British potter Bernard Leach and Japanese enthusiasts, however, the potters were forced to adopt new forms of marketing and production in order to meet the demand for these symbols of their purity, whilst at the same time preserving, for the benefit of the tourists, the appearance of producing works of art untainted by industrialization (Moeran 1984). As is evident from the writing of Hegel, Marx and many later writers, technology itself, as the deliberate imposition of rational will upon the world, may become the foundation for the dominant ideologies of the industrialized world (e.g. Castoriadis 1984: 299–59).

These cases suggest that when manufacture as the signified of the object, becomes reified as having a separate and particular connotation it is not the actual process of manufacture which is of importance, but the ability of the object to stand for a particular form of production and its attendant social relations. The object has always had the ability to proclaim one technological origin while actually deriving from another. The *skeumorph*, in which, for example, a stone blade copies the style of a metal object, is a classic find in archaeological excavations of early bronze age sites. With the development of machinery, the mass produced object intended to disguise its origins and look like the product of hand labour has become well established. In many cases, this symbolism is part of a more general ability to proclaim or deny a distance from nature.

Although the artefact may stand for a particular form of production, it cannot be assumed that it will do so, or that the divisions which appear as significant from one perspective upon modern society will necessarily emerge as the major dimensions of differentiation in the object world. It might be thought, for example, that the major distinction between socialist and capitalist development, terms which are founded in contrasting philosophies of the proper relations of production, would be a prime subject for the symbolic capacity of the modern artefact. In practice, when making a purchase, it is very rare for us to note whether an object is made by a cooperative or a private factory, or in East or West Germany, and extraordinarily this division appears hardly, if at all, within the major symbolic dimensions of the contemporary world of commodities. We do not think in terms of capitalist shoes and socialist shoes. From this example, we can draw a conclusion of crucial importance for the analysis of material culture: divisions which may appear important in language and ideology may be absent from object differentiation, while distinctions within the domain of artefacts may constitute important divisions which would elsewhere be ignored or denied.

Artefacts and Function

In no domain is it as difficult as it is in the matter of function and utility to distinguish the actual place of artefacts in human practices from the particular legitimations and assumptions we have about them. In many societies, the classification and labelling of objects appears to indicate a close relationship between artefact and particular function, and the labels 'kitchen chair' or 'fryingpan' in Britain may be matched, for example, by an equivalent close relationship between pots and their labels in Nepal (Birmingham 1975). Function apears to play a key role in infant recognition and naming of objects (Miller and Johnson-Laird 1976: 229–35), and, in adulthood, continues to play an important, though highly flexible, role in the description of objects in daily life (Miller 1978). What is problematic about this is the common assumption that it is caused by, and in turn indicates, some relationship of efficiency between the object and its use, such that this is the prime reason for its particular form, being either the natural outcome of adaptation, or the product of deliberate design processes for industrial goods.

Although functional purpose must impose a certain constraint on the shape and form of an object, that constraint is generally a very loose one for everyday forms (though obviously not for machine parts). A moment's reflection upon the several hundred different shapes of glass bottle in an off licence, all of which serve essentially the same purpose of containing liquids, or upon the variety of clothing in the high street, or china in the store, indicates this high degree of variability. Even though the individual shopper will often find some functional justification for his or her particular choice, as being especially practical, other reasons, some of which will be analysed in later chapters, may be adduced, relating to social rather than functional considerations which may more convincingly account for the majority of purchases.

While for some this may be evident enough in the society of mass consumption, it has equally commonly been assumed that this degree of variability is an aberrant result of the wastage of modern capitalism, and that the 'pristine' subjects of social anthropology live in a far closer relationship with the given needs of their environment (e.g. Forde 1934). The vast arrays of artefacts to be found in ethnographic museums which serve as simple vessels or clothing are, however, eloquent evidence for the distance between form and function in non-industrial as well as industrial societies. In parts of Melanesia such as the Solomon Islands, for example, relatively homogeneous tropical forest may be the setting for an extreme variety of cultural forms, such as spears or armbands, as one moves across an island archipelago. Detailed observation of the hand-made containers used in a South Asian village reveals a wide variety of forms designed to serve identical purposes, and a very loose relationship between form and fitness for function (Miller 1985: 51–74).

Just as with manufacture, the artefact may be used to express not actual efficiency but an ideal of function. In modern practices, this ideal has been conceived of as a principle of utility, to be embodied in the creation of the artefactual world. With modernism, the strongest assertion of the value of utility is found in the assumption that aesthetics may be subordinated to function. The proper modernist artefact is always held to be aesthetically pleasing precisely to the degree to which it exemplifies the adage that form follows function (Benton and Benton 1975). However, the actual reproduction of modernist form over the last century and a half has revealed exactly the opposite tendency, since objects formed entirely on the basis of utility have proved singularly unattractive (which accounts for their general absence from commercial marketing). This has not in any way curtailed enthusiasm for the principle that good design is based upon utility among its acolytes in London's Design Centre or the Boilerhouse Project of the Victoria and Albert Museum, London, where beauty through ergonomics may still be an avowed aim.

Once again, this division does not accord with political affiliation; Baudrillard attacks Marx and Marxist assertions of natural utility with as much vehemence as contemporary critics attack modernist architecture as an elitist imposition of ideology upon the general public. This embodiment of utility and technological rationality in the object as modernist form may be a powerful example of the much more general tendency towards the legitimizing role being played by technological rationality in the modern world (e.g. Habermas 1970; Sahlins 1976a). In movements such as 'hi-tech', objects most clearly come to exhibit a principle of utility quite detached from any consideration of actual purpose, as the style is applied (as was streamlining in its day) indiscriminately to steam irons or armchairs. With hi-tech style, as with much of modernism, it is evident that the theoretical articulation of these principles is far less developed than their material expression. Indeed, hi-tech could be better understood as a set of principles distilled from a collection of material forms than as objects intended to embody prior principles.

The object form which has always been seen as most clearly exemplifying the utility principle is the tool. Tools, after all, extend the very possibility of humanity as productive agent, and thus make for obvious analogies with biological function. When understood as our 'extra-somatic means of adaption' they have become almost definitional of culture (White 1959). This notion of the instrumental object as an extension of being should not, however, be reduced to a relationship of efficiency, since an agriculturalist may wax more lyrical about a musical instrument than a plough, and the microcomputer's popularity may be greater among those who in common parlance 'waste time' in obsessive programming or games, than among those who use it as a practical means to some other end. It is the object's relationship to the social group which is crucial, rather than its ability to perform a transformation of nature under the sign of utility.

The artefact's capacity to separate itself from the immediacy of a relationship embodied in the concept of utility is most evident in the manner in which it is used for precisely the opposite function, that is, to separate the individual from productive activity. Although one means of detachment from the world is a spiritual asceticism based upon a lack of material possessions, more common has been the desire to accumulate luxuries and objects which themselves signify the lack of any need to engage directly in productive labour. The object's ornate and fragile form is an emblem of the leisure class which is constituted precisely by this distance (Veblen 1970). Civilization is most commonly defined not as greater efficiency in crop-growing and manufacture, but precisely as the preservation of distance from these activities.

Artefacts, the Self and Society

One of the limitations of anthropological investigations of the social meaning of artefacts is the tendency to Romanticize non-industrial societies as prior to objectification in the Marxist sense of rupture. The classic statement on this question with respect to the person was by Mauss (1979), who argued that the contemporary concept of the self is a relatively recent creation, strongly tied to the rise of various legalistic notions of the person in relation to property in ancient Rome and emerging in its modern form after certain developments in eighteenth-century German philosophy. Recent objectivist approaches in the social sciences and philosophy have attempted to equate all reference to the self with a particular and historical bourgeois self inextricably related to capitalism. Anthropologists, in turn, have attempted to argue that, for example, the transition from brideservice, in which labour is performed by the prospective groom, to bridewealth, where objects are given in exchange for the bride, marks a significant difference in the development of a phenomenon whereby objects may stand for human labour, with the implication that this is the first stage towards the conditions of property and alienation as we know them today (Strathern 1985). This theme, which relates the development of individualism and alienability specifically to *homo economicus*, has been a longstanding concern in philosophical and political anthropology (e.g. Dumont 1977).

Although we may find a particularly explicit conceptualization of the autonomous self in certain contemporary societies, this may be only an aspect of the more general separation and autonomy of concepts evident in modernist theory. While some capitalist societies may practise an extreme individualism, it is surely only a Romantic tendency to dichotomize which denies the possibility of this characteristic to all other societies. The specific objectification of a moral and juridical individual through the use of objects may be found in a wide range of societies, including those where kinship rather than the economy appears to be the dominant organizational principle.

The phenomenon of certain mundane objects becoming so firmly associated with an individual that they are understood as literal extensions of that individual's being was discussed in some detail by Levy-Bruhl (1966: 100–27). In many societies, the clothing, ornaments and tools belonging to an individual may be considered so integral to him or her that to touch or do harm to these inanimate objects is considered indistinguishable from taking the same action against the person. Such property is identical to the person and may stand for that person in his or her absence. It may well be burnt together with the corpse as an equal form of the physical detritus of death. The 'self' objectified in the object will be differentially constructed according to the cosmological context. Tambiah (1984) has recently described an example of the transformation from one form of embodiment to another in Thailand, where buddhist amulets objectifying the charisma of forest saints are exploited by certain individuals as a means of gaining material advantage in their business dealings in the city.

As was noted in chapter 4 with respect to recent work on the *hau*, by embodying ancestral links objects may be the basis of an individual's present social identity such that loss of the object would itself constitute a danger to the legitimacy and viability of the personage and the group he or she leads (Wiener 1985). At the other extreme, societies, may allow claims upon that which we consider inalienable. For example, in areas of the South Pacific it is not uncommon for parents to have to relinquish a new baby to admiring kin who have claimed it (Sahlins 1976b; Silk 1980). It is more useful to argue the variable nature of the relationship between the individual and society than to assume a linear evolution towards the autonomous self. Even between societies which may be subsumed under the label of late capitalism, such as the USA and Japan, there may be considerable differences in this regard (Abercrombie et al. 1986).

Anthropological discusion of this relationship between self, object and society is dominated by the more general analysis of exchange. Until recently, emphasis was most commonly placed on the object as gift in the tradition of Mauss, but some consideration is now also being given to what is too often taken merely as the gift's antithesis, that is the commodity. Appadurai (1986) provides a survey of some of the relevant literature, pointing out that in some respects commodities are not necessarily as divorced from wider cultural considerations as is often supposed. Almost all societies have elements of an exchange of objects in which persons are directly implicated, market exchange in which they are not implicated, and separate spheres of exchange which constrain the equivalences between things (e.g. Douglas 1967; Miller 1986).

Mauss's underlying concern was with individualism as an aspect of the fragmentation and disembedded nature of capitalist society. The problem is not, however, unique to capitalism. The fundamental opposition which may erupt between economy and society was noted by Simmel, who observed that the merchant is identified with the relative autonomy and abstraction of flexible exchange and is therefore often, as 'stranger', held in an ambiguous and partially anomalous relation to the host society (e.g. Simmel 1950: 402–8). Indeed, Parry has recently argued that it is only under the conditions of a relatively free market that there is evidence for the entirely disinterested gift, in which calculation should be entirely absent, this being a product of the same emergent duality (Parry 1986).

Any consideration of the relationship between commodities and persons is overshadowed by the concept of property which, as Sartre (1969: 575–600), Simmel (1978: 306), and others have noted, cannot be separated from the basic relationship between being and having. In turn, discussion on this topic often focuses less upon the effect of property relations today than on the links established between property as an institution and Locke's concepts of individuality and natural rights, and, in turn, Marx's critique of private property. Unfortunately, the particular division most often invoked in contemporary political rhetoric concerning private and public property is misleading with regard to this issue, since the concept of private property suggests a close relationship between person and thing, whilst in practice private property is an institution which works to produce precisely the opposite effect. Private property as a notion conflates the direct relationship between the individual and those objects with which he or she is associated in self-construction with those over which he or she has legal rights. As an institution, private property is the foundation of abstract relationships between anonymous people and postulated objects, an extreme example of which is the relationship between shareholder and investment. In terms of the legalistic concept of private property, an individual is able to own an object with which he or she may have no personal relationship, thus preventing others from realizing their potential for achieving such a relationship. The claim to legitimacy of particular possession is based entirely upon the institutionalization of rights.

With respect to the object as objectification it might be better to use a term such as personal property, which assumes a genuinely self-productive relationship between persons and objects. The classic case of private property would than become not home ownership but the ownership of sombody else's home. The confusion of private and personal property as the subject of criticism has led most people, who for good reason wish to defend property with which they are intimately associated also to defend institutions which may result in their alienation from such property. People wishing to own their council house may thereby be led to believe mistakenly, that the present institutionalization of private property is in their interests. Using a concept such as objectification, in which the cultural nature of the subject–object relationship is brought to the fore, the lines of this particular debate might be redrawn with important political conse-quences. Personal property is best linked with communal rather than private property, such as state or kin-held property, since it is a statement of relative inalienability, such that the social subject, individual or collective, associated with the object retains control over the conditions under which it may be alienated.

Artefacts and Space

The relationship between the materiality of the artefact and the materiality of space is especially close. Various authors have attempted to investigate the qualities which pertain to the nature of spatial order as such (e.g. Hillier and Hanson 1984), and many others have investigated the social use of space with particular reference to architecture (e.g. Ardener ed. 1981; Gilsenan 1982: 164–214; King ed. 1980). Berman (1983), following Benjamin and Simmel, gives a vivid impression of the impact of urban form as the media through which modernity was transmitted to become the precondition for contem-porary Western society.

In certain societies, spatial planning has been used to represent a sacred order which is of an ideal form, and within which actual human society attempts to exemplify certain principles, often creating tightly controlled urban populations ordered according to spatial dimensions such as left and right hands, verticality and circumambulation (e.g. Geertz 1980; Wheatley 1971). In South Asia, such religious cosmologies were replaced under colonialism by equally explicit secular images of power and authority, as in the layout of Imperial Delhi (King 1976). These elements of spatial order as representation are complemented by the impact of new material developments such as transport systems, which may affect our sense of space and distance. Much recent geographical research has been devoted to the relationship between space and time (Thrift 1977).

One example of the function of the symbolism of space is the fact that artefacts have always made an impression on us by virtue of their exotic qualities. Lapis lazuli was probably valued in the ancient world not only for its colour, but also because it was derived from a single source and thus always signified its origins as distance. In archaeological literature, goods imported in small quantities have often been studied under the general term of 'prestige goods', and, as such, control over these resources appears to have been a major factor in the rise and fall of early social hierarchies (Friedman and Rowlands 1977). Distance, which increases the problem of access, may be used to emphasize the differential ability of elites to acquire sumptuary objects, or, for peripheral areas such as Anatolia, might signify the awe with which the core civilization of Mesopotamia was regarded. In contemporary societies, goods which are difficult to obtain because of their exotic origins vie with highly priced goods in competing status systems.

As in the previous areas discussed, objects may not merely be used to refer to a given social group, but may themselves be constitutive of a certain social relation. One example is the use of objects, as opposed to the experience of actual peoples, to objectify the dual notions of orientalism and primitivism, which have dominated the way the Occident has historically constructed its self-image. It was noted at the beginning of this chapter that early European travellers brought back objects to represent the peoples of other lands and, through the arrangement of these objects in museums, contributed to the development of early theories of social evolution and diffusion (Steadman 1979). These objects were often used to exemplify the competing images of the Romantic and nobel primitive and the cannabilistic barbarian as suited the arguments or interests of the time. Smith (1960) has shown how images of the Pacific islanders were manipulated in these two directions, and Mitter (1977) has traced the varied history of European interpretations of Hindu sacred statuary, from viewing them initially as images of the devil, to finally incorporating them as works of art. On further investigation of many of the objects themselves, it becomes clear that they not only represent the selection of non-European artefacts by Europeans, but may also themselves be manufactured as objectifications of the relationship between different societies.

One instance of this image-construction is the 'Oriental' style of cloth (Irwin and Brett 1970). Some years ago, research workers at London's Victoria and Albert Museum and elsewhere encountered a considerable quantity of textiles in a recognizable style, composed mainly of exuberant large blossoms with curvilinear stems, sometimes joined to trees which were no longer rooted to the earth. At first, researchers attempted to place this style in the area from which it was assumed to originate – perhaps Persia, China or Central Asia – but through historical research it became clear that this was based on the false premise that the cloth was made in the original style of a certain group of people. In fact, it seems that this chintz was the product of a relationship rather than a society. When Indian cloth was first imported to Britain, it was in great demand because of its enormous technical superiority over British materials, European cloth dyeing being still in its infancy. The actual Indian designs were not, however, to the taste of the British at the time, who had developed a somewhat different image of Oriental peoples. The consumers' hints and suggestions, communicated over considerable distance and thereby often greatly distorted when realized by the manufacturers, resulted in changes in the cloth, which in turn prompted further comments. Gradually, through several cycles of modification and response, there emerged a style embodying an image of what the European consumers thought the Indian manufactures ought to be making for themselves. This design has come to be known as the Oriental style, since it objectifies precisely what Said (1979) and others have termed orientalism. Similarly, much of what has been called primitive art or ethnic art consists of objects made in that style which manufacturers in various parts of the world have perceived to be demanded of them (Graburn ed. 1976; Williams 1985). Indeed, objects used for inspiration by the artists in the nineteenth-century Paris studios were from parts of West Africa which had been making such images for European consumption for centuries (Donne 1978).

The point to be made here is one common in contemporary discussions of racism. Nation-states define themselves, in part, in terms of what they are not; that is, by setting themselves in opposition to alternative degenerate or ideal societies. Both people and objects are then required to exemplify the stereotypes which have been construc- ted. Within the Occident, such a process has been highly influential in the development of genres both in an older literary tradition and also in more recent media such as film. In the recent film *Return of the Jedi*, for example, the imaginative licence of science fiction is combined with a reverence for genres already developed within the film industry in order to offer images of Orientalism and primitivism extended and exaggerated beyond the point of realistic representation of 'other' peoples or goods (for an extension of this argument see Miller forthcoming; for a comparable example see Spooner 1986).

Artefacts and Time

Like spatial position, temporality is an intrinsic property of the object, which always exists in time, and will potentially signify the amount of time elapsed since it was created. As was pointed out in chapter 4 through Lévi-Strauss's example of the Australian Churinga, material objects are often the principal means of objectifying a sense of the past. The historical associations of the object of art noted by Benjamin (1973) pertain almost inevitably to any object which can be said to have passed through the hands of the ancestors, and are often a pivot around which social identity is constructed.

The concept of primitivism enables a society to construct its self-image not only by objectifying its concept of other distanced peoples, but also by conflating the dimension of space with that of time. Thus, contemporary peoples living in distant areas are viewed as though they were relics of one's own past (Fabian 1983). The temporality of the object may also contribute to our sense of identity by evoking the past of our own society. This is crucial for large-scale societies such as nation-states which, by virtue of their size, demand some concretized form such as a monument which can serve as a focus for the populace's identification with the state.

One example of this use of artefacts is derived from the relationship between the discipline of archaeology and the nation-state. Archaeology has as its declared intention the reconstruction of past societies and the understanding of processes of long term social change. In practice, however, its main result is the production of large numbers of ancient artefacts and monuments. One advantage of the fact that it can often produce little contextual information in comparison with this massive material product is that the labels given to this material are often relatively arbitrary. Archaeology therefore has the ability to impose, with relatively few complications, the particular contemporary boundaries of the nation-state upon its findings, and to identify these as the prehistory of Germany or Italy. As prehistory, these are typically based on sequences ranging from paleolithic stone axes through bronze age pottery to iron age swords. Since these are relatively common finds of a mundane form, the highly parochial local museum can often contribute its own sequence which is a version of the overall national pattern, thereby helping to embody in material form, and as an aid in teaching, that sense of history which underlies the collective identity presupposed by the state.

Different objects may serve different purposes in this regard. The large monument is territorially fixed, and, as an assertion of identity, it is commonly the basis of claims to both territory and historical achievement; for this reason archaeological monuments such as Great Zimbabwe and Masada have particular significance in newly formed countries such as Zimbabwe and Israel. The smaller portable artefact, by contrast, lends itself to being exported to areas outside of its site of discovery, and thereby provides evidence for more abstract legitimations; for example, the claim by colonial governments to represent the historical legacy of a sequence of great accomplishments is subsumed and given meaning by the concept of civilization. Thus, Britain as colonial power could represent the achievements of ancient civilizations such as Mesopotamia or Eygpt as the beginnings of a linear historical relationship leading, not to the people who now dwell in these same areas, but to Britain itself. In the museum display of these materials (such as the treasures of Tutankhamun's tomb), stress may be laid on the objects' discovery by British archaeologists, thereby helping to legitimize the implicit pseudo-evolutionary claims of historical advance as civilization (Gidri 1974).

This may also have positive consequences. The Solomon Islands is a new nation-state which may have been created through the imposition of an arbitrary boundary, but has to exist as a viable institution within the modern world. One of the constraints it suffers is the dominance of a history which tends to be reduced to that of either missions or colonial discovery, with the implications that the Solomon Islanders themselves were a stagnant and unchanging people prior to the arrival of Europeans, a view reinforced by some of the dominant synchronic traditions in social anthropology. By tracing artefactual change over several millenia, archaeology can produce materials which are regarded as directly ancestral by the modern population, even though different from those used today. Thus, mundane objects such as clam-shell axes and fish hooks may be used to objectify a concept of self-development and self-created change which may potentially be a powerful force in the rise of post-colonial states (Miller 1980).

Just as objects may come to symbolize time, so time is the context in which the symbolism of the object must be understood. In the case of a large archaeological monument such as Stonehenge, the object acts as a text which may be differentially interpreted, according to the period, as emblem of ritual power, as ruin, as national monument, or as symbol for druid and hippie (a process which is already evident in prehistory, see Shennan 1983). Barth (1975) provides a remarkably clear instance of the alteration of the 'meaning' of a set of objects, in his account of a sequence of initiation rituals within a particular New Guinea society. During the rituals for initiation into each successive age-set the 'true' meanings of certain sacred objects are revealed and it transpires that the interpretations given at the previous stage were false or partial. Almost all mundane objects possess some kind of biography through which their significance may radically alter. For example, the pottery made in an ordinary Indian village may start as a ritual object whose meaning is derived from the ceremony within which it is presented. The same pot may later on serve a specific function, holding only those items appropriate to its name. Later still, it may be dissociated from this role and used for general storage, in which case its previous specific symbolic role is ignored, and it is no longer of consequence whether its ritual status accords with that of its contents (Miller 1985: 172–83). Similarly, a blouse which is purchased from a shop as an alienable commodity may then become so intimately associated with a particular individual that it may not even be borrowed by a sibling, After some time, however, the object may lose this close association, becoming, as jumble, an alienable commodity once again.

These two elements of temporal symbolism, the object standing for time and time controlling what the object stands for, come together in the realm of fashion. What makes an object fashionable it is ability to signify the present; it is thus always doomed to become unfashionable with the movement of time. Fashion usually operates within a system of emulation and differentiation in knowledge, such that it uses the dynamic force of object change as a means of reinforcing the stability of the social system within which it is operating (Miller 1985: 184–96; Simmel 1957). Consideration of fashion, and indeed of markets in general (e.g. Geertz 1979) where the value of the object is related to highly transient knowledge, reinforces the impression of possible instability in artefact symbolism, and its dependence upon wider information-based and other contextual features. The older tradition of semiotic anthropology, in which objects were said to represent fixed denotations for a given society, based only on synchronic structure and with little consideration of when and where the interpretation was taking place, seems to be invalidated by these further considerations. Similarly, once concepts such as alienability and authenticity are re-defined within a general theory of objectification, as properties of relationships rather than of either peoples or things, the place of time in determining the implications of context becomes of major importance.

Artefacts and Style

Up to now, objects have been related to external contextual dimensions in an unmediated form, without consideration of their internal organization. Although the term 'style' is often used to cover a wide range of artefactual properties which relate such artefacts to their social environment (for example in archaeology Hodder 1982a: 125–84, 204–7; 1982b 173–96; various papers in Hodder ed. 1982), here it will be used to refer solely to the relationship between artefacts within a given object domain, such as all windows or all cars.

Little mention has been made so far of those elements of material forms which relate to each other in an ordered fashion, and which may thereby influence the manner in which they are utilized in constituting cultural patterns or acting as systems of meaning. In the latter case, an exact equivalent to grammar in linguistics is unlikely to be found, since, as noted earlier, objects gain their effect from their comparative lack of abstraction and the various bridging functions they can thereby perform. This greater reliance on context means that the branch of linguistics termed 'pragmatics' (e.g. Levinson 1983; Sperber and Wilson 1986) is likely to be of far greater significance than semantics of syntax in those material culture studies which investigate the object's communicative abilities.

The first manner in which objects may be related to each other is as type-tokens. Most artefacts are either the product of mass production, in which case they are identical to all others items produced by the same process, or else are intended as equal copies of a normative cultural notion, in which case, for example, all spears of the same type are intended to look alike. Where objects are deliberately unique it may be that they are intended to signify some generic concept of uniqueness, such as in art; the object is then both an individual form and an example of a larger category to which it must be related. Objects as catagories may, however, be related more to the fuzzy logic of normative and peripheral forms than to the contrastive logical approach of componential analysis and binary opposition (Kempton 1981; Rosch 1978).

At the next level of analysis, every object may usually be organized into a given field within which it contrasts with all others, for example the various types of curtain, canoe, car or ornament. Such a field is commonly organized according to the principle of style, which may be defined as the use of certain limited dimensions upon which the variability of a domain is expressed. Thus, certain aspects of the artefact will be used to create distinctions of flavour, type of lid, colour or length of skirt; but in all these cases other properties will be uniform througout the range. It is this which helps us to recognize that an object is from a certain period or particular place. The thousands of varieties of European shirts may differ in terms of button types and collar lengths, but they remain recognizable as shirts as opposed to garments used in other cultures for an identical functional purpose; and this is because the manufacturers, as it were, agree to differ with respect to these specific and limited dimensions. Such internal order is highly significant, since it reinforces the point that objects are not best understood as merely subservient to social divisions. Social groups may be divided according to the logic of objects with which they associate, which includes the objects' autonomous tendencies towards pattern, as well as their physical constraints.

At the next level, objects in different domains may be organized according to a comparable underlying logic. This principle has been most forcefully demonstrated in structuralist and semiotic analyses (e.g. Friedrich 1970; Humphrey 1971). In structuralism, these formal properties are taken at a relativley abstract level. Lévi-Strauss has recently provided his own examples of the material artefact as pseudo-mythic form. In a study of masks used amongst the American Indians of the north-west coast, he shows the *Xwexwe* masks of the Kwakiutl, with their bulging eyes, protuding jaws and tongues, are the inverse transformation of their *Dzonkwa* mask which have sunken eyes, hollow cheeks, and no tongue, but are the same as those masks called *Swaihwe* of the neighbouring Sailish. He compares this material inversion to the opposite pattern of semantic inversion integrating these into mythic and other cultural forms such as dance and kinship, noting that 'when from one group the plastic form is preserved, the semantic function is inverted. On the other hand, when the semantic function is retained, it is the plastic form which is inverted' (Lévi-Strauss 1982: 93). In such an analysis, the transformations of the cultural forms become almost independent of their social vehicles, as societies themselves are understood as merely variants upon a deeper structural order. In a sense, this inverts the Durkheimian tradition from which it originally stemmed, by representing society as a reflection of style.

As with the other areas discussed above, style has achieved a certain autonomy in contemporary industrial society, going beyond its capacity for ordering to become itself the focus of concern. This was brought out in an incisive account of the impact of the *Bauhaus* on modern society by Baudrillard (1981: 185–203), in whose view this principle of creating order through style has become dominant over social interest, as a kind of structuralism imposed on everyday life. The *Bauhaus* is seen as the symbol of a drive to make all human creations serve the principles of style. In this new world, all architecture, furnishing, clothing and behaviour are intended to relate to each other in a visibly coherent fashion. This works to break down all frames into a universal order of good design. The matching colour scheme is extended to all commodities, so that a given company may prefer to purchase machine tools manufactured by a firm with a reputation for design in microchips, attracted by that firm's modern hi-tech image rather than its reputation for efficiency (Fry 1982). Ironically, that set of ideas and ideals which expressed the legitimacy of form following function was most effective in ensuring that function followed form.

Baudrillard perceives this as the product of multi-national capitalism, but on reflection this principle is not so different from the utility of relations enhanced by the object which was stressed as socially cohesive in a non-industrial society. Among the Kwakiutl, discussed above, all objects may be related through a style expressive of an orality in which humankind achieves significance by its place in a universal cycle of devouring and reproduction (Walens 1981). Religions have also often attempted to reduce all human action to stylistic embrace as an expresion of cosmological pretentions. Modernism must be granted its specificity, but it also has its precursors.

Conclusion

If the implications of the examples surveyed in this chapter can be summarized in a single idea, it is that the medium of objectification matters. It makes a difference what form is used in the process of becoming; and of those media used in objectification, physical artefacts have certain properties and tendencies which, in an age of rapidly increasing material culture, ought to be investigated in their own right. The physicality of the artefact lends itself to the work of praxis – that is, cultural construction through action rather than just conceptualization. The object also acts to integrate the representative individual within the normative order of the larger social group, where it serves as a medium of intersubjective order inculcated as a generative practice through some version of 'habitus'. This order is continually objectified in the pattern or style of the artefactual world.

The object may lend itself equally to the expression of difference, indicating the separate domains to which people or aspects of people belong, and to the expression of unity, connecting otherwise diverse domains. Although conventionally the totalizing property of the artefact is stressed as a condition of the non-modern (e.g. Bateson 1973; Forge 1973), and the commodity is viewed as the fragmenting medium of modernity, both forms in fact exist in both contexts. For example, in several cases in the present text, the object has been shown to be expressive of quite autonomous elements of the dimensions analysed, as function beyond efficiency, image of manufacture beyond actual construction, pure individuality, coherent style and so forth. What is curious, however, is that it is often the same object which does all of these things. The image of modernism as artefact is in this sense a totalizing image using the project of art as its means of accomplishing such totality (compare Gell 1986 for the ability of the commodity to perform this function in a non-industrial context). Thus the high-modernist building was able simultaneously to enshrine a notion of pure rationality in systems-building, pure formalism in its opposition to ornament, pure functionality which was seen as the basis of its aesthetic value, and pure style. It was thus held to be as authentic an image of the society within which it was produced as the gift, whose authenticity was premised upon its own totalizing ability. In practice, however, both are cosmological pretensions which achieve their aim only by virtue of the object's other ability to keep apart the many alternative orders and demands which would threaten the purity of these abstractions.

The deeply integrated place of the artefact in constituting culture and human relations has made discussion of it one of the most difficult of all areas to include in abstract academic discourse. The mundane artefact is not merely problematic but inevitably embarrassing as the focused topic of analysis, a practice which always appears fetishistic. Its study is therefore in its infancy, and the cases presented above provide no more than a glimpse of its potential interest. The flexibility of the artefact indicated in the deliberately wide range of examples provided should not, however, lead the reader to assume an arbitrary or unsystematic use, any more than the flexibility and uniqueness of languages excludes the possibility of linguistic analysis.

PART III

Mass Consumption

8

The Study of Consumption

Introduction

The remaining chapters of this book will all be concerned with the potential application to the understanding of mass consumption of the ideas about objectification and material culture so far developed. The focus of attention will move to contemporary Britain, although examples will also be drawn from elsewhere.

In Britain, our relationship with goods is almost entirely one of consumption. Even those directly engaged in industrial production are more likely to be immediately associated with a complex work process than with an identifiable product. The consumption of goods is quite remarkably neglected as a subject of study outside of formal economics and models of individual purchasing behaviour. This becomes evident if one considers the goods we encounter in terms of some fairly simple criteria. Such goods might be divided into those we possess and those we encounter but do not possess. These may in turn be sub-divided; goods possessed may comprise either the results of private purchase or goods allocated by the state, while goods not possessed tend to fall into two categories: first, those we encounter as material forms, in particular the built environment, the goods of our acquaintances or those in the high street shop, and secondly, goods we do not experience directly, but which appear to us through the media – for example in television, magazines and advertising. It is indicative of the lack of serious analysis of the artefact, however, that even for such a politically sensitive issue as the division between private purchase and state allocation, the implications for the subsequent relationship people have with those goods are quite unknown (with the possible exception of housing). Studies of the impact of production relations on a group's identity have not been complemented by equivalent studies based upon consumption.

The discussion of consumption will be divided among three chapters. In the present chapter, a brief account of the historical background to contemporary consumption will be followed by a resumé of some of the approaches to this issue found in various disciplines, one of which, the tradition stemming from Veblen's work on goods as the expression of social differentiation, will be discussed in more detail. Chapter 9 will be devoted almost entirely to the general question of how active a role should be ascribed to consumers in understanding the meaning of goods in social relations today, and the nature of goods as material culture. The final chapter will attempt a more general model of consumption in terms of the concept of objectification.

Consumption and the Industrial Revolution

The problem in discussing consumption is that our 'common sense' understanding of the phenomenon is often merely a reflection of the ordering of the processes we see around us. An object is manufactured before it is purchased, and we therefore have a tendency to see consumption activities as the result of, or as a process secondary to, the development of manufacturing and other forms of production. In the history of Britain as taught in schools and conventionally rendered, the great event of modern times was the industrial revolution. It is this epoch which has traditionally marked for pupils a break from learning about royalty and politicians to noting the dates of inventions such as the spinning jenny and Arkwright's mule. Industrialization provides the backdrop for the study of the subsequent transformation into modern economic classes: the rise of colonialism is explained in terms of a search for markets, and wars in terms of economic competition.

An exception to this tendency towards a belief in technological determinism is that branch of Marxist history which follows Marx himself in preferring to focus on changes in the social organization of productive relations. Marx provides a clear example of this in his analysis of the period of manufacture during which the social organization of production became concentrated in a variety of ways, such as the bringing together within one workshop of all of the stages in the production of a particular item. Such social changes are shown to be prior to, and necessary precursors of, any technological changes, such as industrialization (Marx 1974: 318–47). More recent literature on proto-industrialization (e.g. Kriedte et al. 1981) continues the same tradition. Marxist writings emphasize the social organization of production as the primary factor in the transformation to modernity, an emphasis continually reproduced in the abundant use made of the term 'capitalism' in most accounts.

Historical documentation in this field becomes more scarce as the emphasis moves towards other aspects of social organization, despite the highly influential work of the French historian Braudel, whose books (e.g. 1981) include lengthy accounts of patterns of consumption in food, textiles and housing, which have been followed up by the Annales school of historians (see also Elias 1978; Sombart 1967 for alternative traditions). A variety of recent studies provide a glimpse of possible alternatives to the hegmony of technology and relations of production in popular conceptions of the nature and cause of modernity. There has been no general attempt to rewrite the history of the period from a perspective based on changes in consumption and material culture (though see Mukerji 1983), but two examples may be suggestive, the first derived from historians and the second from studies of material culture.

Several recent works on British history have examined the development of craft production, consumption and the increase in material culture, with volumes concentrating upon the seventeenth century (Thirsk 1978), the eighteenth century (McKendrick, Brewer and Plumb 1983), and the results of the industrial revolution in the later nineteenth century (e.g. Fraser 1981). Particularly important are a series of changes which took place prior to the development of industrial technology. The main argument is summarized by McKendrick: 'In a society in which the social distance between classes is *too great to bridge*, as say between a landed aristocracy and a landless peasantry, or in which the distance is *unbridgeable*, as in a caste society, then new patterns of increased expenditure on consumer goods are extremely difficult if not impossible to induce' (1983: 20). It follows that the break up of the *ancien régime* and the impact of the Enlightenment gave rise to a radical transformation of the nature of objects in society.

In a period of strong social stratification, objects tend to reflect given social hierarchies. At such a time, sumptuary laws may be passed which forbid the use of particular goods to those who are deemed to be below a certain station in life (e.g. Braudel 1981: 311; Mukerji 1983: 179–82; Sennett 1976), a form of regulation common to a large range of societies (e.g. Srinivas 1966: 16), which may be associated with limited spheres of exchange (e.g. Douglas 1967; Salisbury 1962), and restrictions on mercantile practices. The process of signification between material object and social station in this situation strives to remain relatively uncomplex and controlled. When, however, this breaks down, goods can change from being relatively static symbols to being more directly constitutive of social status. Under these altered conditions, emulation is increasingly significant as a strategy by means of which people lower in a given social hierarchy attempt to realize their aspirations towards higher status by modifying their behaviour, their dress and the kind of goods they purchase, since it now becomes possible to mistake a poor nobleman for a wealthy trader. Emulation in turn stimulates the desire to retain differentials, which often becomes based upon access to knowledge about goods and their prestige connotations. By this process, fashion emerges as the means for continuing those forms of social discrimination previously regulated by sumptuary rulings. In other words, demand for goods may flourish in the context of ambiguity in social hierarchy.

Behind the industrial revolution were a series of major historical transformations, including the abandonment of popular culture by the European elites after 1500 such that the concept of culture itself became more closely related to hierarchy, but was combined with a growth in literacy and other resources by means of which lower status groups might also gain access to the new high culture (see Burke 1978: 270 and Mukerji 1983 for pre-1800; Williams 1961 for post-1800). New exotic prestige goods were used on a much wider national and international scale, contrasting with regional and local styles, which became more consciously preserved. Inventions such as clocks, new transport systems and printing were also influential in expanding communication about such innovations and their implications.

Mukerji focuses on the early modern period of the fifteenth and sixteenth centuries as marking a highly significant rise in material culture, so that peasants and ordinary town dwellers who had remarkably few personal possessions in late medieval periods (Braudel 1981: 283) were becoming familiar with many more products, and from a much wider area (Burke 1978: 246–8). Following on this, the more general impact of Enlightenment ideas which questioned the legitimacy of the *ancien régime* allowed goods to begin to play new constitutive roles, which in turn led to a substantial rise in demand. Mukerji (1983) also challenges Weber's concentration upon the link between Protestantism and capitalism, and argues rather that this period sees the rise of both asceticism and hedonism as more explicit and abstract attitudes to goods themselves. This is closer to Simmel's arguments concerning the relationship between the rise of money as abstraction and material culture as specificity. Mukerji is not dividing off consumption from production, but showing how it is impossible to account for the development of the latter without considering the history of the former. As noted by McKendrick et al. (1983), these changes led to substantial shifts in the nature and pattern of demand in eighteenth-century England prior to the main developments in machine technology.

To follow this argument in more detail, it is worth turning to the product which is most intimately associated with the earliest period of the industrial revolution, that is cotton cloth. Braudel's work has a problematic tendency to regard certain societies as changeless, especially the so-called 'traditional' civilizations (e.g. 1981: 285, 312). This view stems, in part, from the difficulty in perceiving in an unfamiliar society that degree of micro-differentiation which is so important in appreciating the subtleties of consumption patterns in one's own society. Other equally influential modern forms of historiography have tended to develop still further this European ethnocentrism, with other societies viewed either as the passive victims of the European search for markets (e.g. Wallerstein 1979), so that the rest of the world is seen as peripheral to a West-European core, or else as active players in what is still, however, a story dominated by European desires (e.g. Wolf 1982).

Such histories tend to ignore the extraordinary extent and longevity of certain earlier trade patterns to which Europe itself was merely peripheral. It comes as something of a shock, therefore, to realize that there were other areas, such as South Asia, more developed in technology and the articulation between production and trade, and highly dynamic in mercantile organization, which might have possessed equal potential to have become the centre for an industrial revolution, if these factors were indeed the primary causative variables (Perlin 1983). One of the problems the European traders encountered early on in their attempt to develop longer trade routes, was that peoples in South-East Asia who produced spices highly regarded in Europe did not, for their part, show any great desire for European products. Britain could only obtain these goods by intervening in an already well-established trading pattern, taking much-desired cotton cloth from South Asia and using this to purchase spices from the East Indies.

One effect of this intended trade in spices was the probably largely unintended arrival in Britain of quantities of South Asian calicoes. These were of a markedly superior quality to anything which could be produced in Europe at the time; indeed, by comparison, the British had not by then developed any significant dyeing technology. South Asian calicoes in both silk and, later on, cotton became an increasingly desirable commodity in Britain, first as a luxury item but subsequently as a widely used material. Britain had perhaps never faced such a large demand for a product which, since cotton could not be grown in the country, it was incapable of producing itself. A previous influx of linen in the sixteenth century had been countered by government sponsorship of the linen industry and the growing of coarse flax and hemp, part of a larger tendency in Britain towards the development of local projects to counter foreign imports (Thirsk 1978: 72–4). The industrial revolution, which began with machinery for cotton textile production, should therefore be understood, in part, as an exercise in import-substitution (Chaudhuri 1978; Mukerji 1983: 210–42). By means of an unprecedented policy of increasing its manufacturing efficiency through technology, and putting pressure on South Asia to export raw cotton, a trade which it had never previously engaged in, at the expense of calico, which was subject to high import duties, Britain was able to turn the tide against India, and later to flood that area with cheap cotton goods.

The impact of this arrival of South Asian calico can only be understood in terms of those wider social changes already referred to. London was a crucial site for such developments, since with a population of 900,000 it was unique in the Europe of 1800 (McKendrick 1983: 21). During the eighteenth century, the older categories of difference in goods, that is locality, occupation and so forth, appear to have become overwhelmed by more flexible and creative differences. McKendrick provides examples of the hundreds of hairstyles on offer in 1772, or a pattern book for garments with 1,370 designs. Textiles are admirably suited to the dictates of fashion, which guarantees continuous demand (1983: 34–99), and the same period saw the rise of women's fashion magazines (1983: 47). In this period there was also a retailing boom; by 1817 there were 153 fashion shops in London's Oxford Street. Certain social groups began to be regarded as consumer target populations. Plumb (1983: 289–315) and Forty (1986: 63–91) document the rise of goods aimed at specific consumer groups such as children, later developed as youth groups demanding particular age-based products.

In complementary essays on Josiah Wedgwood, McKendrick (1983: 100–45) and Forty (1986: 13–41) chart the strategies which fostered new patterns of emulation and marketing, and the birth of the modern professional designer. Forty suggests that the attraction of the neo-classical, which emerged from a somewhat wider range as the most successful of Wedgewood's styles, was that it provided an acceptable facade for the introduction of the advances being made by ceramic science, the most modern techniques thereby being employed in the improvement of reproductions, a tension in commercial styling which has been strongly asserted ever since.

Once again, it is striking that these transformations, which include the development of many of the forms of marketing, design and distribution characteristic of mass production, ocurred before the rise of machinery in this industry. They were principally organizational, being based on handmade products. With this in mind, the new findings of scholars working in the Marxist tradition to show the importance of putting-out systems of production such as the Verlag in proto-industrialization, take on a new significance (e.g. Kriedte et al. 1981:101–7). The Verlag system is one in which patterns may be supplied by merchants to household-based manufacturers from a wide variety of markets, and are then copied by people who have no direct contact with these markets. This system is finely attuned to new ventures in marketing and distribution, and is probably quite similar to the major South Asian forms of production which had previously established the foundations for large-scale international trade, in the absence of industrial machinery; although, in that case, divisions in the production process, which allowed for control by merchants and middlemen, were more closely articulated by social divisions such as caste and *purdah*.

Machine-based production began, not only in textiles, but in a range of goods which were particularly sensitive to this type of flexible demand, and only later on concentrated on the heavier industrial goods we now particularly associate with factory-based machine production (McKendrick 1983: 31–2). It is these goods which provided the material for the 'nation of shopkeepers' image of Britain held by her contemporaries. In other areas where similar changes occurred at a slightly later date, the rise of mass material culture and retailing was the subject of some incisive commentary. The aura of the emerging high street was captured by Simmel and Baudelaire and later reconstructed by Benjamin in his arcades project (1983). The processes of emulation and democratization were to extend these into the large department stores as harbingers of the modern retailing world of today (Fraser 1981; Miller 1981). Recent work by Williams (1982) in analysing a dynamic and important debate about the nature of consumption in France suggests that a century ago there was a far more balanced view of changes in the relationship between consumption and production as historical transformation than exists today. There is an explicit concern in the writings of Zola, Gide, and Tarde, not only with the effect of mass consumption, but also with the proper response of the worker as consumer. These authors were situated within a more active public debate centered on displays such as the world fairs (Benedict ed. 1983) and movements such as the consumer cooperatives and programmes for a 'socialism of consumption' (Williams 1982: 287–98)

Criticisms have already been made in chapter 3 of Marx's tendency to overemphasize production as opposed to consumption, but this was in relation to abstract theory. It is interesting to note a similar problem with attempts to put some of his ideas into practice. An illustrative case may be found in the work and practical impact of William Morris, who sought not only to recognize but also to ameliorate the social and aesthetic impact of the machine, partly under the influence of socialist ideas. Through the emergence of the arts and crafts movement, Morris succeeded in establishing a craft tradition in which the individual could retain some control over every stage of manufacture from design to execution, and thereby gain a far more satisfactory relationship with the product. Unfortunately, because this tradition tended to ignore the problem of consumption, the main impact of this craft revival was to promote a conspicuous handmade image, explicitly separate from the products of mass consumption, and immediately recognized as a quality or luxury product which signified, and thereby helped reproduce, the new moneyed elites. The impact of Morris's ideas as channelled through the sphere of consumption, provided an effective means for the further development of precisely those class differences which in turn helped reproduce the conditions for the exploitation of labour. Given the history of socialist economies, it is doubtful whether even a far more radical and complete transformation of the relations of production would, of itself, have removed this basis for class differentiation, and for this reason Morris remains a problematic model for contemporary socialism.

The second example of how the historical transformations underpinning modern society may be examined from unconventional perspectives which emphasize consumption as well as production comes from a series of studies in American historical archaeology. These have been concerned with documenting changes in American colonial society, from its inception to recent times, through the analysis of material culture, mainly derived from archaeological excavations, but also from extant buildings. A summary of the main argument is provided in a slim volume by Deetz (1977) who compares changes in pottery, gravestone design, and house construction, with asides on music and eating patterns, during the seventeenth and eighteenth centuries (see also Glassie 1975; Leone 1984).

At the start of the period, following the traditions of Stuart yeomanry, custom demanded a mainly communal use of a variety of household materials, with pottery playing only a minor role, mainly in dairying. From 1660 onwards, pottery was more frequently used in food preparation and consumption, and there was the first ceremonial use of plates in parlour display. After 1760, mass produced English wares were in use, with a large increase in plates, cups, saucers and chamber pots. These marked a shift from communal use to individual use, although individual items were connected at a household level by a common pattern, as found in the modern set of china. Gravestones also underwent a three-phase change. In the early period the death's head was the predominant motif used in churchyard-based cemeteries, in which by no means every individual received a grave marker. Through stylistic development, the death's head was gradually transmuted into a cherub in line with the revivalist period of Christianity, and inscriptions show a concern to separate the mortal body and immortal soul. By the third period, there was a new fashion for urn and willow motifs, which had become commemorative symbols on graves marking the achievements of the individual in life. Such motifs were particularly common in well-ordered separate family cemeteries.

The next set of materials, house forms, has been most fully studied by Glassie in an analysis of eighteenth-century extant folk housing in Middle Virginia. These dwellings belonged to the poorer white small holders, and were built without consultation with architects or planners. Through a sophisticated structural analysis of features ranging from window position to door latch, Glassie reconstructs a major change taking place around the late 1870s (1975: 182, 185), in which chimneys and central halls became incorporated into the main building, and a new concern with symmetry appears, along with a homogenization of the exterior around a more conspicuously ordered façade. Similar analyses indicating new ordering principles have been carried out on the gardens of aristocrats (e.g. Leone 1984), furnishings, the disposal of rubbish and forms of cutlery (Deetz 1977). Overall, these studies mark the emergence of what has been called the Georgian style, which employs bilateral symmetry, the individualization of personal space and property, and the specification of discrete elements reunited in a cohesive unity. The style is interpreted as a new form of conservatism based on an alliance between poorer white farmers and an aristocracy beleaguered by a combination of factors, including a fall in tobacco prices, a rise in slavery, and a shift in local identity.

Whatever the particular context of such changes, these studies demonstrate that a set of transformations in material culture which may be found to permeate almost every trivial domain, from chimneys to rubbish disposal, can be understood as a largely unconscious and unintentional response by a variety of social groups, which produced new forms of demand and new means of incorporating the emergence of mass produced items. Many of the familiar aspects of modernization, such as a rise of individualism and of specification in material culture use and scientific-rational order, may be traced in these studies, but the evidence provides a means of analysing such changes in terms of the structural organization of everyday objects for the population as a whole, and acts as a balance to the more common literary and self-reflective accounts of these changes. This balance is important, since, for example, some accounts whose critical focus is the rise of the individual, private, property-owning self, almost appear to conspire with that reification of the self which they seek to criticize in contemporary culture, by isolating and concentrating on this single factor. In these studies, by contrast, this transformation is understood as one of a whole series of cultural changes, heading towards new forms of abstraction and specificity. From certain unusual perspectives, history may therefore complement the standard picture of the industrial revolution to provide a basis for the study of the mass consumption which dominates contemporary life.

Studies of Contemporary Consumption

Several of the more extensive areas of analysis of modern consumption will be dealt with quite briefly, since they lie largely outside of the scope of the present work. First, and perhaps most bizarre, is the field entitled design history. As conventionally studied, this is clearly intended to be a form of pseudo art history, in which the task is to locate great individuals such as Raymond Loewy or Norman Bel Geddes and portray them as the creators of modern mass culture. The analysis is usually based on the strict modernism which was the ideology of the professions involved, and is epitomized in comments such as 'we seem to find that the aesthetics of an industrial product will take care of themselves automatically after we have provided a balance between function, simplicity and utility' (Bayley 1979: 71). This approach has recently been subject to an effective critique by Forty (1986), who points out that designers have always been handmaidens to the business interests they serve, and to separate them out as self-determined arbiters of cultural form is even less convincing than in the case of high art which strives for such autonomy. In effect this design history is a study of the industrial artefact which quite ignores the consumer. A more recent critical tradition in this field, as in the journal *Block*, provides an alternative approach much more closely concerned with the social context of cultural innovation. Forty provides abundant examples of the complex manner in which commerce developed new goods around perceived divisions in the target population and a series of beliefs about the nature of hygiene, domesticity, science and modernity which become enshrined in and reproduced through the appearance of everyday objects, although again the transformation of goods in consumption is largely ignored.

Within anthropology, there has always been a tradition seeking to locate underlying and generalizable processes and patterns in material culture studies. Kroeber and his followers devoted considerable effort to studies ranging from changes in skirt length over several decades to the diffusion and diversity of artefact styles amongst Californian Indians (Kroeber 1939). More recently, studies of modern objects by archaeologists working in the sub-discipline of ethno-archaeology have sought to provide 'general and testable' laws of stylistic behaviour, strongly influenced by an extreme and exquisitely inappropriate form of positivism which took hold of the discipline in the 1960s, and appears to have been retained long after most other social sciences threw off its shackles (e.g. Binford 1972; 1978; Gould and Schiffer eds 1981, see Hodder 1982a and b for a critique). Such studies exemplify the kind of fetishism to which material culture studies are always prone, when people are superseded as the subject of investigation by objects, and become essentially labels for their movement or pattern.

By far the most extensive research into the relationship between society and mass consumption objects has been conducted in the world of commerce itself, and its offshoots in marketing and advertising, which are strongly linked to the discipline of economics. In common with ethno-archaeology, such research tends towards an abstract positivism, using complex mathematical models to predict the behaviour of certain social groups in response to a new product. Societies are divided, not only by conventional sociological categories such as occupation and housing, but also in relation to psychological attitudes and other aspects of known consumer performance. There is a large number of books and journals devoted to different aspects of such research, which may be employed, though with some caution, for other purposes (e.g. Engel et al. 1973; Crimp 1981). Conventional economic approaches to consumption tend towards a macro-scale of analysis whose assumptions about the nature of society, demand, and the actual relationship between goods and people can generally be reduced to certain highly simplistic and dubious notions, with the social demand for goods being replaced by the quite insufficient symbolic equation with price. Douglas and Isherwood (1978) provide a useful and informed critique of this literature.

At one level, the total separation of such research from anthropology is quite artificial, given that these studies are often directly parallel to anthropological concerns with social organization and stratification. There are, however, highly specific concerns in business-oriented research, which limit its more general interest. First, it is almost always concerned with the point of sale; there is no reason for researchers to be concerned with the social value and longer term implications of products. Secondly, business studies tend to affirm a consumer passivity in response to marketing initiatives. People working in these professions often take pleasure in describing a sales campaign in which surplus stocks of milk were dispersed by persuading the public that it had a taste for a new mass product, such as yoghurt, or in reminding us that ploughman's lunches could be invented to persuade a new group to patronize pubs. Such stories, and they are legion, are quite accurate with respect to the intention and perspective of business and marketing interests, but it will be argued in the next chapter that they may be a poor foundation for an understanding of the nature of consumption. Business literature is therefore vital for understanding business, which is one of the major forces in modern culture, but it is more limited when it comes to a study of the consumer and his or her relation to the object. Connected with these studies, though quite different in emphasis, is the rise of consumer protection and associated legislation, which is more concerned with the implications of goods, but tends to be restricted to functional efficiency and safety, rather than wider social relations.

One approach which is curiously similar to business studies in its view of the populace is that of some contemporary Marxism. This tradition tends to focus upon mass consumption as the instrument of capital for which the individual subject is created as consumer, and provides important critical accounts of the mechanisms by which producers construct their markets (e.g. Haug 1986). Capital is devoted to the creation of desires and needs which can only be fulfilled by the latest developments of the market. Needs are always related back to capitalism's demand for the social reproduction of its labour force. Preteceille and Terrail (1985) provide a recent elaboration of this position, taking into account the various approaches emerging from cultural anthropology, but they retain the classic Marxist conception that modern 'needs' can only be accounted for in terms of the search by capital for greater profits, and that consumption is always subservient to production interests (e.g. 1985: 37–81). In many current studies, it is the state which is abstracted as the complementary prime mover in the development of new collective forms of consumption (e.g. Castells 1977), and largely functionalist arguments are derived to indicate how any changes which appear to have occurred can always be found to have accorded with the 'interests' of these two forces, capital and the state, which are usually in harmony as 'state monopoly capitalism' and always in direct conflict with the interests of the population as a whole.

A modern twist to the Marxist critique of the commodity has emerged with the application of semiotics. Although often associated with structuralism, semiotic analysts is involved in the details of representation and signification, while structuralism proper eschewed this concern with a drive towards more abstract models of cognition and culture. The results of the application of these techniques have been varied. Sometimes objects are perceived merely as alternatives to words, as signs to be used in pseudo-linguistic formal analysis. In the hands of writers such as Barthes (1973) semiotic analysis becomes an extension of the critique of the commodity and bourgeois culture, a series of denunciations Barthes termed 'semioclasm'. Objects are analysed as myths which provide artificial resolutions to real contradictions in society. The process of signification is what accomplishes the task of the myth; it subverts simple denotation through its wider connotation, it naturalizes culture as the given order of the day, and it utilizes the ambiguities and tendencies of the process of signification itself in order to effect its apparent closures.

In the later development of Barthes' work, and in the work of others who followed similar trajectories (e.g. Coward and Ellis 1977), this analysis moves further from the specific contents of the objects and their social impact, to address the problem of the media itself, and the nature of the sign. The older style of semiotic analysis is replaced by the post-structuralist tradition in which the subject is constructed in terms of a larger discourse, and analysis is devoted to topics such as narrative structure and deconstruction. In chapter 9, this will be reviewed in relation to the earlier critique of mass culture.

In opposition to the above studies are those which have been carried out by anthropologists, who have applied traditions more central to that discipline. One of the most important recent examples of such a study was the result of joint work by an anthropologist and an economist, and focused on critical appraisal of many of the assumptions about goods current in economics (Douglas and Isherwood 1980). In this work, rather than being reduced to utility or competitive status display, goods are examined in terms of their expressive and symbolic function, and the central thesis with respect to this is one which has largely been assumed in the present work. The references by Douglas and Isherwood to conventional economics are complemented by Sahlins' critique of similar assumptions in Marxist economics (1976a), which in part extends the work of

Baudrillard; and both of these works use symbolic analysis in order to attempt more general assessments of the relationship between divisions of goods and divisions of peoples.

The work of Douglas and Isherwood may be related to that Durkheimian pre-structuralist tradition which sees objects as aiding in the creation of a cognitive order based upon social divisions. They argue that goods are used to make 'visible and stable the categories of culture' (1980: 59). These cognitive categories are, however, themselves derived from a deeper base: social structure. Thus, 'It would seem then that the clue to finding real partitioning amongst goods must be to trace some underlying partitioning in society' (1980: 907). The authors' stress on cognition has the advantage that it leads to an appreciation of the importance of the distribution of knowledge about what goods should represent, rather than merely of the distribution of the goods themselves. They tend, however, towards what Sahlins has castigated as a 'sociability fetishism' (1976a: 120), in which social structure is often treated as both prior to, and ontologically superior to, its appearance in goods.

Despite his critique of Douglas, Sahlins' own attempt to construct an approach to consumption (1976a: 166–204) is subject to quite similar limitations. In their enthusiasm to criticize economistic assumptions concerning utility, both works tend to overstress the autonomy of the features they assert. The result is that in perhaps, too stark contrast to the approaches above, they entirely ignore the interests and power of commercial institutions. They tend to assert the overwhelming desire for cognitive order, and thus offer an unrealistically cohesive model of cognition itself which ignores the problems of ideology and framing. Most importantly, they fail to acknowledge the genuine lessons of Marx's work, as, for example, reflected in Bourdieu's *Outline of a Theory of Practice* (1977), in which the significance of artefacts is seen to consist in their simultaneous operation in both the material and cognitive worlds, thereby exposing the artificiality of a dichotomous approach. In short, these anthropologists tend towards several of the dualisms which the concept of objectification has been used to oppose, while nevertheless providing important assertions and exemplifications of the process of consumption as culture.

An ethnographically-based study set in Chicago (Csikszentmihalyi and Rochberg-Halton 1981) provides an example of a very different approach to an anthropology of consumption. This work is based on the examination of the goods used by some three hundred individuals in eighty-two households. The limitations of this study as an approach to consumption in general derive not only from a rather unbalanced subjectivism in the authors' theoretical models, but also from the particular selection of objects of concern. The analysis undertaken is not of goods in general, but of those selected as the most 'cherished' possessions by the informants. Not surprisingly, the pattern of reasons given for such a selection tends to be highly personal and particular, with emphasis being placed mainly on the objectification of personal relations, for example, with deceased friends and relatives. The self to whose development the authors relate this process tends to be a highly individualist subjective self, of the psychological rather than the anthropological tradition, with given psychic needs. Although Simmel is quoted, there is none of the subtlety of his analysis of the necessary contradictions of industrial society, and the emphasis on goals of happy homes and cohesive families appears cut off from the wider realms of social action. A far more satisfactory, if idiosyncratic, account of the cultural contexts within which modern commodities operate is provided by Appadurai (1986), especially in the introduction to this varied set of essays and examples, which follows from traditional anthropological concern with the nature of exchange.

Consumption as Social Differentiation

After these relatively brief accounts of a variety of approaches to the study of consumption as a social phenomenon, one particular perspective demands more substantial resumé and analysis. This perspective is here distilled out of the similarities between two major studies of consumption, one of which may almost be credited with initiating such studies, while the other provides the most extensive contemporary survey. These are Bourdieu's recent book *Distinction* (1984) and Veblen's *The Theory of the Leisure Class* (1899, here 1970). Although the former makes no mention of the latter, and despite a number of differences, the two share certain central assumptions.

One of the distinctions between these two works is that Veblen's goal is more limited; he is not concerned with consumption in general so much as a specific type of consumption which was of particular importance in the period during which he was writing, a period which may be seen as marking the transition to the age of mass consumption. Veblen, like Simmel, had the advantage of seeing as new and shocking many phenomena of mass consumption which today are regarded as commonplace and natural. Veblen's particular interest in the leisure class determined the direction of his argument. Leisure is to be understood as the ability to absent oneself from work. Thus, for a particular segment of the rich it was less wealth *per se* which was of importance, than wealth displayed as a conspicuous distance from the world of practical necessity. The class of people for whom this may have been of paramount importance was not the traditional aristocracy which had never been involved in work, having merely inherited their estates, but those termed the *nouveaux riches*, the use of which term implies a much more direct involvement in the work process as the basis for capital accumulation.

Veblen portrays this class as determined to create a distance between themselves and that world of necessity which was the foundation of their fortune. They also desired to emulate that other class for whom time and birth had provided legitimacy, and for whom wealth appeared as a natural attribute rather than a possibly transient accretion. The rise of industrial work processes and domestic labour, both of which appeared as particularly servile pursuits, only encouraged the capitalists' desire to distance themselves from their origins. However, just as they had formerly worked to obtain their fortune, so also the *nouveaux riches* were obliged to employ material goods to assert their social pretensions.

It was this *nouveaux riches* strategy which so jarred with those such as Veblen who had been raised on the more general American ethic that work itself was a highly moral activity in which pride should be taken, as in the case of Weber's Protestant ethic which valued utility and austerity. Veblen's achievement was to capture the strategies of the leisure class in a series of classic phrases and categories and exemplify them clearly and in detail with a masterful sense of irony. He showed that the mere absence from work or possession of wealth was translated into highly exaggerated forms which he termed conspicuous consumption and conspicuous leisure. The individual being insufficient for the expression of these values, they might be extended in vicarious forms such as footservants who had nothing to do but to display their own superfluity, or pets, which provided surfaces for the further display of luxury.

As well as outlining the ways in which the leisure class expressed their status, Veblen clarified the two major means by which such strategies were extended into society in general. The first of these was through control over matters of taste. Good taste became associated with the expression of distance from the world of work, the practical or the natural world, and was termed 'refined' or 'cultivated', being dissociated from that which could be regarded as 'cheap' (1970: 112). This became extended through the process of emulation, by which lower groups in the hierarchy sought to copy the higher groups, a strategy so fundamental that Veblen believed it to be the foundation for the concept of private property (1970: 33–40). In America, where there was a comparative absence of a long term aristocracy, these social hierarchies took on a particularly strong pecuniary emphasis. Through these processes the leisure class, which might itself represent but a small fraction of society, could extend its influence over the whole. Wealth was, however, not the only factor discussed by Veblen, and it is of particular interest that he ends his account of the leisure class with a chapter on 'The higher learning as an expression of pecuniary culture', and with an emphasis on Classics as the key at that time to the concept of high culture. Unfortunately, Veblen's emphasis upon particular strategies related to very particular segments of the population has tended to become generalized in popular accounts as a basis for understanding consumption *per se* (Douglas and Isherwood 1979: 4)

The tradition which links Veblen and Bourdieu is evident in their mutual emphasis on the area of taste as the key dimension controlling the significance of ordinary goods, and their common location of the source of taste in distance from work. Bourdieu, though less witty and stylish, achieves a large number of advances over Veblen's account in terms of the sophistication of his analysis and his ability to move this critique away from the characterization of a particular segment of the population to the analysis of French society as a whole, and from simple emulation and display to complex forces of strategy and social reproduction. These moves are necessary, given both the democratization of mass consumption and the growth in sophistication and subtlety of the ideological practices of dominant groups in the intervening period.

Bourdieu's first task is to rescue taste as preference from essentialist doctrines of aesthetics, and thereby free it as a potential tool for the contingent historical analysis of society. He achieves this by taking a central pillar in this tradition, Kant's concept of the aesthetic as distanced contemplation which transcends the immediacy of experience, and demonstrating that this is only a single perspective, that of the dominant class. The Kantian aesthetic is one of refusal, a forgoing of the immediate pleasure of the sensual and the evident in favour of a cultivated and abstracted appropriation through an achieved understanding. It therefore tends towards a rejection of representation of the signified or naturalistic, in favour of the principles of convention, the esoteric and formal. The overt display of wealth and consumption by Veblen's leisure class is challenged by a more subtle, detached and inconspicuous form to be appreciated only by those sufficiently cultivated or civilized. It is an aesthetic clearly expressed in the cool, detached and 'difficult' forms of modern art.

The Kantian aesthetic achieves its meaning only by contrast to what Bourdieu terms an anti-Kantian aesthetic. This is the aesthetic of popular culture, a preference for immediate entertainment, pleasure, the gut feeling, a regard for the sensual and the representational. Here, it is the substance and the signified which are of importance. A telling illustration resulted from questions concerning suitable subjects for photography. The Kantian perspective prefers cabbages and a car crash, the anti-Kantian favours sunset and first communion (Bourdieu 1984: 34–41). For the former, beauty is created through the mode of representation; for the latter, it is inherent in the subject. These differences in taste, which are equally evident in a wide range of media – for example, a preference for 'difficult' as opposed to popular music – provide the basis for unearthing a deep classificatory device which Bourdieu identifies as an example of that 'habitus' described in chapter 6.

As habitus, this distinction between the Kantian and anti-Kantian aesthetic is both derived from material conditions, and in turn provides an insight into a classificatory scheme which may be applied to an infinite number of actual material and consumption domains. The term 'taste' provides a clue to its deep rooted nature. When faced with what we regard as consummately bad taste, or people who seem to revel in exactly the behaviour we abhor, we often feel revolted, nauseous or acutely embarrassed, as when parents say the wrong thing in front of a child's peers, or that child is forced to wear clothes whose image he or she rejects.

When mapping these differences in taste, the sociological criterion used by Bourdieu tends to be either occupation or educational level, but both are related to the common conception of class, as upper, middle and working. Taste is then seen principally as the cause of 'classism', which can be defined as the kind of distate the middle and upper classes feel for the vulgar in fun fairs, cheap commodities, artificial copies, or lack of style, and the contempt working people feel for the pretentious, cold and degenerate middle and upper classes.

The source for the basic difference in taste is traced by Bourdieu to the different experiences of these classes in modern society. The immediacy of working people's tastes derives from the immediacy of their work experience, and the pressure imposed by their needs. A person who provides manual labour, and whose access to the basics of sustenance and comfort is not guaranteed, has a respect and desire for the sensual, physical and immediate. An individual who has been brought up in the abstractions of education and capital, and who is certain of obtaining daily necessities, cultivates a distance from these needs, and affects a taste based in the respect and desire for the abstract, distanced and formal. These objective conditions are interiorized through habitus as desire expressed in taste. Habitus thereby mediates between material conditions including, but not entirely reduced to, productive relations, and the observable practices of the social group.

Although in Veblen's time dominant groups could flaunt their birth or wealth, these were already undergoing the crises of legitimacy indicated in the venom of Veblen's writings. Much of Bourdieu's work in *Distinction* and other books is concerned with how these legitimatory principles have been replaced by others based on the education system. Education is used to support current social differences, since it claims to generate distinctions based on merit rather than birth or wealth, being itself the means by which differential ability is identified. Along with other sociologists (e.g. Goldthorpe et al. 1980; Halsey, Heath and Ridge 1980) who have used statistical analyses of education and occupation over several generations to question assumptions concerning increased social mobility, Bourdieu is able to demonstrate the largely illusory nature of this claim (1984: 135–68). The rise of mass education saw a decline in social mobility and merely an inflation in employers' demands for qualifications.

The basis for education's ability to bring about this process of social reproduction lies in what Bourdieu terms cultural capital. Cultural capital is based on time invested in obtaining certain kinds of knowledge. Learning Classics or memorizing the year by year achievements of a football club will enhance the individual's reputation in certain environments, but will prove a poor investment if used in the wrong circumstances. Bourdieu's main original contribution to analyses of education is to distinguish between that which is directly inculcated in the education process and that which is indirectly absorbed.

Some capital may be obtained through direct transference, as when an acquired skill for keeping in touch with the latest developments and information in a given academic field is then applied to the world of fashion. Less obvious is Bourdieu's evidence that education fosters a general tendency towards the use of high culture. His surveys indicate that the likelihood of visiting the theatre, art galleries or museums will depend not upon subjects studied or grades of qualification achieved, but simply upon the length of time spent in a higher academic institution.

One possible reason for this relationship between education and culture is brought out especially clearly in an earlier article by Bourdieu (1968). The increasing abstraction of modern art has tended to extend this distance from the immediacy of forms, and to make such art increasingly difficult to interpret for those not familiar with the conventions and history of the field. This is true for abstract modern theatre, painting, avant-garde music, literature and so forth. In a sense, if cultural products are regarded as a code which must be interpreted, this code has become increasingly difficult to decipher without access to some key. Education, on the other hand, has become increasingly important as a discriminating variable, that is, in terms of the level of education achieved. It also provides the key to the translation of high culture by emphasizing the importance of attaining knowledge about abstract and esoteric subjects. Thus, the difficulty of deciphering the cultural code has been compounded by the difficulty of gaining access to the devices for its decoding. These two factors act together to create and reproduce social hierarchy. At the top of the scale there is a close relationship with high avant-garde arts and esoteric social theories, the best current example of which is the relationship between post-modernism and post-structuralism (e.g. Foster ed. 1983).

The relationship between the two kinds of capital – cultural and economic – is uneasy. On the one hand, education provides a means by which business capital may reproduce its social order. The children of the rich may work in health food shops or other faddish and esoteric pursuits which utilize their educational experience and may provide a more acceptable form of class reproduction than simple inheritance. There is, however, also an antagonism between the two orders, as the holders of cultural capital deride money capital as mere wealth and its conspicuous expressions as high vulgarity, while the holders of money capital regard the pretensions and esoteric forms of high cultural capital as parasitic and irrelevant. In modern British society, this often takes the form of a left–right political division between fractions of the upper classes. Bourdieu's own analysis of politics, however, stresses rather the division between the 'knows' and the 'don't knows', in relation to the pressure put on the general public to have an informed opinion on often very distant issues (1984: 397–465).

Society, then, is not to be understood in terms of a simple hierarchy, but as a continual struggle over the hierarchy of hier-archies; that is, whether, in this case, that of wealth should prevail over that of knowledge. In a sense, this is the modern version of ancient struggles between church, state, military and trading concerns, and the continuance of the French court traditions studied by Elias (1978). Each group attempts to project its interests, its 'capital', as the proper source for social reputation and status. In the main, the holders of cultural capital can be regarded as the dominated fraction of the dominant class.

Although the examples above related to the arts, the importance of using the concept of taste is that it applies equally to the world of mass consumption. Bourdieu provides a fascinating array of domains divided according to the criteria of taste. An obvious case is that of food, which may be graded according to the social position of the consumer. Working people are found to prefer the immediacy of abundance, a plentiful table proclaiming its sustenance, strong red meats, solid breads and cheeses, an unfussy array of quantity wherever possible. Middle class food becomes cuisine. Taste is here based on knowledge of the proper methods of preparing and presenting foods, and there is a moral interest in food as wholesome, healthy and sustaining. Food for higher classes is increasingly split between the two fractions of the dominant class. The food associated with economic capital is characterized by rich sauces and desserts, and rare and luxurious items such as truffles. The ultimate food for the display of cultural capital today is the *nouvelle cuisine*, which refuses any suggestion that food might be for sustenance, a minimalist food which emphasizes the aesthetic of presentation, an austere but cultivated pleasure.

A similar set of divisions can be identified in a vast range of goods. The middle-class children's toy is never intended for mere amusement or pleasure; its prime interest is its educational value, the child must absorb the toy as a challenge, something from which it will learn in order to improve itself. Similarly, there is an array of products for producing the body beautiful, a tall elegant figure disdainful of practical or even biological constraint. In every consumer domain, fashion provides opportunities for differentiation, in terms of speed of access to knowledge. Through such examples, it becomes clear how the habitus acts both to generate the diversity of forms and, in turn, to classify these same diverse fields. It provides a set of dispositions promoting self-recognition and the creation of relationships such as friendships and marriages with others who share that set of prejudices concerning the correct nature of things; but the individuals concerned rarely possess any awareness of the social origins of these tastes.

It is this structuralist mode, through which the particularities of the object world at a given time may help generate the objectifications by which a set of social relationships comes to know itself through an array of everyday taxonomies which makes Bourdieu's work such an advance on previous analyses of consumption. It accounts for the way in which goods not merely reflect distinction, but are an instrument of it. It indicates the power and importance of consumption trivia, both in everyday social encounters and at the level of meta-social alignments. Bourdieu's habitus is as deeply rooted in material culture as in cognitive orders and social divisions, and it provides the means for combining an approach to all three. It also accounts for the extraordinary ability of shoppers to select from a huge array those goods most appropriate to themselves and their close friends or relatives.

As a modern social analyst, Bourdieu is exemplary in his refusal to reduce his model of society to any single social attribute. Although he often uses occupation and length of time in educational institutions as the axes for his displays and charts, in the text he attempts to encompass a far greater range of differences based on gender, age and expectation. He clearly regards these as always interconnected; the meaning of gender depends upon one's class, and vice versa. He provides a polythetic perspective on social position, exhibiting the structuralist preference for relationships over entities, so that all social attributes are understood primarily in terms of their co-variant properties. This relational approach is opposed to Marx's theory of class, conflating a theoretically constructed concept with a given body of people defined largely by economic position; although Bourdieu recognizes that such has been the impact of Marx and Marxism that class as representation has by now been realized, through sheer symbolic efficacy, to an extraordinary degree (Bourdieu 1985).

Bourdieu also attempts a balance between relativism and moral judgement. One of the work's main strengths is that it covers all social positions. A radical lesbian whose main concerns are CND and South Africa is as likely to be placed in terms of education and occupation (e.g. teaching or social work), as the home-loving, conservative, television absorbed, do-it-yourself enthusiast might represent the aspiring white collar working class. The work is, however, clearly intended to expose the pretensions to a superior rationality of middle- and upper-class taste.

Although *Distinction* is surely the most significant contribution to the study of consumption made by any anthropologist, and one of the major resources for obtaining a better understanding of our own culture, there are certain important limitations to the work. Perhaps the main weakness in the text, which accounts for a number of others, is the methodology employed. Despite having worked previously as an ethnographer, Bourdieu makes no attempt to employ the ethnographic method in this work, relying instead on a lengthy questionnaire reproduced at the end of the book. Although highly inventive and productive, this questionnaire can provide only explicit responses, rather than insight into actual practices, and, through processing, has created a normative characterization of the diverse social fractions involved, which are seen as an exemplars of a larger, statistically-based model of class. The actual brilliance often displayed in the art of living in modern society by people of all classes, and the use of ambiguities, inconsistencies, resistance, framing and such devices in individual and social strategies are thereby lost.

What is especially curious is that this questionnaire is strongly reminiscent of others which are well-established as a marketing technique, and are supplemented by actual marketing surveys. Like marketing, it classifies informants according to sociological classes combined with consumption patterns. It is not unacceptable for an academic to employ a technique developed in industry, but what is strange is that this is combined with a remarkable lack of consideration for the impact of marketing itself. However welcome Bourdieu's analysis of consumers may be when contrasted to the more common attempt to explain the same material as a simple expression of business interests, the book's impact is not enhanced by its entirely ignoring the sphere of production. Bourdieu's habitus does not spontaneously generate a world of goods, only a set of dispositions. To understand how the congruity between the two is achieved demands an investigation of marketing, designers (as by Forty 1986) and other distributive agencies. It is not sufficient merely to talk of the articulation of two independent spheres (Bourdieu 1984: 230).

Despite the striving for the autonomy of consumption activities, resulting in an exaggerated separation from business interests, in some respects Bourdieu's major source of analogy tends to fall back, not on to an economic, but perhaps on to an economistic model. Capital both economic and symbolic appears as an investment open to calculation, and social hierarchy tends to be reducible to these two main linear strands through which capital can be exploited in social positioning. The result is very different from the ideas expressed in chapter 6, where it was suggested that one of the many results of the rise of material culture as a mode of cultural form was its ability to multiply and keep apart a plethora of hierarchies and diverse spheres.

Also surprising, given Bourdieu's work as an ethnographer in Algeria, is the lack of consideration for the nature of mass consumption as an historical phenomena. The world of *Distinction* is 'given', and the sense of modernity as a dynamic form found in the writings of Simmel (1978) or Berman (1983) is quite absent. As a result, the corresponding differences between these societies are not underlined, and this ahistorical representation lends itself to a simplification of both subject and object. The subject as agent of strategy appears as highly constrained and normative. The actual complexities of modern working-class life, the use of distancing or parody, as emerges, for example, from studies of popular culture, is lost in the drive for a consistent congruence through habitus engendered by class interests and constrained possibilities. Working people are reduced to a relationship of immediacy from which they cannot escape. This is much less subtle than the characterization of strategy given in Bourdieu's *Outline of a Theory of Practice*, and is consistent with a simplification of the concept of the object. Despite the exemplary use of material culture as evidence, there is no discussion of its nature and growth as compared to other media.

Distinction tends to revert to a notion of objectification which consists mainly in the external sedimentation and subsequent reproduction of class interests. To locate objects in relation to interest and power, however sophisticated and non-reductionist, is only one perspective upon mass consumption. Other aspects of culture are ignored. The problems of alienation and estrangement are reduced to problems of access to knowledge. Projects based on religion, morals, the nature of the self and so forth cannot be fully incorporated within this framework. The focus on class fragments is, however, often based less on the problem of exploitation than on a Romantic vision of the working class as an authentic humanity, whose sensuality and desires are preferable and proper. Ironically, such a view rests on an aestheticization of labour. Bourdieu implies the same Romantic preference for the work ethic and antipathy towards abstraction as Veblen. As in many similar Romantic writings on the left of the political spectrum, the working class is considered authentic by virtue of precisely those attributes which have been forced upon it by oppression from above. Despite his structuralist methodology (and abstract style of writing), Bourdieu does not appear to perceive the neccessary relationship between abstraction and specificity and the contradictory nature of modern culture brought out by Simmel.

For these reasons, however valuable Bourdieu's work may be in identifying the patterns and relationships of the society of mass consumption, it is limited with respect to the present project. *Distinction* does not provide a theory of either consumption or material culture as the form of modern culture. Many of the areas most fully developed theoretically in Bourdieu's earlier work are simplified in the interests of achieving an understanding of the underlying structure of such a complex phenomenon as modern French society as a totality.

When Bourdieu's approach is set against the range of other approaches discussed in this chapter, certain highly divergent tendencies become evident. Some approaches, including the conventional account of the industrial revolution, certain Marxist analyses and business-oriented researches, appear to emphasize productive forces as the prime mover, and are concerned with consumption only as the outcome of capitalist interests and the problem of ensuring that desire and demand correspond with the needs of industry. Other approaches, including those of Douglas and Bourdieu, are concerned with consumers themselves as groups with interests, both cognitive and material, which are projected in patterns of objects, and in this case it is industry which is seen as handmaiden to the pattern of consumer group demands.

This difference is crosscut by one of the major questions addressed by Bourdieu in his earlier work (1977) but largely ignored in *Distinction*, which is the balance between objectivist approaches such as those found in archaeology, and subjectivist approaches, the most extreme of which would be design history or the study of Chicago homes. The intention of the next chapter is to examine, through actual cases of consumption, the means by which some balance may be achieved between the relevant factors. What, however, should already be evident as a result of both the historical and anthropological materials investigated in this chapter is that, just as with material culture in general, in many social studies (with the conspicuous exception of economics) a stress on consumption is a necessary corollary to its previous neglect. The development of a study of consumption may then be integrated, not as dichotomous to relations of production, nor as a universal social function, but as a continually growing element of modern culture, which must therefore play an increasingly prominent role in attempts to understand the nature of contemporary societies.

9

Object Domains, Ideology and Interests

Material Ideology

Bourdieu's *Distinction*, in common with several other approaches to consumption, such as that of semiotics, is largely based upon the mapping of differences between goods on to differences between social groups, which, in the more reductionist instances, are often treated as prior social divisions unaltered by this process of signification. An alternative approach, which will be adopted in this chapter, is to concentrate rather on the possibility of identifying divisions which pertain to particular object domains and which may not be consistent with any cohesive representation of society. In such cases, the significance of the social divisions associated with objects is most evident from the study of the goods themselves.

Within such an approach, objects may not be reducible to the workings of a central hierarchical principle, or be directly related to what are otherwise considered the most important social divisions. In at least one example, the distinction between goods is more closely related to contradictions within one given set of individuals than to differences between social groups. As mass consumption, a particular array of objects may be found to represent and assist in the construction of perspectives relating to control over production or rivalry between consumers, but also to wider issues concerning morality and social ideals. As external forms, however, objects may also be independent of the interpretation of any one particular group, and their consistency as a material presence may belie the actual variety of meanings they evoke.

To set any analysis of the styles of artefacts within the social context of contemporary Britain would appear to require consideration of a wide range of agents and relevant factors. These include forms of production and comerce and the demands of profit, the interests of and constraints on manufacture, design, marketing and advertising, whose role it is to create the images of industrial goods in relation to specified target populations, and the interests of and constraints on the consumer population, who use and in their turn manipulate the meaning of these forms through differential selection, placement, use and association.

As an initial example, one of the most fundamental ranges of objects in contemporary British society will be examined, that is the variety of house styles found in residential developments. Fortunately, major contemporary building styles have been subject to detailed analysis in terms of their social significance. There is the work of Muthesius on the terraced house (1982), of King on the bungalow (1984), of Oliver et al. on the semi-detached house (1981), and of a multitude of authors on the leading architects of the modernist styles, which emerged as the dominant from taken by council properties.

The major distinctions emerge clearly from these accounts. On the one hand (Oliver et al. 1981: 78), there are the attributes held to be exemplified in the half-timbered, suburban, semi-detached, middle-class house: an ambivalent position in relation to town and country, an expression of individualism extended in the modern do-it-yourself tradition, a concern with compromise and a rejection of extremes, all set within statements about tradition and nationalism. Some of these are further extended in the detached bungalow analysed by King (1984), as part of an opposition to elements of modernity and urbanization which constitute the major transformations of the environment over the last two centuries. In stark opposition to the values of suburbia are the images projected by the council estate, which appears on the landscape as a powerful expression of the ideals of communality, of technological supremacy over the slum, and of modernist statements on the possibilities of present and future society, often tied to concepts of socialist planning as formulated by the Bauhaus and promoted by a number of British local councils. Muthesius documents in detail the interests of the professions involved in building streets of terraced properties: the speculators, suppliers of materials, planning controllers and architects. Jackson (1973: 145) shows that these interests were hidden by the demands of style, as in the semi-detached properties which employed a basic frame but added a spurious individuality on the façade in order to make the house more attractive to prospective buyers, or the modernist- style buildings, which proclaimed their scientific nature to the degree that elements of the internal construction which would not normally have been visible were externalized onto the façade to display a commitment to the appropriation of new technologies.

The symbolic function of the different styles present in the built environment which is the context for everyday action suggest that they might fuel an apparently active and sustained debate between suburban individualism and inner city communalism. The implication, however, that these differences represent actual conflicts in society or the emergence of competing and alternative traditions is quite false. This becomes evident when consideration is given to the processes by which these styles are produced and consumed. The modernist council properties have long been one of the strongest fiefdoms of professionalized architecture, being extremely closely linked to development planning and local political interests, and subject to the intervention of both civic authorities and the state. These links are evident in modernist style which extends also to the large blocks used for government administration and the offices of major commercial organizations. The development of this style, then, should be credited not only to architects, but to the whole range of bureaucratic and business interests, academics, developers and systems builders, and the various strata of decision makers. When taken together, these amount to a large part of one of the dominant interests of contemporary British society: the professional middle class. As a style, modernism visibly lends itself to this appropriation. It projects an ethos based upon the advances of science, the adaptation to systems technology, and the destruction of tradition, which accords well with those elements of technological dominance discussed by Habermas and his Frankfurt School predecessors in their critiques of modernist rationality and the ideology of technological efficiency.

What is curious is that the members of this same dominant group which may be held responsible for the emergence of modernist architecture, and its appropriation by the state as an authority, do not, by and large, choose family homes of their own built in this style, which is clearly incompatible with their personal desires and images. Instead, their own households are more likely to be typical of the larger examples of the detached, the semi-detached and the bungalow, which are extended, in part through emulatory processes, to other sectors of our society with similar aspirations, to such a degree that these styles virtually command modern private development. The consumption of modernist architecture as residential form is almost entirely through state allocation. The consumers of this architecture, the council tenants, have been notoriously restricted in their ability to transform the façade of these dwellings. The suburban dwellers documented by Oliver et al. (1981), who are able to alter the appearance of their homes, tend not to use modernist styles, which, in any case, do not lend themselves to such appropriation.

What this implies is that a group of people who, as consumers, constructed and sustained this image of the individualist tradition also, as producers, constructed the very image of change, community and modernity to which it is opposed. The source of the apparent opposition between these two styles then becomes evident. Clearly, they represent a structural polarity through which the semantic power of the 'semi', as traditional, ambivalent and individualistic, gains its full resonance only by contrast with modernism. To put it the other way around, it is through the state appropriation of the language of change and urbanicity that the construction of an opposite which is perceived as unchanging and surburban becomes sustainable. The representation of the interests of a particular group is greatly clarified if that group is also able to construct an antithetical image (for the details of this argument see Miller 1984). King provides evidence of the power of this structural logic in his example of the attempt by bungalow builders to 'invade' the countryside to such an extent as to threaten the forces which had, until then controlled the spatial distribution of various styles. The result was legislation curtailing any further extension of this form into 'inappropriate' areas (King 1984: 184–92).

This suggests that in studies of material representation it should not be assumed that the consumption of a given group will be represented as a coherent and consistent set of forms. The same segment of the population working as producers and consumers here creates quite contrasting images, although analysis reveals them as emanating from a consistent set of interests. This separation allows for further twists in the nature of representation, since the failure of the modernist council estate could be (and was) manipulated by the media to appear as evidence for the failure of the ideals of communality such estates appeared to represent. It was indeed a failure of such imagery, but it must be remembered that the very image of society, and in some cases of socialism, the council estate embodied was that imposed by academics and professionals, and never that of the residents, who have neither a place in the construction of that image, nor the means for its appropriation.

This analysis of the dominant building styles of our society suggests that a set of representations derived from the interests and perspectives of a particular group in society not only denies access to this aspect of culture to alternative perspectives, but at the same time causes these representations to appear to be the image of those who have been excluded. There are comparable cases in other areas of culture studies (e.g. Williams 1961), where what appears to us as the image of one section of society is actually fabricated by a quite different class. In such cases, the object, in this case building form, may act as a kind of material 'ideology', but the meaning of this term is open to considerable dispute.

The root of the modern use of the term ideology lies with Marx. The theory of value which was the cornerstone of *Capital* asserts clearly that the very terms and their accepted connotations used in conventional descriptions of the political economy of the time, mystified and suppressed the true nature of, for example, exchange value, as an outcome of the dominance of capitalist interests. Marxism invented itself as the proper understanding of the nature of history seen from the perspective of labour, and should therefore have become the perspective and consciousness of labour. In the later history of Marxism, the re-education of the peasantry and workers, along with the transformation of production processes, has always been a prime instrument in the securing of revolutionary goals (Hinton 1972). This practice is saved from its apparent idealist overtones by its claimed congruence with inevitable historical transformations whose roots lie elsewhere.

This argument was refined by Lukács' (1971) suggestion that only certain historical transformations could bring the proletariat to realize their true interests and thereby allow them to commence revolutionary action. In view of this, Marxist teaching can be seen as a kind of catalyst. Not surprisingly, this doctrine has become especially important to those who feel as a matter of Marxist science that the proletariat ought by now to have enacted a revolutionary response to the crises which are seen as always present; and their failure to do so is therefore commonly explained as an aspect of false consciousness, which prevented them from recognizing their proper historical duty.

Recent criticisms have been made of several aspects of this approach. Historical analysis suggests that the argument that the perspectives of dominant groups are so pervasive as to permit no alternative or popular forms of representation is untenable (Abercrombie, Hill and Turner 1980). Marxists influenced by Gramsci's analysis have also often asserted the impact of dominant ideas, but, in their view, acquiescence has been always problematic; it has to be worked for through the establishment of hegemony and can never be simply taken for granted. Furthermore, it is commonly met by diverse forms of resistance (e.g. Hall et al. 1976).

One approach to this problem may be derived from the theory of objectification according to which access to culture, as the externalization through which the social group is constructed, is the basis for social development. In so far as society is divided into different interests, of which labour and capital are the prototypical examples, it may well be that some interests have more control than others over the development of representations which accord to their perspective and thus their interests. As Foucault has shown (1981: 92–102), the power they hold is productive, not merely suppressive, of culture. The concept of perspective implies that understanding is derived from a particular position in the world. If two groups have different perspectives, then, in so far as they are able to create the world, they naturally attempt to do so in accordance with their own perspective, or 'habitus'. In as much, however, as the cultural forms thereby produced become the external environment through which emerge other groups whose interests are not identical, and indeed may be contrary, to their own, we are faced with the situation described in the discussion of building styles above, where the dominated group is forced to attempt to invest itself in the domain of culture represented by the built environment in terms of a set of objects whose initial meanings are antagonistic to its own interests.

What this suggests is that despite valid criticism of their pretensions as theoretical perspectives, the notion of both a dominant ideology and a false consciousness do have at least some place in a theory of ideology. One group may dominate large areas of cultural production, while another, through lack of access to cultural form, may be less clear as to the nature of its own interests. The problems arise when these are reified as essential attributes of an entire spectrum of cultural form. The class which is defined in relation to buildings, essentially that of private as against public tenure, is not the same as that defined by another division such as profession. Although dominant as far as building styles and the press are concerned, this same social segment may be less influential in the areas of trade unions and popular culture. Following this expressivist logic, if a group is unable to objectify its interests in certain domains it may attempt to create its own cultural forms in some other field, although some groups without any resources are bereft of both power and prospects in virtually all spheres. One of the results of the quantitative increase in material culture, providing new domains of representation all working in particular ways, is to complicate further the problem of what may be termed material ideology.

The Limits of Objectivism

This complexity is ignored by many of the approaches to ideology which have in common a tendency towards what may be termed 'objectivism', a term which emphasizes a general antipathy towards a subject- or agency-centered perspective. Where the question of ideology is paramount, the concern is with the manner in which control over cultural forms is used to suppress contradictions or conflicts (Larrain 1982: 15). In recent years, however, analysis based upon a given concept of ideology has been complemented by other projects, some of which also analyse buildings as repressive mechanisms or authoritarian representations (e.g. Foucault 1977b), but whose overarching concepts such as 'power' or 'discourse' imply a still greater distance between interests and representations, and thereby a greater commitment to objectivism.

Critical objectivist approaches have tended towards a totalizing perspective, by virtue of their style of analysis which tries to rise above culture. When applied to the world of goods, such approaches therefore tend to subsume the whole spectrum of industrial commodities under a variety of notions of cultural dominance. In most cases, this is simply inferred in a phrase about the evils of commodity consumption. There has been, however, a range of attempts to emphasize the place of commodities in exemplifying some general condition of dominance, which goes beyond the more particular implications of ideology. Examples of such studies might include aspects of Marcuse's *One Dimensional Man* (1964), the earlier work of Lukács (1971), Barthes's *Mythologies* (1973), Lasch's *The Culture of Narcissism* (1979), and studies by Ewen and Ewen (1982) and Haug (1986). Although these works commonly refer to the bourgeois world as a specific interest group within society, the actual material analysed, such as blue jeans, soap operas or boxing, often represents the cultural forms adopted by the whole spectrum of society.

As an illustration of what appears to be the inevitable result of a strongly objectivist analysis which presupposes its equal relevance for all commodity forms, there follows a brief summary of the trajectory taken by one of the more sustained attempts to focus on the commodity as the central object of research, by the French social theorist Baudrillard. Baudrillard began his studies in the earlier tradition of symbolic analysis, with an attempt to examine the significatory properties of modern mass consumption (e.g. 1981: 29–87). From the beginning, however, he was concerned to overturn one of the most important of the assumed signifieds, that is utility as defined on the right and use value as defined on the left (1975, 1981: 130–63). His critique of Marx's concept of use value helped to open the way for anthropological studies of the cultural construction of need (e.g. Sahlins 1976a), and suggested that the ideas of 'true' and 'false' needs sometimes used in critical studies (e.g. Marcuse 1964) were severely problematic. In time, however, these ideas developed into a much more general critique, in which objects not only did not signify use value but were found not to signify anything outside of themselves. In the modern world, they were held to have become so totally interchangeable that there was no value which could not be reduced to this cycle of exchange. In contrast to Bourdieu, Baudrillard believed that people have become merely the vehicles for expressing the differences between objects. Rather than representing, the sign becomes the front behind which the actual disappearance of the signified goes unnoticed, and we are left merely with the medium itself.

The resulting argument is typical of that current in post-structuralism (e.g. Sturrock ed. 1979); that is, we think we create objects in history which we use to communicate/signify/represent/constitute, but actually today there is simply a world of objects in terms of which our notions of self and society are created. In short, our identity has become synonymous with patterns of consumption which are determined elsewhere. Taken to its logical conclusion (and the advantage of Baudrillard is that he does just this), this view entails a denial of all signification. Baudrillard's argument becomes highly convoluted, as in his *The Precession of Simulacra* (1983), which postulates the annihilation of all content, but the outcome of this contention is clearly nihilistic, since any opposition to this trend, or any radicalism, would be simply subsumed by this subversion of the sign. Che Guevara, Marx and Baudrillard himself himself are therefore destined to become merely a set of surfaces to play with as commodities which have lost the possibility of any further depth. In the case of Baudrillard, this appears to have been a self-fulfilling prophecy, and he is mainly quoted today within the avant-garde arts, where he is indeed very much in vogue (Frankovits ed. 1984).

Baudrillard's biography provides a clear example of the limits of extreme objectivism as an approach to mass commodities (compare Anderson 1983: 32–55 on post-structuralism in general). In a less sustained form, this is still a much used line of attack. Indeed, some of the ideas developed by Baudrillard in the early 1970s recently resurfaced in a critique of the culture of late capitalism by Jameson (1984; see also Foster ed. 1983). Jameson puts forward the familar argument that society has lost any possibility of depth or effect, and is reduced to mere pastiche and superficial self-comment. We are left with a play on signs which has no ultimate reference point other than the commodity. The cultural forms of late capitalism have thus become entirely pervasive and able to subsume any attempt at opposition.

The context for this argument is a critique of post-modernism. This term usually refers either specifically to a movement in architecture which emphasizes a return to a popular façade based upon the design of mass commodities (e.g. Jencks 1977; Venturi, Scott Brown and Izenours 1972), or else to the more general movement towards pluralism and primitivism which followed the critique of modernism. In Jameson's critique, it is precisely this populism and celebration of kitsch which is denigrated. This results in a quite misguided emphasis. Jameson seems to object to the fall of modernism and the decline of a critical aesthetic, and fails to learn from the quite genuine failure of modernism itself with regard to its popular acceptability. What he thereby misses is that post-modernism represents simply a new façade or twist to architectural style as ideology discussed earlier. It serves to hide the professional, that is elite, structure through which it continues to operate by assuming the mantal of the popular for itself. It purports to be an appropriation of the public building by the people, when it is actually an appropriation of a particular version of the populist by one dominant group.

Jameson's approach is typical of that conservatism which regards all other periods of history as authentic, but the present as the final inauthentic state. It is a Romantic version of modernism which is viewed as genuinely progressive and critical, rather than merely the means by which capitalism destroyed any tradition which might have opposed its hegemony. A similar point is made by Anderson (1984) with respect to a still more eloquent defence of modernism by Berman (1983). Modernism certainly had its place in the destruction of the *ancien régime*, but it is only one particular form of social change and has recently been most conspicuous in its failures. Furthermore, modernism created a considerable degree of misery and frustration by insisting that only one particular dominant style had the right to be considered the appropriate form for the expression of socialism.

In relation to the object world, all analyses based on strong objectivism tend to produce similar results. They act to reproduce what has been called the mass culture critique (which may come equally from the political right or left, see Hebdige 1981a), in which the objects of mass consumption today are treated as so tainted, superficial and trite that they could not possibly be worth investigating. There may also be the tacit and covert implication that those people who have to live in and through such an object world are equally superficial and deluded, and are unable to comprehend their position. This implies a rejection of any activities undertaken by the mass of the population (always with the exception of direct revolutionary action) as a possible basis for learning about the future development of our society. The argument is that people cannot construct socialism out of kitsch (sometimes with the equally problematic implication that they can out of art). In the terms of Bourdieu's *Distinction*, these often esoteric academic critiques tend to align closely with the avant-garde arts as holders of cultural capital.

There are many varied precursors to this modern branch of the mass culture critique, for example, the work of Morris, Adorno and Marcuse (e.g. Horkheimer and Adorno 1979), as well as several early versions of the notion of false consciousness. A typical contemporary assumption is spelled out by Gortz, who claims that 'working-class demands have turned into consumerist mass demands. An atomised serialised mass of proletarians demand to be given by society, or more precisely the state, what they are unable to take or produce' (1982: 240). Such a position does not lend itself to anthropological analysis, since one of the objectives of the discipline is to learn something of value from the practices of the people one is studying. The argument that there is a thing called capitalist society which renders its population entirely pathological and dehumanized, with the exception of certain theorists who, although inevitably living their private lives in accordance with the tenets of this delusion, are able in their abstracted social theory to rise above, criticize and provide the only alternative model for society, is somewhat suspicious. The clear lesson of the history of modernism is that the academic left is quite capable of fashioning a central instrument for the reproduction of the interests of the dominant class at precisely the moment when it is making the most strident claims to the contrary.

Recontextualization

It was suggested earlier that the potential for a balance between objectivism and subjectivism in social theory has been demonstrated by a number of recent models (e.g. Bourdieu 1977; Giddens 1979). The problem is then how to translate this balance from the more general issues of social theory to the particular context of mass consumption, and certain limitations in the book *Distinction* with regard to just such a translation have been noted. The extreme objectivism which was rejected above is expressed through a variety of images of an overarching class interest or subsuming discourse, usually related either directly to production or to the general term capitalism, which is used to eliminate the possibility of dominated groups as arbiters of cultural form. Clearly, some fields of material culture, such as that of building style, are compatible with such an approach. If other examples can be located which appear to suggest an alternative conclusion, then this raises the more general question as to what appears to determine the suitability of different theoretical emphases to various material forms.

There is a clear tendency for the more anthropological accounts of consumption, such as those of Bourdieu and Douglas, to concentrate on consumer interests. Another anthropological study based on an analysis of a particular domain of objects is by James (1979), who analyses the sweets which are purchased by children themselves, as opposed to those bought for them by adults. The suggestion is that these 'kets', as they are called in north-east England, although they are found throughout the country, are generated as an inverse transformation of the acceptable qualities of adult foods. They are, in symbolic terms, systematically 'inedible', for example through the use of strong artificial colours avoided in adult food, the portrayal of 'inedible' animals such as beetles and snakes, 'inedible' objects such as machine tools, bootlaces or flying saucers, and subjects disapproved of by adults, particularly ghoulish representations of corpses, blood, vampires and death. Indeed, since the article was written there has been a considerable increase in the number of skulls and corpses in white chocolate which ooze red when bitten into, and a set of candy bones which form skeletons and are purchased in small plastic coffins for ten pence.

The implications of this example are quite different from those of building forms. Here, a social group which is in a relationship of inferiority to the dominant adult world is able to objectify a perspective which asserts clearly the potential opposition of its interests to that world. This suggests a degree of autonomy in cultural production on behalf of dominated groups. While the sweets are produced by industrial processes for mass consumption, and according solely to the demands of profit, it would be equally hard to argue that the result is the responsibility of either some evil genius at the production end, or some demonic child at the consumption end. Rather, we have the emergence, over a considerable period of time, of a children's culture. This in not simply the product of a dominant ideology or control over cultural representation, nor a pure act of resistance, but the mutually constituted relationship of two sets of interests and self-images. This example, then, although opposed to the objectivism of the mass culture critique, could not be termed subjectivist in orientation.

Assessed in terms of mass consumption, a balance between subjectivism and objectivism can be seen as a balance between the weight assigned to the two main forces of production and consumption. The relationship between these two forces must be seen as constantly interactive, not largely autonomous as implied by Bourdieu. Despite the enormous efforts made through advertising, design and the media to create markets for given products, well documented by writers such as Galbraith (1969) and Haug (1986), profits are always dependent upon the reciprocal ability of marketing staff to interpret the changes in the way in which goods are used in social relations. Advertising for items such as children's sweets may confirm and help expand the process of objectification of the child's image of the world, but it could hardly be said to have initiated it. If it is the case, as suggested by various studies (Leiss, Kline and Jhally 1986: 33), that advertising, despite all its resources, has little power to affect long term purchasing trends, then this is an extraordinary finding of contemporary research. While there are other grounds for criticizing the advertising profession, and evidence for a cumulative effect upon social expectations and concepts of lifestyle in general, the failure of any simple correspondence theory should alert us to the complexity of this articulation between production and consumption.

An article by Hebdige (1981b, see also 1983) examining the changing meaning of the motor scooter provides an unusually clear picture of the dynamic interaction between the two forces of production and consumption. The development of the object as image is followed through three 'moments': those of design, distribution and consumption. The argument, in very condensed form, is that the motor scooter was developed in Italy as the feminine equivalent of the more macho motorbike. These gender terms stand for a wide range of associated connotations of industrialization and commodification, through which the childlike scooter, with its enclosed machine parts, reproduces in its relationship to the motorbike the basic asymmetry in the status of the sexes. These images are, however, transformed in a manner not intended by the producers (though later picked up and encouraged by them), but which is established rather through articulation with emergent polarities in British youth cultures. The motorbike takes on an association with the rockers which is then contrasted to the motor scooter's place in the construction of the mods' sense of style; the latter representing a more continental 'soft' image against the rocker's American 'hard' image. The new grouping is consistent with, but not determined by, the original image created by the industry. Obviously, such a brief account omits all the subtlety of the original, which is considerable.

Hebdige's article provides a bridge between those analyses termed 'anthropological', which appear to ignore the direct interests of producers, and those, mainly marxist or commercial, which assume an entirely passive reaction by consumers. It demonstrates both industry's careful reading of the market to try and differentiate material forms on the basis of a prior social division, in this case gender, and also the fact that the transformation of these objects in

Britain provided the foundation for the formation of new social groups, to whom consumer style was so integral that they could not be considered prior to those material changes through which they expressed and thereby created themselves (see also Willis 1978: 11–61). Hebdige's article also permits the reintroduction of elements of intention, and what Giddens (1979: 5) terms 'discursive penetration', to both producer and consumer, while retaining a sense of the larger historical forces emanating from social and technological change.

The three examples so far discussed appear to lend themselves to different theoretical perspectives and conclusions, yet they are all drawn from contemporary British consumption patterns. One factor which might be responsible for the differences between them is the properties of the objects themselves as material culture. It is no coincidence that the three sets of objects can be arranged according to a scale of size decreasing from buildings, through motor scooters to sweets. Buildings are enormous artefacts, immovable, extremely expensive, highly visible and highly durable. Their material importance has led to the extensive involvement of the state in their production and allocation, and their status as major purchases affords opportunities for conspicuous consumption. Such artefacts may tend towards the representation of dominant perspectives, made most explicit in the concept of monuments.

By contrast, there is the vast array of what may be termed 'portable industrial artefacts': the contents of the high streets, supermarkets and shopping catalogues, objects ranging from saucepans, to skirts, to three piece suites. Compared to buildings, they are cheaper, less durable and therefore more amenable to short-term fashion. They may be less likely to attract the interest of the state or the overall image of industrial production, though many are affected by parallel contrasting images of modernity and tradition. They are, however, the subject of mass marketing and advertising, and the source of much immediate profit. Their very variety suggests that a dynamic interplay between the worlds of business and consumption results in a plethora of relationships and divisions.

Within this area are many objects which are so small, cheap and transient that comparatively little research and investment is likely to be put into the active promotion of new forms determined by production, and the producer may be reduced to a more or less passive respondent to apparent shifts in demand. Obviously, no simple correlation will be found between size of object as a single factor and the nature of the object as representation; but when size is taken as a general gloss for a number of those factors relating to framing, consciousness and triviality discussed in chapter 6, it is clear that the nature of material culture itself may be a much underestimated factor in accounting for the patterns and relationships of modern style. The key dimension may not be whether the object is received through the market or some alternative distributive mechanism, but rather its place as a consumption item in constructing social images.

The complexity of the articulation between producer and consumer interests is further illustrated by the case of advertising in women's magazines. In recent years, criticism has been made of the tendency in such magazines to occlude the distinction between text and advert, on the grounds that this is a form of distortion which betrays the trust of the reader in the independent objectivity of editorial content (e.g. Earnshaw 1984). Clearly, many magazines contain articles merely as a front for the dissemination of the advertisements from which the vast bulk of their income is derived, and in so far as they have editorial comment this reflects those messages (Curren 1986; Ferguson 1983). Thus we find advertising features such as articles on holiday resorts and wines in which it is impossible to separate objective opinion from advertising pitch. Does it follow, however, that the readers 'put up' with the bulk of advertising merely because of their interest in the incidental articles?

So evident is the high proportion of adverts in such magazines that the critic who believes that readers are simply fooled by the lack of clear demarcation, must credit them with a remarkably low level of perception. The alternative possibility is that both editors and readers are actually far more interested in the adverts than the rest of the magazine content, and collude in the use of this additional material largely as a legitimation for this practice. The implication that, despite the vast presence of advertising, many people actually want still more of the stuff, is not all that surprising, given the previous arguments for the importance of material goods in modern social relations. After all, having possibly spent a great deal of time in unpleasant and unremitting labour, the wage earner may be forgiven for considering the translation of these wages into an act of consumption as being of some importance; obtaining the right object may considerably enhance a reputation or signify membership of a social group, while making the wrong purchase may lead to exclusion and frustration.

This argument is not intended as a defence of the extent of modern advertising, whose interests are clearly derived from company profitability rather than the enhancement of the welfare of the purchaser. It does, however, demonstrate that there is an activity centered on relating goods to larger concerns about the nature of self and society, which may emerge particularly clearly in advertising. Goffman (1979) has demonstrated how central aspects of social inequalities and concepts of self-presentation may be identified through advertisement analysis. The critic who points out that the advertisement appears to have noting to do with the material and functional nature of the product is merely reproducing the general illusion of vulgar functionalism enshrined in modernism. It is the secondary, often social, but possibly also humorous, moral or sexual connotations which represent the actual value of the 'aestheticized commodity' (Haug 1986: 72) to the purchaser.

Modern feature writing has started to become far more explicit in this collusion. Certain new magazines (and not only free ones) are now distributed explictly as consumer guides. These magazines have been joined by the colour supplements with long explicit consumer features, and series where potential peers are presented in their own rooms with the full cultural regalia of furnishings, decorations, cars and so forth. Winship's (1983) analysis of Options, a recently launched women's magazine, suggests that this close liaison with the modern commodity world plays upon the fantastic in terms of goals which are largely unrealizable in a material sense, but which are clearly lived as fantasy. Fantastic does not, however, mean vicarious, nor does the construction of myth imply mere illusion. The projection of images of possible worlds and cosmologies has always been central to the development of social relations. Neither should this collusion between consumer and producer be seen as always implying an individualistic competitive consumer practice. Adverts may be used as much to help an individual accord with a set of communal values and feelings of social responsibility, as in the explicit advertising of socialism.

The case of advertising complicates another common assumption in critical writing on modern culture, which is that the evaluation of consumption patterns is to be assessed entirely on the basis of hierarchy and the strategies of inclusion or exclusion. Bourdieu is a clear case in point. As a contemporary example, there has been an impressive recent rise of a series of commonly linked 'healthy' practices. These include the wider cultivation and use of wholefoods, organic and pesticide-free crops, homeopathy, acupuncture, biorhythms and other alternative medicines, jogging, areobics and new sporting activities, all of which appeal to the general desire to prolong individual life. These are linked with a wide diversity of other tastes; for example, many of these consumers tend to be left wing, socially concerned, feminist, well-educated, and obviously able to afford these generally expensive alternatives to both the supermarket and the national health service.

If this set of practices is to be condemned as a new form of middle-class oppression through differentiation, then by the same logic many forms of mass culture which have no connection with any 'traditional' working-class regime, but are essentially the results of mechanization and mass production, may become identified with a positive image in the writings of critical sociologists. This tendency emerges in the important body of research entitled popular culture studies (e.g. Bigsby ed. 1976; Waites et al. eds 1982), which has developed in Britain as a major instrument of left-wing cultural politics. The perspective taken in most of these studies is closely related to that represented here, in so far as many of them, including the work of Hebdige, are specifically designed to rescue the possibilities of mass materials from the derogatory attitude of the mass culture critique. The subject of such analysis is usually cultural pursuits such as leisure activities and the mass media, rather than material objects *per se*, and mass activities such as shopping have received relatively little critical attention (Mort 1986, though see Williamson 1986a on consumption). Popular culture, however, tends to be ambiguous with respect to actual mass culture. It often attempts to deal specifically with working-class culture or with sub-cultures which are seen as resistant to the dominant forces in society, so that, as with Bourdieu, though in a somewhat different way, the analysis tends to reduce the material to its place in reproducing or opposing given social positions and conflicts.

The association of the cultural practices of dominated groups with a heroic image is clearly problematic, with writings increasingly assuming that popular means positive (Williamson 1986b). Modern critical texts often contain contradictory evaluative stances. Should, for example, the hard, macho image of some youth groups be positively evaluated as working-class, but negatively evaluated when examined from the perspectives of feminism and racism? Strongly influenced by the pioneering work of Stuart Hall, both the Centre for Contemporary Studies in Birmingham and, more recently, the Open University have produced an extensive literature on these subjects, in which such contradictions are explicitly addressed.

The problem with reducing the analysis of specific material domains to their place in social differentiation and the reproduction of dominance is not only distributive, in that these may crosscut the given social divisions, but also interpretive, in that this approach may tend to ignore all the other projects in the development of which goods are employed. This is argued by Douglas and Isherwood

(1979), who stress cognitive demands in the stabilization of categories through their material expression. Objects have always formed an important part of religious and other similar expressive activities. Asceticism, despite its prominence as an ideal, has played a relatively restricted role in most of the world religions, the actual experience of the mass populace having been oriented more towards certain buildings or monuments and the performing of defined, and often elaborate, ritual activities, so that the opposition commonly assumed between materialism and spirituality is based more on an ideal than on a practised dichotomy.

The wider projects encompassed in material appurtenances may be exemplified through an examination of two studies of fashion. Simmel's analysis (1957: 308–15) focuses upon the relationship between individual and social expression not only as posing problems for social theorists, but also as a lived contradiction for the subjects of such theorists. Simmel argues that fashion plays a major part in many people's attempt to live out the contradictory pulls of this perceived duality. Typically, Simmel does not present these as alternatives, a trend towards isolation as opposed to a trend towards integration, but as necessarily contradictory elements of the same actions. Fashion demands an individual conception of a conventional style, thereby allowing the preservation of a private world, a self-conception which is saved from exposure by the expediency of convention. In obeying the dictates of style, it is the social being which takes responsibility for choice, yet there is simultaneously an arena for personal strategy. Fashion then provides a surface which is partly expressive, but which also in part protects individuals from having to expose their taste in public. This study provides a clear exemplification of the concept of consumption activity as a means of living through necessary contradictions.

In a recent more general study, Wilson (1985: 228–47) argues strongly for the viability of the project of creative recontextualization of these products of mass production, against the particular form of the mass culture critique espoused by some feminist perspectives. The approaches discussed above, which tend towards extreme objectivism, are associated by Wilson with a search for authenticity as some natural 'true' female image outside of the context of consumption and patriarchy, leading in practice to a puritanical moralism. Against this, Wilson posits fashion as a mode of modernity providing a more fluid and flexible form of feminist expression which may promote active criticism of the forces it wishes to oppose, but is also creatively self-defining for feminism, employing modes such as fantasy, parody, and humour in this project. The reason why Wilson's modernism, unlike either classic architectural modernism or the claimed populism of post-modernism, is acceptable as positive recontextualization, lies in the difference between the practitioners. Within architecture and art, the image of both abstract science and high-street commercial 'pop' is always imposed by professionals, who are in effect interpreting the image of another class. With fashion, on the other hand, there is the possibility of mass participatory modernism, in which images provide groups with a vehicle for appropriating and utilizing cultural forces themselves. Fantasy here may or may not be a mystifying force preventing the housewife from attaining an objective understanding of the forms of her oppression, but like religion before it, it is a world either of idealized morals and possibilities, or else of outrageous alternatives against which everyday life may be both evaluated and understood, and, as such, it has attractions of its own for the consumer.

Conclusion: The Birth of the Consumer

All the examples given above have been used to complicate the problem of analysing the meaning of specific domains. In some cases, the nature of the objects themselves is firmly implicated, as in children's sweets; while in other cases, such as that of motor scooters, the form of the objects stays the same and it is their connotations which radically alter. What underlies this complexity is less an appeal for pluralism than a recognition of a pluralism which already confronts us. All the objects discussed are the direct product of commercial concerns and industrial processes. Taken together, they appear to imply that in certain circumstances segments of the population are able to appropriate such industrial objects and utilize them in the creation of their own image. In other cases, people are forced to live in and through objects which are created though the images held of them by a different and dominant section of the population. The possibilities of recontextualization may vary for any given object according to its historical context, or for one particular individual according to his or her changing social environment. Hebdige's work indicates that motor scooters were transformed according to the conceptions of youth groups, but the original distinction promoted in the initial design and marketing of these goods was that of gender. There is nothing in the later trajectory of the images of these goods which suggests that the ability of the bikes and scooters to reproduce gender asymmetry was in any way deflected by the transformation represented by these later shifts.

Simultaneous with the insistence that recontextualization may be possible has been an avoidance of the other extreme, which is that all such recontextualization is a form of resistance which should be regarded as inevitably positive in its consequence. The term recontextualization implies the concept of text which is itself open to many readings, and several parallels may be drawn with discussions concerning the death of the author (here perhaps the death of the producer), in the sociology of art (Wolff 1981: 117–37). Just as modern sociological theory has suggested that the meaning of the text is not simply reducible to the intentions. perspectives or interests of the author, so also the emergence of the object from the world of capitalist or state production does not make it of necessity a direct representation of the interests of capital or the state.

The concept of the death of the author in sociology has, however, rarely led to what might be called the 'birth of the reader'. Most of the writers who have used such ideas (e.g. Barthes 1977: 142–8; Foucault 1977a: 113–38) have tended to work within that form of post-structuralism and strong objectivism in which the attack on the author is part of a more general critique of the subject, such that the rejection of the highly individualistic autonomous subject of the liberal tradition develops into a denial of any degree of autonomy or individuality in social relations. The problem with the objectivist foundations for this approach is that the critique of capitalism too often becomes a critique of mass industrial culture *per se*, which has had the effect of stifling any positive advocacy of a potential popular alternative which remains within the context of industrial culture. To that extent, the academic advocates of socialism may be partly responsible for rendering it increasingly unattractive to those sections of society for whom a direct increase in material wealth remains a primary concern.

In contrast to this nihilistic conclusion, the material presented here suggests that the notion of recontextualization permits a more positive reading of the possibilities for the receptor of the commodity. The change from user to consumer is not necessarily the kind of fall from freedom suggested by Raymond Williams (1980), but may lie closer to possibilities which are addressed in other trends within the sociology of art, where interpretation is understood as recreation (Wolff 1981: 95–116). In the study of mass consumption, this becomes translated from abstract theory into a continual interaction mediated by the specific form of industrial commerce through which the material manifestation of this relationship is continually being recreated. Any approach to mass consumption must therefore deal directly with this same mass of objects.

The complexity and contradictions which have been illustrated in contemporary material culture may be accounted for in terms of the general characteristics of this media noted in chapter 6. Objects as diverse concrete forms may be used to create simultaneous but highly diverse representations whose very materiality acts to prevent them coming into direct conflict at the level of open and conscious dispute. Material forms therefore lend themselves admirably to the workings of both ideological control and uncontested dissent. This reconfirms the problematic nature of the relationship between culture and society noted in the first part of this book. Rather than postulating some relatively consistent phenomenon called 'society' that is distorted or misrepresented by culture, we may dispense with any such assumptions concerning prior subjects, and deal directly with the actual contradictory and complex phenomena of cultural form within which and through which social relations operate. If this argument is not to regress into the objectivist attack on society and the subject, however, it can only be by reaffirming the essentially positive nature of culture as objectification and the possibilities it provides for social development, which will be the aim of the next chapter.

10

Towards a Theory of Consumption

Introduction

The argument which began with the abstraction of a concept of objectification from Hegel has led to the analysis of specific cases of contemporary mass consumption such as semi-detached housing and clothing fashions. The purpose of this final chapter is to complete the circle by using the implications of the case material on consumption as recontextualization to reformulate the concept of objectification as an approach to contemporary consumption. The term objectification was considered initially in relation to a set of ideas concerning the resolution of the subject–object dichotomy derived from an aspect of Hegel's *Phenomenology of Spirit*. The abstraction is only partial, however. Unlike the term dialectic, which signifies the use of a particular form of logic, the concept of objectification, as developed here, is always grounded in some notion of culture. Hegel represents only one source for the meaning of this term, which was later transformed through its exemplification in a variety of studies of human development and cultural relations, all of which were concerned with the development of a given subject through its creation of, or projection on to, an external world, and the subsequent introjection of these projections.

In this chapter, an attempt will be made to associate modern British society with a particular phase in such a Hegelian scheme. It will be argued that, during the period since Marx, social conditions have changed to such a degree that any translation of Hegel must advance a stage beyond Marx's original reformulation. As with Marx's analysis of capitalism, the present analysis will be compared with periods in the *Phenomenology* such as the unhappy consciousness, which are marked by an inability to recognize the social nature of social productions, and a series of competing philosophies and practices which threaten to submerge human and social interest beneath several over-autonomous and reified abstractions. Finally, some suggestions will be made as to how we might progress from this period of unhappy consciousness and regain the possibilities immanent in the development of the subject, that is, society.

The return to Hegel is based on the premise that perspectives he developed may still be enlightening today. His work provides the foundation for an examination of subject–object relations which avoids reductionism to either of these two, and at the same time captures the dynamic nature of the historical context in which these relations operate. Hegel subsumed the Kantian concept of an external world which is, in part at least, only constituted through the particular manner of its appropriation, but he did so without reducing this merely to the static mechanisms of mind. He provides for the dynamic construction of these structuring mechanisms within the process of appropriation itself. The spectrum covered by the *Phenomenology* ranged from the individualist psychology of the expanding consciousness, through to the objective context of laws, history, morality, and social relations. In terms of the particular problems of today it did so in a manner which echoes the helter-skelter thrust towards diversity and variability characteristic of modern life.

Perhaps the most attractive feature of Hegel's ideas is that they are essentially positive. They assume the development of the subject as desirable, and although their pseudo-evolutionist implications may now seem antiquated, they allow us to identify with a subject as progressive. They thereby provide the foundation for a form of critical analysis which opposed the status quo not merely by representing it as repressive, but also by comparing it with what could be, with the immanent possibilities of the present. Although in their original form they sometimes tended towards conservatism in their appraisal of the Prussian state, when abstracted as objectification their critical potential was indicated most forcibly by the early writings of Marx. When developed further as a concept, objectification may become highly atypical of modern theory. It places emphasis on a cultural context for its realization, but its dependence upon some concept of a developing subject refuses the allure of extreme relativism lost either in theory or empiricism. It provides for a progressive development which feeds on diversity without tending towards nihilism. Its insistence that the products of culture will ultimately be known as our own creations which can be encompassed at some future stage, resists the attraction of the tragic.

In brief, the model insists that a subject cannot be envisaged outside the process of its own becoming. There is no *a priori* subject which acts or is acted upon. The subject is inherently dynamic, reacting and developing according to the nature of its projections and experience.

As an intrinsic part of being, and in order to attempt an understanding of the world, the subject continually externalizes outwards, producing forms or attaching itself to the structures through which form may be created. All such forms are generated in history, which is the context within which that subject – generally some social fraction – acts. As a cultural theory, these forms may include language, material culture, individual dreams, large institutions or concepts such as the nation state and religion. In time, depending upon historical conditions, these externalizations may become increasingly diverse and abstract. Although the subject may at certain periods appear lost in the sheer scale of its own products, or be subject to the cultural mediation of a dominant group, and thus fail to perceive these cultural forms as its own creations, the tendency is always towards some form of reappropriation through which the external can be sublated and therefore become part of the progressive development of the subject.

Although not necessarily implied in Hegel's own use of these ideas, such a return to the subject may be taken as a return to essentially human values from a period in which goals, values and ideas are dominated by a logic stemming from the interests produced by the autonomy of external forms created as culture. This interpretation will be applied in the present work. Society progresses through the creation of external forms, which may be either, as with the Australian aboriginals of the ethnographic literature, concepts or complex institutions embedded in ritual and social structures, or else, as in Britain, of an increasingly material nature. In the former case, the model of objectification as culture, while not static, does not have the element of modernization which leads to ever increasing expansion, as is found in post-industrial societies. These externalizations always threaten to develop autonomous momentum. Within the concept of objectification lurks a Frankenstein image of a model, once externalized, turning away from and then against its human creators, as in Marx's theory of capitalism as rupture. Society in its various manifestations is always striving to reappropriate culture, and thereby progress, a drive sustained by the feelings of estrangement generated by such a condition of rupture. The term 'human values' is defined tautologically as that which contributes to the progressive tendency of society.

Marx and Simmel

The attempts by Marx and Simmel to use Hegel as the basis for a theory of modernity were investigated in the first part of this book. In the case of Marx, the privileging of production as the sole site of self-alienation was rejected, as was the notion of communism, which, along with Hegel's original concept of absolute knowledge and all other Romantic versions of the end of history, was argued to be spurious as both a theoretical and a practical solution. Simmel, by contrast, used Hegel to provide a model of the increasingly abstract nature of modern culture based upon the quantitative and abstract nature of money. He also addressed the issue of increasing diversity in terms of the quantitative rise of material culture and its implications. Although Marx is far more explicit about his use of Hegel, Simmel comes closer to the transformation envisaged here. This comparison is misleading, however, in so far as certain central tenets of Marx's moral philosophy, and the attack on class and exploitation, had, by Simmel's time, become firmly integrated into the more general humanistic outlook, and are implicit in, for example, the comparable works of Durkheim and Weber. These are goals which the present work attempts to espouse, notwithstanding the critique of some of Marx's more academic structural reasoning.

The views of both Marx and Simmel concerning the progressive nature of capitalism are clear, though the latter tends to reduce this to the impact of money and impersonal relations. They agree that it has reduced the obligatory ties of the feudal era and is, by implication, the necessary foundation for any modern concept of freedom. In Marx's case, the freedom promised by capitalism is an illusion, since it is wrested away by the capitalist from the people and becomes merely the freedom of the wage labourer to be exploited by the capitalist. I take the stress in Marx's analysis to be based largely on an opposition to the illiberalism of the bourgeois, rather than, as in much contemporary Marxism, mainly an assault on its liberalism. Simmel also notes the alienation consequent upon the rise of abstract relations, but sees this as the inevitable contradiction in abstraction itself, both freeing and estranged. Some of the differences between Marx and Simmel may be the result of the period of time which separated them.

The single historical moment clearly dominating Marx's entire perspective is the industrial revolution. He and Engels witnessed the extremes of degradation and trauma this produced, and, although they could perceive more clearly than their contemporaries the progressive implications of such a transformation, this insight was correctly subservient to the immediate dilemma of the suffering and exploitation which had been the particular means of its accomplishment in Britain. The resulting bitter condemnation of the dehumanizing practices of the day resulted, however, in support for an essentially conservative view of the place of production. Its paramount importance in the construction of social relations was simply inferred from recent history. The supersession of the present condition was embodied for Marx and many writers of the time in a series of utopian notions which, in many cases, looked back for their models to pre-industrial relations between the people and the means of production, there being no alternative guide to the future.

At the time Simmel was writing, although it was before the major scientific revolutions of this century, the image of the industrial revolution was less immediate than the overwhelming sense of its products. Although many of the conditions described by Marx and Engels still obtained, the possibility of an industry which did not extract the maximum work out of labour for the minimum wage was evident. Simmel was more impressed with the extent to which mass consumption had become a feature of modern urban life, expanding the material environment beyond all expectations. He describes this moment of modernity as a new diversity and abstraction, which perhaps only became evident when the middle class, rising in size and scope, began to create its distance from commerce and from the physicality of production. The taste complexes described by Elias in *The Court Society,* evolving from the ancient court regime with its princes and aristocracy, were being replaced by that mass struggle over reputation and social position which would emerge as the society described by Bourdieu. With Simmel, then, a similar concern with estrangement and abstraction took the form of the problematic use of this new commodity world, rather than being based entirely on the exploitation of labour.

Today, in the late 1980s, we are still further in time from Simmel than Simmel was from Marx. The changes which have taken place in this century are at least as great and have had consequences at least as important as those which overwhelmed Marx and Simmel. Although many governments continue to assert the direct applications of Marx's philosophical and political perspectives, the very concept of praxis indicates that these must be subject to transformation through the impact of historical change. Taking a global perspective, there are areas today which may be seen as analogous with that part of European history experienced by these writers. The profundity of Marx's model is perhaps greatest in the context of revolutionary movements in the Third World. As a theory of multinational or local exploitation of a labour force, it is perhaps more important in these contexts today than it ever was in Britain in 1850, since the sophistication of international capitalism is such that there seems little possibility of much of the world escaping from its position as underdeveloped, except through violent revolution. This is not always the case. India, for example, has resisted the pressures which would have made it merely the working ground for external capitalism, but India has vast resources on which to draw in such a struggle.

In Britain, however, many of Marx's assumptions appear to have been greatly weakened by the praxis of historical change. The idea that wages are merely intended to cover the demands of social reproduction is unconvincing, as are those functionalist analyses which regard the welfare state as simply the latest extension of capitalist instrumentality (e.g. Castells 1977). The labour theory of value, which, as employed by Marx, postulated productive work as the sole source of value, is even less convincing today than it was when it was first formulated. The idea that surplus value is merely the appropriation of human labour takes no account of the vast impact of the scientific revolution, since it cannot be applied to the age of the microchip, of machines which often make the physical nature of human labour itself entirely redundant. Indeed, at one point in the *Grundrisse*, Marx perceived this consequence of the imposition of science on to his own equation (quoted in Habermas 1972: 48–50). The worker as de-skilled machine appendage is increasingly replaced by the robot. If a quarter of the population still works in direct manufacturing, this leaves a large majority who probably never have, and there is little prospect of industrial production expanding its use of human resources. This is not to deny the continuity of class and inequality, which have made increasing use of the education system for their reproduction; but even such evidence of continued inequality as, for example, the demonstration that the welfare state has continually provided proportionally more aid to the better-off (Le-Grand 1982) does not contradict the general rise in material prosperity of society as a whole over the last century, such that the average contemporary industrial worker may possess a greater wealth of material goods and machines which perform servile tasks than the average member of the middle class in the nineteenth century.

Any progressive developments since the time of Marx have arisen from several causes, among which the beneficent attitude of capital is not numbered. Capital itself attempts to serve its own interests as greedily and as totally as it has always done. Three factors of particular importance may be singled out. First, the trade union movement has achieved enormous advances in the interests of labour, but only through continual struggle and the ability of working people to undergo self sacrifice and deprivation to ensure the representation of their interests. The second factor is the impact of socialism itself, stemming from Marx, but also from more pragmatic and reformist inspirations, which have provided models and goals. These have tended to operate through the growing power of the state as the instrument through which certain excesses of capitalism could be countered, and, in the case of the fully socialist state, radically transformed. Today, therefore, the academic writings of Marx are complemented by the histories of a large number of explicitly socialist states and mixed economies, in their successes and their failures.

The third, and for the present argument most important, factor is the central contradiction of capitalism in which the labourer represents, in his or her other role as consumer, the market necessary for the goods produced by capitalism. However opposed capital and labour may appear in the struggle of wages against profit, for capitalism to achieve its goals, and its sales, it is necessary for the labourer to buy and to continue to desire more goods. When the labour force does not represent the market, the interests of the two groups are totally antagonistic, but when the labour force is the market the relationship becomes more ambiguous. In this respect, the labourers' fight against capital has always depended upon their acquiescence in the capitalist's desire to sell; that is, they 'agree' to fight for higher wages which may then be used for purchasing. With the decline of colonialism, British industry has had to take particular cognizance of its own people as its major market. The desire to repress wages is offset by the profitability achievable through economies of scale in mass production. When this happens, a certain identity of interests between capital and labour may appear. This may be illustrated by postulating a scenario in which capital is always forced merely to produce that which its own labour force as consumers demanded from it in the way of goods. This subservience of capital to the demands of the labourer could still serve the interests of capital, since it would no longer produce unprofitable, in the sense of unwanted, products, providing that consumer demand continued to expand. This potential identity of interests may have proved as important historically as the much more accepted historical antagonism between labour and capital, and is an essential premise for the possibilities of socialism.

The Unhappy Consciousness

The concept of unhappy consciousness denotes periods of dichotomized subject–object relations resulting from the inherently contradictory nature of a number of aspects of modern society. This may occur, in part, because these contradictions are not perceived as such, but are merely experienced as the kind of oppression signified in the anomie of Durkheim or the blasé and cynical attitudes described by Simmel. This makes the roots of that oppression harder to identify, and we become unable to recognize our own place either in the creation of these oppressive structures or, potentially, in their partial resolution (since the contradictions are inherent, resolutions are always partial and must always be maintained rather than simply achieved).

The first source of this modern dilemma is the continued rise of mass industrial production and commerce. The contradiction lies in the nature of industry as revealed by history. On the one hand, industry has created all those products upon which modern life is based. Without the car or bus, the phone, the paperback, the health service, the television, the mass produced architecture, modern urban life is impossible to envisage. The twentieth century has seen the original industrial revolution enormously expanded, as scientific advances are continually translated into new goods. There is little sign that most of the populace wish for anything other than a continual increase in the availability of such products and the benefits felt to be received by their possession. Such benefits are by no means limited to material or technological advances, but, as is evident in all the anthropological investigations of mass consumption, are mainly based on the possibilities they present for the expansion of society, its forms and relations. There is little reason to think that a return to craft production on a large scale would produce more than a radical restriction of the availability of goods to elite sections of society. With growing ecological constraints future expansion will come increasingly from scientific innovation rather than new physical resources.

The extension of industry is complemented by that of commerce and monetarization. The importance of money as part of the general expansion of quantification and abstract logic is such that it is probably the main medium through which we think mathematically in everyday life. Simmel's argument that money is the basis of modern freedom and that the complexities and choices represented in our society are impossible even to envisage without it, seems entirely applicable today. Also still evident is the contradiction that money goes beyond serving evident human interests and becomes, as 'capital', an interest in itself, in which people are reduced to questions of profit and efficiency. The instrument of capital is industry run on the logic of profitability, and the accepted criterion for successful industry is almost entirely the expansion of capital rather than the impact of its products. Marx showed clearly that, left to itself, this logic tends to separate the market of consumers from its own wage labour, reducing the latter to the minimum wages necesary for social reproduction. This situation is most clearly developed through a new international division of labour, where workers in certain countries may be paid minimal wages since the market for their products is abroad. Where this separation could not be sustained, as in Britain, capitalism may still work towards a highly unequal distribution of its products.

The contradiction posed by industry, which lies in the positive nature of many of its products set against its historical tendency to follow its own autonomous interest rather than the interests of the people who create through it, has been partly responsible for the transformation of the second powerful contradictory force in modern society, that of the modern state. Whether or not the state developed to ensure the efficient working of capitalism as it expanded internationally, or to preserve the hegemony of a class, today the state appears as the only force large enough to attempt to redirect the aims of large-scale industry away from pure profit towards the interests of the population. Whether this is done on the massive scale of state socialism, or by means of the more limited but still extensive economic and social policies of the so-called mixed economies, the state appears in the twentieth century to have developed an increasingly large-scale interventionist role.

Just as money is the foundation for freedom, the state is the essential mechanism for the creation of equality. Although in certain societies it may serve as the instrument of capital, it is the only force which has the potential, given certain historical conditions and the requisite social agency, to restrain capitalism's natural tendency towards inequality, and, through redistributive mechanisms and legislative means, to create the conditions for the achievement of equality. Equality should not be defined in Rousseauist terms as a natural order intrinsic to humanity, a primitive condition. Rather, it is a highly abstract concept which probably could not be envisaged as a practical (as opposed to a theoretical) proposition without the prior development of a strong democratic state. The achievement of even a degree of equality is an extremely complex task requiring an enormous investment in bureaucracy, taxation and planning. It is, therefore, as essential to retain the services provided by the state, as the products provided by industry. Again, there appears to be a consensus of opinion in countries such as Britain in favour of some form of essential state services such as education and health, although arguments continue over degrees of intervention and the balance between state and private control.

Though a means to human progression, the state is as liable as capital to become an autonomous institution which turns against society. In some socialist societies, equality amounts to homogenization and the complete suppression of liberal advancement or pluralistic diversity. The welfare state in Britain has also been increasingly regarded as an authoritarian force which suppresses the interests of precisely those it is intended to aid. This contradiction which is inherent in the state was most forcibly expressed in the writings of Weber on the development of bureaucratic authority (1974: 329–41), and during this century has appeared as an increasingly intractable dilemma.

If money is the basis of modern freedom, and the state for modern equality, then a third force which has seen commensurate growth, and which is promoted as an attempt to gain some modern understanding of these historical processes, is what might be called cultural modernism. The rise of science and quantification, and the continued destruction of previous ties, are all marked in the emergence of new modes of expression. These are most explictly promoted in the arts, that is, modern literature, theatre and cinema, but are equally prominent in the styles of modern commercial goods. This force not only contributes to the rise of diversity and abstraction, but is increasingly the medium through which these are expressed and understood. For a considerable period, modernism seemed to be equated with largely benign and positive forces, such as the sciences, which were eliminating disease and poverty, or the avant-garde, which expressed the possibilities of the new age. Over the last two decades, however, the social disaster of the new built environment as the major expression of modernity, the image of an inaccessible modern art, plus the general perception of the amorality of the white-coated scientist dealing with the incomprehensible, have contributed to an overall sense of the other side of modernity as alien abstraction so brilliantly described by Simmel.

Although attempting to capture the advances of science in its notions of design, function and progress, modernism as an image may again lead to reification and lose any sense of the human nature of these creations. Hi-tech objects can become so functional in appearance that they no longer function particularly well for the user; art as high taste and education as knowledge become not instruments for understanding, but, as Bourdieu has shown, merely forms of obfuscation acting as instruments for the maintenance of class dominance. Knowledge is no longer used to develop, but to differentiate. Today, the negative side of scientific advancement is so forcibly expressed in the destruction of the natural environment, and in the threat of annihilation though atomic war, that it is doubtful whether the older positive image will return.

These three forces are illustrative of all these changes in society which have combined to create the condition of the unhappy consciousness of today. In all cases, these changes are based upon largely progressive and essential developments which provide the foundation for the unparalleled possibilities of modern life and the promise of socialism. The constant fight for higher wages by members of the work force at all levels cannot simply be reduced to a demand for the paypacket. It must always imply a demand for the purchases represented by those wages; that is, a continued demand for goods. For all the verbal attacks on modern goods, the more effective critique of practised asceticism is rarely encountered; that is to say, the private practices of many academic critics, amongst whom there are very few Gandhis and Tolstoys, may well contradict the substance of their argument. As anthropologists who have examined consumption have affirmed, it is impossible to isolate a range of 'authentic' goods serving 'real' needs (e.g. Douglas and Isherwood 1979; Sahlins 1976a). The political interventions made by the left may almost always be translated as a demand for services for a wide variety of social groups, and for state intervention in the redistribution of resources, which implies the continuance of a mass industrial base and bureaucracy to secure the means for such provisions.

The period of unhappy consciousness is one in which we recognize the negative and abstract nature of these forces as oppressive, but fail to realize that these negative conditions are the outcome of a whole series of historical developments which we otherwise regard as positive and essential to our well being. Certain of the most evident signs of alienation, such as the pressures of mass advertising, the level of inequality and the imposed modernist form so contrary to mass aesthetics and desires, might all be altered through positive political action. This would not itself counter our inability to be reconciled with the deeper contradictions by which a bureaucracy demands some anonymity to act fairly, and in many other areas institutional practices have to consist in compromises rather than resolutions. Following the Hegelian logic, a recognition that the estranged conditions and feelings of alienation created by the rationalism and abstraction of the present are, to a considerable degree, an inevitable consequence of positive developments, might itself be a first step (though only a first step) towards the reappropriation of culture, but this implies a recognition that we are facing contradictions which have to be lived rather than removed. While the form taken by the contradictions outlined here are specific to contexts such as contemporary Britain, they relate to contradictions which are intrinsic, as Simmel indicated, to culture *per se*, and their equivalents may be found in quite different societies, such as in New Guinea or India.

Modern Consumption

Like the mass of material goods, consumption is examined at present in most of the critical social sciences only as an aspect of the general problem of commodities. Goods are seen, as indeed Simmel in part understood them, as part of the ever growing problem of abstraction and differentiation. Objective culture has become unimaginably vast, producing goods largely as symbols of wealth and fashion, often modes of oppressive social differentiation. The processes leading towards autonomy described above, command virtually all the channels through which we obtain such goods. The vast majority are purchased and are pure commodities in that the money spent on them could equally well have been spent on some other item out of the vast array. Baudrillard and the critics of post-modernism provide the clearest account of this sense of the complete interchangeability of things, implying also a reduction of human relations to this exchange cycle of style. In those cases when we do not obtain goods through direct purchase, the most common alternative source is the state, which may provide the house we live in, the range of furnishings, our education, the libraries, the sport facilities and so forth. Depending on one's place in class and society, the state may be far more important than money as a source of goods. It is, however, comparable to money in making those goods symbols of an estranged and autonomous force which imposes itself on us as people who are eminently exchangeable one for another.

If this is the nature of the commodity, the interpretation of objectification it implies would still largely follow the two authors so far discussed. Wage labour may be more rewarding than it was, but the place of the labourer as part of the market – that is, as nothing more than the consumer of commodities bombarded by marketing and advertising (e.g. Williams 1980) – appears to follow a similar logic of estrangement. This increase in external form merely advances the first phase of self-alienation, extending the abstract and diverse nature of culture, which thus appears the more alien and the harder to assimilate. Whether because, following Hegel, we are unable to perceive, or, following Marx, objective conditions prevent us from achieving the conditions which would allow for the sublation of goods, the situation is clearly one of incomplete objectification as rupture, rather than of social development.

This is the approach to goods I wish to reject. It is an approach predicated on reducing consumption to the nature of the commodity, and the consumer to the process by which the commodity is obtained. In opposition to this argument is that perspective with focuses upon the same problem, but sees it as one faced also by the consumer of goods, and which emphasizes the period of time following the purchase or allocation of the item. This alternative perspective is only possible because of the changing historical conditions in the period since Marx wrote, during which the mass of the population have reduced their time spent in labour and enormously increased their time spent in consumption.

As consumers, we confront these abstractions of money and the state most fully at the moment of obtaining goods. In the process of shopping, we have to immerse ourselves in this vast alienated world of products completely distanced from the world of production. We cannot while shopping relate a packet of potato crisps to the factory where it is made, in terms of either the people working there or the machines. At the moment of purchase, or allocation, the object is merely the property of capital or of the state from which we receive it. The individual may feel either estranged from this world of the shopping centre or public institution, or else excited by its scale and potential. Either way, the situation is radically transformed upon obtaining the goods in question.

On purchase, the vast morass of possible goods is replaced by the specificity of the particular item. The extraordinary degree of that item's specificity becomes apparent when it is contrasted with all those other goods it is not. Furthermore, this specificity is usually related to a person, either the purchaser or the intended user, and the two are inseparable; that is, the specific nature of that person is confirmed in the particularity of the selection, the relation between this object and others providing a dimension through which the particular social position of the intended individual is experienced. This is the start of a long and complex process, by which the consumer works upon the object purchased and recontextualizes it, until it is often no longer recognizable as having any relation to the world of the abstract and becomes its very negation, something which could be neither bought nor given. If the item is allocated by the state, then all specificity is a result of work done upon the object following its receipt.

Thus, consumption as work may be defined as that which translates the object from an alienable to an inalienable condition; that is, from being a symbol of estrangement and price value to being an artefact invested with particular inseparable connotations. Commerce obviously attempts to pre-empt this process through practices such as advertising which most often relate to objects in terms of general lifestyle, but this does not mean that advertising creates the demand that goods should be subsumed in this way, and these images should not be confused with an acutal process performed as a significant cultural practice by people in society. Work in this sense does not necessarily mean physical labour transforming the object; it may signify the time of possession, a particular context of presentation as ritual gift or memorabilia, or the incorporation of the single object into a stylistic array which is used to express the creator's place in relation to peers engaged in similar activities. The object is transformed by its intimate association with a particular individual or social group, or with the relationship between these.

Clearly, such work is not to be understood in the narrow sense of that which happens to a particular object after it is obtained, but has to include the more general construction of cultural milieux which give such objects their social meaning and provide the instrument employed in any such individual transformations. The work done on a pint of beer includes the whole culture of pub behaviour, such as buying rounds, as well as the development of an often long term association between the consumer and a particular beer, which excludes all other types of drink or brands identified with other social groups by gender, class, parochial affinity and so on. Such cultural practices cannot be reduced to mere social distinction, but should be seen as constituting a highly specific and often extremely important material presence generating possibilities of sociability and cognitive order, as well as engendering ideas of morality, ideal worlds and other abstractions and principles. Although, for some, the age of the pub and the authentic nature of the 'real ale' may be important, others may perceive an atmosphere of plastic facades, parodied images and the products of international breweries as more proper, unpretentious and tasteful. The aesthetics may be entirely relativistic; it is the social practices to which they are integral which make such activity consumption work. The ability to recontextualize goods is therefore not reducible to mere possession, but relates to more general objective conditions which provide access to the resources and degree of control over the cultural environment. As demonstrated in chapter 9, an ability to appropriate cannot be assumed, and relates to the more general inequalities evident in contemporary society. On occasion, as shown in the example of children's sweets, the act of appropriation starts with the creation of the array of goods themselves.

In short, the modern process of consumption is a much neglected part of the great process of sublation by which society attempts to create itself through negation. Thus, far from being a mere commodity, a continuation of all those processes which led up to the object – that is, the mass abstractions which create objects as external forms – the object in consumption confronts, criticizes and finally may often subjugate these abstractions in a process of human becoming. If a commodity is defined as the product and symbol of abstract and oppressive structures, then the object of consumption is the negation of the commodity. Although the object's material form remains constant as it undergoes the work of consumption, its social nature is radically altered. This is not, of course, a description of all consumption or a realizable aim of all the participants in the modern economy, but what must be recognized is that it is immanent in consumption itself. That is to say, we must know that the work we do on the goods we purchase, or obtain, and the cultural networks with which we associate ourselves, can be understood in a similar vein to the work we do on the natural world. In consumption, quite as fully as in production, it is possible, through use of the self-alienation which created the cultural world, to emerge through a process of reappropriation towards the full project of objectification in which the subject becomes at home with itself in its otherness.

In our society, these two moments are inseparable; the same circumstance which constructs production as a moment of estrangement provides the conditions under which consumption as reappropriation appears possible. Even if work conditions are improved, the scale of production must make it unlikely that this could ever become again the main arena through which people can identify with self-constructed culture. In turn, the possibility for consumption emerges once goods are no longer perceived as mere commodities, but are understood as a major constituent of modern culture. From this, it will be shown that, ironically, it is only through the creative use of the industrial product that we can envisage a supersession of any autonomous interest called capitalism, and that only through the transformation of the state's services can the state also be reabsorbed as an instrument of development. In short, consumption is a major factor in the potential return of culture to human values. As is explicit in the work of Hegel, progress cannot be through recapturing something simpler and past, but only through a new mastering of the enormity of the present.

To argue the necessity of goods is no more than to argue the necessity of culture. It is not, however, to assert the autonomy of culture. In chapter 3, it is argued that Marx, in attempting to redress Hegel's emphasis on the high culture of philosophy and intellectually appropriated forms, and to ground these ideas in a wider notion of social relations of which social and economic conditions were an intrinsic feature, in practice subsumed culture as form within the play of social differentiation. This tendency has been taken still further by writings in the Durkheimian tradition and by later Marxists, which have reduced culture to merely the external reflection of the history of social conflicts and distinctions. In proposing consumption activity as the continual struggle to appropriate goods and services made in alienating circumstances and transform them into inalienable culture, the aim is to readjust a balance, but not to reduce the subject of history to a world of objects. The manner in which consumption is reformulated here as a process in terms of their place in which objects are always understood, does not permit a return to the simple study of individuals or objects *per se*. It continues the tradition of studying society in relational terms, but insists on a wider totality in which social relations are always cultural relations, and as such are always constituted within the sphere of what Hegel and Simmel argued were necessarily contradictory circumstances existing over and above social division and conflict.

In contemporary British society, and indeed, as well be argued later on, in any feasible socialist society, culture is generally purchased or allocated in the first instance, but this does not make it inferior to culture physically produced by the appropriation of nature. That is to say that society may construct itself in the appropriation of culture as much as in the transformation of nature. To refer to society as 'constructing itself' is to signify that these activities are based on historically given forms and peoples, and that both the suject and the object of this process are cultural, rather than natural, forms. This notion of the self as a cultural form constantly re-evaluated by social criteria is opposed to the concept of an essentialist natural self masked by the artificial nature of culture as commodity. This may be illustrated with reference to cosmetics. It is commonly argued that the real self is represented by the natural face which provides direct access to the person as he or she truly is, while to cover the face in cosmetics is to mask it in terms of a set of unrealizable ideals generally manufactured by the capitalist market or patriarchal society in which the authentic person has become submerged. Certain of these assertions relating to the predominantly single gender use of cosmetics and the interests of the market are undeniable (e.g. Myers 1982), but what is questionable is the implication that the effect of cosmetics is always to hide the 'real' person.

In contrast to this may be set the attitude of New Guinea highlanders to their own considerable use of self-decoration, including face painting, as analysed by Strathern [1979]. Here we have exactly the opposite conjecture. For the New Guinea highlander the natural face is relatively arbitrary; they see no reason why the fact that they are the equivalent of freckled or blond, pockmarked or conventionally handsome should be a direct representation of their real selves. It is only when the face is something worked upon, through elaborate cosmetic preparations which provide an expression of the self constructed by the self, that they appear in their true guise to the observer. The moment when the British critic regards us as most covered up is precisely the moment when the New Guinea highlanders see themselves as lying naked before the world; it is here that aspects of their true self such as their cohesion with the community, or their state of health, will emerge, as revealed by their ability to construct an acceptable cultural self on the external face. The act of self-construction is therefore not totally controllable, but will reveal aspects of their relationship with the wider society which they might have wished to remain hidden. Although a self-construction, it is a social being which is made evident.

The Briton assumes an essentialist given self; the New Guinea highlander a culturally constructed self. But it may be noted that the New Guinea conception is not of the self as constructed entirely by external forces, as in the post-structuralist reading of the body as text; the medium may be conventional and historical, but it is the particular nature of its manipulation by a given individual which is significant for the future development of that person in society. Nor does it appear of great consequence if some of the items obtained, such as feathers and shells, are purchased with cash rather than salt, or are from birds shot with guns rather than arrows. For the highlander, therefore, culture is an objectification through which social relations are developed through being made manifest. This view is closer to that of Wilson (1985: 228–47), discussed in the last chapter. Wilson also rejects that notion of natural authenticity which is the premise behind a wide range of critical discussions, in favour of the active projection of the social being upon the body, and argues for the possibilities of pleasure as a radical activity against the implied asceticism of these critiques.

Returned to the context of modern Britian, this example shows the limitations of the debate between individualism and communal or social expressions (see also Abercrombie et al. 1986). Britain has a far larger mass culture, with far more extensive communal forms, than any New Guinea society, and probably also more explicit concepts of individualism. These are conventionally seen as alternatives, but they are actually both products of one set of differences between Britain and New Guinea. The image and extent of modern individualism is predicated upon the image and extent of communal mass society. They achieve their strength of imagery through contrast, which is merely the product of the inherent contradictions resulting from a process of objectification, that is, the making explicit through externalization of a self-understanding of individual and society in history. Attempts to create societies which are entirely promotions of either individualism or communalism are therefore both disastrous, since they reify one element of a single abstraction. Both extremes tend towards the dualism of subject–object relations which Hegel attempted to resolve.

The large-scale institutions which dominate industrial societies tend to create a sense of an encroaching force which retains control over us, and since such institutions work on the basis of superordinate decision-making which regulates our lives, they conflict with the equal sense of individual autonomy and freedom which is produced by that same force. It is the sense of institutional anonymity which provides us with our most potent image of the struggling, free individual. Indeed, the productive communality of a local or self-constructed community may be achieved in large part by the necessary subsumption of the individual to a group, in the interests of doing battle against these vast institutional forces. Just as these two sets of values are the results of two moments in the same productive process, so their resolution may in part be affected by examining them in terms of two moments of the consumption process.

The processes at the highest level of state organization must be those of quantitative assessment, technological efficiency and social control. Industry and the state could not be reduced to the small-scale, immediately accountable and approachable, without losing their ability to meet the vast demands of modern planning (which is not to say that they could not be more accountable than they are at present). These institutions can only be broken down to sufficiently small-scale elements to be able to fulfil the requirements and reflect the interests of, as well as being a locus of affectivity for, the population, if there is an increased concentration on the work, not of the bureaucracy, but of the people themselves on the products of the state and industry. It is at this stage that we find the extreme expressions of plurality, specificity and diversity which, although conceived of as the opposite image of the central productive sphere, are actually premised upon its very abstraction. These are often directly related, since the larger the plurality of interests served, the larger the scale of planning and organization required. In short, individualism and pluralism are premised upon their antithesis: the autonomous homogenized bureaucracy. A concern with the diverse populace is therefore served not through privatization – that is, switching from one abstracted institution, the state, to a far more invidious one, capatalism – but rather by concentrating on the articulation between the producers and consumers of goods and services.

The diversity of the products of this process of consumption is unlimited, since goods which are identical at the point of purchase or allocation may be recontextualized by different social groups in an infinite number of ways. If we assume the continued existence of large-scale industry employing people *en masse*, of large-scale institutions providing services *en masse*, and of a massive market for distribution, we must then consider the means by which people may find new ways of relating to these institutions and recontextualizing their products without reducing the scale, or altering the necessarily distanced nature, of these projects. Analysis of cooperatives, share allocations and so forth has provided abundant discussion of the implications of this problem with respect to the control over production, and, increasingly in recent years, with respect to welfare state services – that is, the consumer influence on the health service, education and involvement in local government. However, it is in the work done on goods at the level of mass consumption that this recontextualization has gone furthest in practice, and this area is the least studied and the least understood. This praxis may well offer lessons, however, for attempts to project plans for these other domains.

Mass Consumption and Equality

In evaluating the role of goods in the production of social relations, a difficulty arises from the common assumption that mass consumption is inextricably linked to the commodity form and is thereby supportive of only one particular social form, usually termed capitalist. This is despite the equal suitability of the label 'mass consumption' to societies as diverse as Britain, the Soviet Union and Japan. Embedded in a similar network of connotations is the supposition that, while activities such as work may provide the foundation for communal values, it is through consumption that individualist and competitive social relations, the 'bourgeois' private world, emerge. This forms part of the general critique of consumption as materialistic and individualistic. Although, in a society dominated by the market, private individually-oriented consumption practices based on the pursuit of money and affluent lifestyles are common, it is useful to question the degree to which the assumed links between consumption, individualism and inequality are intrinsic to the nature of consumption as an activity. The relationship between capitalism and individualism has recently come under scrutiny (Abercrombie et al. 1986). Clearly, leisure is commonly used as a means of expressing a distance from the estranged conditions of work, and, by analogy with the building styles discussed in the last chapter, it can be argued that the enforced and artificial communality of the workplace is likely to produce an overtly private, self-controlled response in leisure practices. It does not follow, however, that this tendency is a necessary outcome of mass consumption.

The image of consumption as private and individualistic is closely tied to a further concern with its place in the production of social differentiation through taste, which has been emphasized in the tradition of consumption analysis represented by Veblen and Bourdieu. This major consequence of mass consumption is, of course, a thoroughly social activity, but its social nature is here predicated only upon its place as an agent in class oppression expressed through goods. In the following examples, by contrast, consumption can be examined as an intra-class phenomenon used in establishing social cohesion and normative order. These therefore serve to indicate a potential for consumption as a social practice contrary to that stressed in most accounts.

From the work of Engels in the nineteenth century to the long-running television soap opera *Coronation Street* today, the Lancashire town of Salford has been used as a model for the conditions of working-class life in British industrial centres. This more than justifies the title of Robert Roberts' (1973) description of growing up in the area as *The Classic Slum*. In a chapter on possessions, Roberts makes clear that, despite some of the worst poverty seen in Britain, there was a major domain of consumption in Salford which refused to be eliminated by the vicissitudes of the time. Over a long period of time, there had developed among the working class a concept of the parlour. Despite lack of space, this room was not used except on special occasions, but was reserved for displaying goods such as ornaments. The parlour does not seem to be a result of recent emulation of the middle class, but may rather relate to much older traditions. There is evidence of a similar concern with display in medieval Europe; in some cases it would appear that half the commoner's house was set aside for display purposes (Burke 1978). In the history of European house interiors, display appears generally to have been predominant over comfort (Braudel 1981: 306–11). Such evidence, based on a record of an industrial slum, is quite contrary to Bourdieu's representation of the 'true' worker as only interested in consumption of a very immediate nature, directly connected to basic demands.

Roberts describes the importance of the parlour, its care, furnishing, cleaning and decoration, among people who were pawning clothing to get by from week to week. Indeed, it may be that working people were devoting at least as high a proportion of their much more limited free time and cash to display purposes as the contemporary middle class who are more commonly associated with such activities. This was not entirely undivisive, as it pertained to that section of the working class who saw themselves as 'respectable', as against those who were beyond the pale, but this is only to say that they were next to the bottom of the social ladder. Recent work on the transference of working-class families to new towns such as Harlow in the 1950s suggests strong resistance by the occupants of these properties to the plans of architects and designers, which imposed a quite different and more restricting, spatial order, which the residents had then to adjust for their own purposes and in terms of their own traditions (J. Attfield, personal communication).

Such practices emerge with particular clarity in a recent ethnography of the lives of working-class Norwegian women in the town of Bergen (Gullestad 1984). Gullestad describes a world in which men play a relatively small part. The women control the aesthetics of furnishing and household arrangements, spending some considerable effort on these, with the men helping through do-it-yourself work and repairs. The women often undertake part-time work as childminders, cleaners or shop sales staff, otherwise working as housewives and mothers. They associate themselves with a particular social fraction opposed to the values of both the 'trendy' left-wing students and the 'posh' middle classes, but are to some extend emulatory of the wealthier business classes. As in Salford, they have a strong sense of respectability and oppose those who fail to keep up standards through heavy drinking or failing to look after children. They appear to have much stronger social networks than the men, and although married, they go out to discos, and have parties and their own clubs from which their husbands are excluded. This social network is centred upon the custom of regularly meeting to 'chat' around the kitchen table in mid-morning. Furnishing is a major part of the context of these meetings, and they all work hard to present their homes as suitable settings. There are, however, limits. The women seem well aware of the possibility of furnishing and cleaning becoming a vicarious and thus anti-social activity. Anyone who carries on tidying in company, or is said to have 'dust on the brain' is held as culpable. Furthermore, although there is clear interest in evaluating different abilities in terms of home furnishing, there are strong normative limits. An individual possessing more than average money and ability would be cautious about overdoing her furnishing in any way which would transform her from being a good example of her social group to being apparently above and beyond her peers.

In this case, mass consumption goods are used to create the context for close social networks of which they are an integral part. They help to provide equalizing and normative mechanisms promoting solidarity and sociability. There are elements of this 'housewifery' which are clearly problematic, just as class as context is problematic in other analyses, but these cases do at least suggest that the quantitative increase in material culture does not itself, even when purchased through the capitalist market, mean that goods can only signify wealth and therefore the competition of conspicuous consumption. It is commonly ethnography, immersed in the everyday lives of the people while being used to exemplify some academic argument, that appears to counter the assumed 'truths' about, for example, the nature of new suburban towns (e.g. Gans 1967). It is mainly those groups who identify themselves entirely with the abstraction of money as quantitative division, and thereby with goods as largely an expression of wealth, which then engage in the kinds of strategies described so wittily by Veblen in his account of the leisure class.

These examples lead not only to a questioning of the materialism and individualism thought to be intrinsic to the process of consumption, but also to the equally common assumption that it is a direct expression of capitalism which extends capitalist values into the private domain. In the Bergen study the women's normative and egalitarian practices could hardly be seen as a form of resistance to capitalism given their general emulation of the values of the business classes. The more basic question as to what forms of distribution and consumption mechanisms might be considered as fundamental components of capitalism may perhaps be most clearly posed in terms of a possible alternative socialist society.

There are enormously diverse images of what socialism might be, and each has different implications for the ideas being explored here. Clearly, if the aim is to establish a critical position in relation to the status quo in countries such as Britain, these models need not be restricted to those governments currently claiming to represent socialism, although equally it would be wrong to ignore the experiences of such countries. One study which offers clear evidence from the history of socialism in practice, as well as examining the possibilities for a more ideal socialist society which has not yet appeared, is that by Nove (1983) entitled *The Economics of Feasible Socialism*. Just as it was argued in chapter 7 of the present text that socialism need not result in the elimination of individual property, though it would eliminate private 'collective' property, Nove's work shows that the advent of socialism as the end of class oppression might not mean the destruction of the market as the major means of distributing goods, only its elimination as a means of producing inequality. The better part of the present vast array of goods which are often claimed to be solely the result of capitalism might therefore be preserved under a socialist system.

Nove examines the implications of a new situation in which control over production is no longer in the hands of capital and the class it serves, but has devolved to a version of the cooperative, the state or another collective mechanism. He assumes that such a socialist society would retain the heavily industrialized base which provides for the production of mass commodities. His socialism is not, then, a conservative return to a kind of Morris craft tradition. In these conditions he argues that:

> To influence the pattern of production by their behaviour as buyers is surely the most genuinely democratic way to give power to consumers. There is no direct 'political' alternative. There being hundreds of thousands of different kinds of goods and services in infinite permutations and combinations, a political voting process is impracticable, a ballot paper incorporating microeconomic consumer choice unthinkable (Nove 1983: 225).

Nove refuses to accept that central planning and a free competitive market are mutually exclusive alternatives but argues for the essential place of both. The details of his discussion (see also Kellner 1984, Nove 1985: 24–7, 34–5) providing a picture of the complex logistics of such an economy, which would have to deal with the vast problems of a large modern state, give an often more profound understanding than that available in abstract philosophy of the necessary articulation between the philosophical ideals of liberal freedoms and egalitarian justice, the former enshrined in the abstraction permitted by money, the latter in the abstraction of the state. Although Nove notes the faults of a market system, his argument is that for a *feasible* socialism, any alternative to it has far greater drawbacks and more invidious consequences. The model allows the consumer a measure of choice of goods, but proposes state regulation of their social implications, in order, for example, to ensure adequate safety standards and to guard against the misleading representations so common today.

If Nove's model of the distribution process were extended to consumption, goods would be returned from the necessarily regulatory and homogenizing domain of central planning, through the state, back to the parochial, transient and diverse needs of the populace. The state itself might well have to increase its regulatory activities in order to counter practices which appear to favour only private interest or marketing geared to producer 'created' demand. This seems more credible than the attempt by Offe (1984) to argue a case for returning consumption decisions to the workplace. There is no reason to assume that factory workers who produce pig troughs or aids for the disabled are in any respect better judges than management today of the necessity or quality of such products. Nove may be mistaken in his estimation of the importance of the market as the appropriate mechanism for relating goods to people; although it will inevitably play a role, the threat of capitalist autonomy where profit serves only itself is extremely evident at present. What is currently absent is the kind of dynamic debate over alternative distributive mechanisms starting from the nature of consumption, which Williams (1982) suggests operated in France a century ago. The precise models of, for example, consumer cooperatives, may no longer be the best available, but a change in our understanding of what consumption is about as a social activity should provide a starting point for a re-examination of this key question. In socializing mass material culture, debates over the forms of distribution should properly follow rather than precede decisions concerning the desired form of consumption.

It is hard to derive from historical example any support for the argument that involvement in cooperative production produces a direct association with production and, through production, with culture itself. In the kibbutz of Israel, the one long term case of free collective production (that is where collectivization is clearly derived from social choice rather than political pressure) at present available, a cooperative approach is taken to the production of commodities such as plastics, fruit and vegetables or micro electronic components. Since the kibbutz is a cooperative, all members take a turn at the excessively boring task of overseeing, often at night, the machines spewing out plastic buckets, soap dishes and so on. It is highly unlikely that the socialist nature of the production scheme provides for a new identification between the worker and either the form or the result of production. While these aspects of the original cooperative continue today, the total communal ownership of goods has generally faded away. Although meals and child rearing facilities continued to be collective responsibilities for some time, individuals did not feel able to support a system in which a blouse they had hand crocheted might be redistributed to someone they did not like. Such a system is probably unsustainable except through highly authoritarian structures or Messianic beliefs. A more reasonable outcome is a continued dissociation from the mass production of plastic buckets though an equitable share of work, but combined with a market which allows for the actual distribution of such products between these localized production units ensuring equal availability, and a free area of equitable consumption which allows for the assertion of control by the consumer, with all the resultant pluralism. Communal consumption as sublation arises through similar desires concerning the specific nature of goods and services; that is, consumption as a participatory normative activity. It is not solely the outcome of communal work or an equal share in profits, which remain on the plane of abstraction.

Such discussion offers two important lessons. The first is that, even if we envisage (somewhat optimistically) the destruction of inequalities, class divisions, profit-based distortions of claims to public welfare, and all the other iniquities of contemporary society, certain central problems integral to the contradictions, and essential to the production of the material conditions of modern life would remain to be faced. We would still have a vast scale of industry, a vast (probably far more vast) state bureaucracy, and a massive population in huge urban conglomerates, all requiring the powers of flexibility, rationalization and quantification which would be essential to such increased planning operations. The second lesson is that this contradiction is relevant for thinking about politics today, and not just in some future society, because it radically affects the image of possible alternatives to present social conditions. If the intention is to stand by a commitment to the reduction of oppressive inequalities, then mass consumption appears as a key area in the resolution of the alienatory consequences of the mechanisms necessary for the achievement of such goals.

This presupposes that the expansion of goods and services seen in this century is a largely positive development, tied to some historical recollection of the constraints and suffering which this expansion ameliorated. This is suggested by the general support for a struggle for higher wages. No populaton having fought for generations for an increase in their pay packets is likely to give up all the material advances such wages represent without some evident and plausible reason. Although new considerations might influence a decision to vote for a 'green' political party committed to raising electricity prices as the only means of eliminating dangerous nuclear power stations. Such material advantages should not be confused with functional efficiency. It is not that workers have fought for some basic or necessary level of attainment after which all further material additions are superfluous. For those with secure work, most increases in wage levels relate today to possibilities for holidays, and a new diversity in food, clothing and house facilities which, however desirable, are hard to define in terms of finite basic needs. Although poverty continues unabated (and indeed has recently clearly increased) in countries such as Britain, it is not (however much it ought to be) the main pressure behind demands for material increase.

These contradictions in modern society posed by the vast and abstract nature of modern institutions might emerge more explicitly under socialism, since many of the more evident and in a sense 'simpler' causes of social strife would have been eliminated; that is, the regulation of society for the social advantage and the identifiable interests of a few. For this reason, any social practices which can be identified today as having arisen in part as the population's response to these contradictions, become of still greater consequence when considered as models for a possible socialism tomorrow.

Within contemporary Britain, examples of a reabsorbtion of resources back from the autonomous and massive state through to smaller-scale communal or popular bodies which then distribute them locally may be found in diverse circumstances. There are cases of government bodies such as the late Greater London Council actively pursuing a policy of pluralistic redistribution, often to groups such as extremely orthodox representatives of minority religions who may be quite opposed to the council's particular political persuasion. Indeed, to a degree, this is true of all modern governmental services. Bodies such as the National Childbirth Trust and the Hospice movement may arise at the consumer level and seek to re-order the impact of national services in the interests of given consumer groups. Other groups, such as the miners' wives committees formed during the 1984–5 miners' stirke to redistribute supplies and keep up morale, come from within a group acting in direct confrontation with the government of the time. All of these serve to transform welfare provision into something appropriable on a local level. These examples accord with the older liberal tradition of self-creation, rather than the imposed or philanthropic authoritarian image of welfare provision. The Greater London Council was a particularly interesting case of an avowedly socialist body which presented an image based on the diverse possibilities of mass culture forms such as public entertainment, as opposed to the generally rather austere image of socialism, whose opposition to capitalism is thought to demand an opposition to mass consumption taken as synonymous with materi-alism. The GLC also made considerable use of advertising, marketing and the structures of the market to transform itself from a populist to a genuinely popular body. There has been a considerable increase in concern with this area of cultural/commercial activity amongst the British left, as reflected in the pages of journals such as the *New Socialist* (e.g. 1986: 38) and *Marxism Today*.

The above account suggests a reworking of the various critiques of consumption subsumed by the term fetishism. The traditional uses of this term are problematic. First, fetishism is used to assert in a very broad form a general discontent with consumer culture and the nature of goods, accompanied by an asceticism conveyed as a feeling of the general malaise of materialism. Obviously, a book devoted to the subject of material culture will in a sense place undue emphasis on the relationship between people and goods, rather than directly on the relationships among people. The argument of the first half of this book was intended to indicate, however, that all such social relations are predicated upon culture, that is objectification, and that material goods are merely one, though an increasingly important, form of culture. The blanket assumption of fetishism is therefore predicated on the false notion of a pre-cultural social subject.

The narrower and more reasonable accusation of fetishism comes in the form of an argument related to the very particular conditions of modern mass consumption, in which it is said that goods are used vicariously. That is, instead of engaging in social interaction, people become obsessively concerned with their individual relation to material goods. Clearly, this describes an actual condition in modern life and is a further example of that reification which defines the unhappy consciousness, in which the forms of culture become abstracted interests in themselves, preventing rather than generating the development of social values. This is to say that, like those other institutions already discussed, such as the state and monetarization, consumption may be seen as having tendencies towards antisocial autonomy and exclusivity of interest. While some goods such as private art collections or guns may indeed favour antisocial orientations, other such as the telephone and bus do not. The examples given in the last two chapters were intended to indicate that such fetishism is not a necessary outcome of mass consumption, but rather a reification of goods comparable with other examples of reification. Mass consumption may also be seen as a key instrument in exactly the opposite tendency; that is, the creation of an inalienable world in which objects are so firmly integrated in the development of particular social relations and group identity as to be as clearly generative of society. In this sense, the productive capacity of the object as exemplified in Mauss's account of the gift may be retained in the very different social context of a highly extensive division of labour, in which objects can no longer be viewed as directly related to social totalities, but may nevertheless remain an instrument of objectification.

A third form of the critique of fetishism, and the most precise, is that derived from Marx's original use of the term in *Capital*. Marx noted how both the structure of the political economy and the language of business as a particular form of representation tended to make the manufactured object appear, not as the work of the people, but as an alien form confronting them only as a commodity to be purchased by them. This notion of fetishism follows from the arguments of Marx's earliest writings, as explored in chapter 3. Marx stressed, however, in this later work, the manner in which these problems of representation were closely articulated with the mechanisms of class and the manner in which a class reproduces its interests.

This critique may still be germane, even if, as has been argued, the site of potential communal self-creation has moved increasingly towards the sphere of consumption. Fundamental conflicts of interest between social classes might still create analogous conflicts in the way in which the relationship between goods and people appears to us. Much of the evidence presented in this book suggests that there is commonly a close relationship between possession, the construction of identity and the adherence to certain social values. This suggests in turn that deprivation with respect to goods is not to be judged as mere loss of physical resources. If the identity of the peer group is formed, in part, through its association with particular items, then the individual's inability to afford those items reflects directly on what may be for them a disastrous split between their desired social identity and their actual self-projection. Such close articulation between social group and object possession is encouraged by advertising and design (e.g. Dyer 1982; Forty 1986), one of whose aims is to create unprecedented desires. In the context of present inequalities, with unequal distribution of goods and unequal access to forms of ideological control, these may exacerbate class and status differences.

The market, which might work to express general consumer desire in a socialist society, often does exactly the opposite today, as shown by those studies of media such as newspapers, which have demonstrated that the importance of advertising revenue creates biases in favour of the wealthy, whose views are disproportionately represented (Curren 1986). At present, then, some classes are consumers to a far greater extent than others, and their interests are therefore unduly represented. This is compounded by the more subtle influence of ideology discussed in chapter 9, which determines that these goods are made according to specific perspectives and interests which results in a material culture constructed for one group in the image of that group held by other dominant forces. This could result in what might be described as a lack of access to the means of objectification.

Fetishism as a representation of an apparently autonomous world of goods outside the context of human self-creation may also be a feature of certain academic positions which might otherwise be related to Marxism itself. The critique of post-modernism discussed in chapter 9 appears to adopt a similar position, in which goods are understood as entirely the result of the dictates of late capitalism, and all the human work of consumption which goes into them is ignored. The reification of concepts such as 'myth', 'discourse', 'deconstruction' and so forth is as effectively dismissive of the actions of the mass of the population as are the more conspicuous languages of capital. Indeed, as with Marx's critique of capitalist practice and representation, we are in a situation today where goods are often regarded as mere commodities and their place in social development therefore goes unrecognized by the very people who use them.

Equally problematic is that form of socialist philosophy which was so skilfully demolished by Baudrillard's earlier critical writings. This was the assumption that these goods possess some basic 'use value' relating to a constant and evident need, and that stylistic diversity is mere waste promoted by the branding policy of capitalism. One of the major failures of socialist practice is that it is has attempted to embody this modernist approach to function. A popular opposition to vulgar functionalism as a criterion for which goods should be produced, often emerging as consumer concern for style or fashion, is neither the result of capitalism or the operation of middle-class values, but simply an assertion of the nature of goods as culture. If put into practice by some naive socialism, the functionalist perspective would threaten the very means by which goods may be reappropriated by the consumer, and this may well already have occurred in the socialisms of Eastern Europe. A problem with all these uses of the term fetishism, however, is that they specify too narrow an area for what goods do, mainly related to class relations. In contrast to this, when goods are treated as an element of culture itself, we find a much wider spectrum of contradictions and strategies within which objects are implicated.

Learning from Consumption Practices

The attack on Romanticism for its derision of the mundane and tainted practices of everyday life could easily translate into an alternative Romanticism about modern consumption as always acting to create inalienable, highly sociable communities. Clearly, this would be a travesty of the social relations observable today, and would ignore all the uses of goods for social oppression documented in such detail by Bourdieu and contemporary Marxists. The argument for the potential progressive importance of consumption is one based on a historical tendency, as over the last century populations have attempted to overcome the problems of industrial society; but it is not a general description of the world today. Such a Romanticism is based on the assumption that populism is right simply because it comes from the mass populace, and ignores the clear ability of mass movements to favour antisocial politics such as fascism, or self-destructive private practices. At a lesser level, this Romanticism may lead to an undifferentiated treatment of popular culture as intrinsically positive (Williamson 1986a), an attitude which leaves no room for principle or discrimination. The problem is to avoid either a blanket condemnation or blanket populism, and instead to investigate the key issue of what conditions appear to generate progressive strategies in consumption. It is evident from examples already given that such tendencies may be identified in some aspects of present day consumption activity, and these might provide insights into the strategies by which people are able to recontextualize cultural forms. The limits to philosophical and theoretical discussion of these questions are evident in the extent to which what should be relevant critical social theory appears to lead only to an extreme relativism, nihilism, and anti-humanism. Although something of this trend emerged from a particular branch of social anthropology – that of structuralism – traditional anthropology may provide a means of extricating social analysis from this tendency, because of its commitment to the close observation of everyday human practices as the basis for its generalizations.

Since the world of practices refuses the separation of variables and factors required for the development of most economic theory, an answer to the question of the conditions favourable to particular kinds of consumption is best searched for in the same areas to which any implications drawn from it will in turn be applied. There are many distinctions which are clearly of crucial importance, but about which we know relatively little in terms of their social impact. The example of the distinction between the allocation of services by the state and the effect of private purchase has already been noted. Since there are relatively few studies of long term consumption and its place in the construction of culture, it is difficult to take account of such practices in the development of planning. This deficiency of modern academia becomes still more acute if the desire is to move towards a greater reliance on planning as part of some varient of a socialist society.

Such an anthropology presupposes that we regard the activities of everyday life as a form of praxis; that is, a working out of philosophical conundrums by other means. This in turn implies a respect for the philosophy implicated in mass activity, according to which suburbia, the council estate and the consumption patterns of housewives, as well as more obvious alternative cultures such as youth groups, are understood as active constructions of particular cultural forms from which we can gain some understanding, if we can learn how to read what Berman (1984: 114) has called the 'signs in the street'.

Compared to the purity of theoretical academic positions and dichotomies, the practices of households as observed in ethnography appear as a kind of mass kitsch whose pretensions articulate at the level of practice so much of that which is carefully kept apart in academic study. Consumption at this level cannot be seen as concerning simply one thing, and self-construction by society cannot be reduced to two dimensions; rather, it is the site at which the whole range of often self-contradictory and unbalanced desires, constraints and possibilities come together in that very incoherent process often glossed as social reproduction.

Material culture contributes in specific ways to the possibilities and maintenance of this kitsch contradictory nature of everyday culture. There are abundant examples of oppressive ideologies established through the dominance of certain groups over material production, enormous inequalities or taste as classism. Yet at the same time, and in the same society, examples may be found of goods used to recontextualize and thus transform the images produced by industry, or goods used to create small-scale social peer groups by reworking materials from alienated and abstract forms to re-emerge as the specificity of the inalienable.

As noted in chapter 6, material culture promotes framing, which provides for the maintenance of diversity, while keeping contradictory forces operating without coming into conflict. Reduced to the level of individual furnishings, these are often divided into a variety of styles designed to fit different circumstances from formal presentation to informal relaxation, different moods, or simply the use of small-scale controlled environments to reproduce different possibilities in a manner which extends the notion of play also discussed in chapter 6. Consistency of self or object is not a noticeable feature of the modern age.

This raises the question of what is indicated by such inconsistency. Although many philosophies and theories appear to assume that a homogeneous and totalizing ego is the goal of psychological development (e.g. Greenberg and Mitchell 1983), while any fragmentation or splitting is pathological, and that by analogy the same is true of society as expressive totality (see examples in Jay 1984), these assumptions should be treated with some caution. As indicated in chapter 6, there are alternative models of the person in which contradiction may become an essential element of the developmental process. If the modern personality appears as a kind of counter-factual self, which keeps afloat several possible characters, aided by a range of goods which externalize these into different forms, this may be a positive response to a necessarily contradictory world. It may not be socially desirable to act in relation to a work situation in the same way that one interacts with a family at home, not because of some fault in either situation, or the greater authenticity of one, but because the possibilities of modern life have developed from such divisions and frames. A refusal of quantitative rationality as embodying attitudes which impose too great a distance from human values is not necessarily a progressive stance when directed, for example, against a computer used for redistributing resources. Nor is this element of contradiction solely an aspect of modernity; it may be identified in communities such as rural India, where the logic of the market is systematically separated from that of ritual exchange (Miller 1986).

These attributes of material culture may be used to counter the pessimism in Simmel's view of the tragic nature of modern culture · itself. Despite the enormously powerful and revealing quality of Simmel's writing in this area, he tended to develop from his analysis of the necessarily contradictory nature of modern life, a common frustration with its apparently fragmentary consequences. The massive form taken by material culture, and its extreme diversity, suggested to Simmel that, despite the liberating nature of its possibilities, it would overwhelm what he called subjective culture and would always tend to remain the abstract, quantified, oppressive and inappropriable presence of an unsublated objective culture.

What Simmel could not include in this argument, because they have developed largely since his time, are the myriad strategies of recontextualization and consumption which have been used to overcome the alienatory consequences of mass consumer culture. The sheer profusion encouraged by the transience of fashion was expected to overwhelm us in its very diversity, but in practice there is the building up through bricolage of specific and particular social groups which define themselves as much through the rejection of all those cultural forms they are not as from the assertion of their particular style. Small sections of the population become immersed to an extraordinary degree in the enormous profusion of hobbies, sports, clubs, fringe activities, and the nationwide organizations devoted to interests as diverse as medieval music, swimming, ballroom dancing, steel bands and fan clubs. The building of social networks and leisure activities around these highly particular pursuits is one of the strangest and most exotic features of contemporary industrial society, and one which is for ever increasing. There is no more eloquent confrontation with the abstraction of money, the state and modernity than a life devoted to racing pigeons, or medieval fantasies played out on a microcomputer. All such activities, whose adherents may be widely dispersed, depend upon the paraphernalia of mass consumption such as telephones, trains, and easy and relatively cheap access to relevant goods from commercial markets.

This plurality suggests a growth in the use of time for activities which are seen by the general population as self-productive. In this sense, the older dichotomy between production and consumption is challenged. The workplace is not, and, indeed, never has been the only site for self-production through work. This challenge is echoed in the economic sphere itself. Gershuny (1978, 1983, 1985) has written extensively on recent developments which enables processes previously considered as the sphere of production or service industry to be performed at home – for example, the flourishing do-it-yourself tradition, car repairs and house extensions. Today, even semi-industrial processes strongly identified with the workplace are part of a home economy, not paid for by wages, but saving the household considerable amounts of money. Gershuny points out that this means that the expected increase in demand for service provision in developed industrial societies may well not occur. Anthropologists have also analysed the way different resources may be looked to in dealing with problems and crises (Wallman 1984), and Gortz (1982) provides a more extreme view of the significance of a decline in waged labour as the definitional pivot of class relations.

These observations served as some of the points of departure for an ethnographic study of certain related trends in contemporary British society, based on fieldwork on the Isle of Sheppey (Pahl 1984). Although not primarily concerned with consumption, Pahl's work follows through the argument that one particular kind of work, that of waged labour, has been over privileged in academic discussion at the expense of the wide variety of activities which are articulated by the household as strategies both for producing monetary income and for providing opportunities for non-monetary work with which household members can identify.

Pahl notes that his fieldwork on Sheppey is complemented by studies in Hungary, New Zealand and the Soviet Union (1984: 331). The key point of agreement between many such observers is the perceived failure of modernism, with its particular variant of the image of participatory collective action, as a means of emancipation. Instead, there has been a growth or return of the small-scale, household-based strategies of obtaining and dispensing resources. This has also been a clear trend in the economic structure of a number of socialist states (Nove 1983). Pahl tends to overemphasize the particular level of household organization in a manner comparable with others privileging either collective bureaucracy or autonomous individuals, but the small-scale level of organization is clear.

An important conclusion from Pahl's evidence (1984: 317; Pahl and Wallace 1985), and that of others working on the 'informal' economy (e.g. Mingione 1985) is that self-provisioning is not an alternative means by which resources may be obtained, and is only available to those who have a basic level of income in the first place. As a result, there is developing a new polarization between those who are involved in both work and informal self-production, and those without resources to be involved in either. This suggests that under present economic structures the development of positive consumption strategies by the majority is often supported by a worsening of conditions for a large highly oppressed minority. Consumption is by definition concerned with the utilization of resources; it is not an alternative 'leisure' arena which compensates for their absence. An uncovering of the positive potential in consumption should not detract from the struggle to eliminate poverty and inequalities. On the contrary, what has been insisted upon is that it is absurd to call for the end of poverty and simultaneously imply that this would represent the end of authenticity. Consumption as portrayed here is not a return to a simple 'enclosed' world, but a highly sophisticated historical development predicated upon the articulation between small- and large-scale spheres of involvement.

The evidence may be used to suggest a potential balance between a strong state which might intervene to ensure some level of equality and preserve public control over major resources, and activities which encourage flexibility and plurality at the level of consumption. Both need to be stronger, and the condition for the strength of one is the power of the other. Pahl is correct to stress the importance of primary fieldwork in order to provide policy-making with insights gained from the actual practices of the population at the micro-level. He points, with caution, to writers who have started to move from production to house ownership as points to identity formation, but fails to appreciate that one of the major reasons for the present importance of the household is that it is one of the sites of modern consumption where these activities, as much as different kinds of employment, are articulated (see also Young and Willmott 1973).

Problems which arise from this stress on the household include the danger of a 'neo-familism' ideology (Godard 1985: 324–7), and also of ignoring the rise of an isolated and anomic part of the population, especially in the larger cities. A more general ethnography might reveal a series of levels of cultural construction through recontextualization. For example, television is clearly a home-based activity, but the appropriation of the media may not be centred on the household as a group. Soap operas, which are often condemned as providing vicarious neighbourhoods, are typical of a nationwide production system that provides material which can be dissected and commented on for its moral and social implications in a wide variety of circumstances, as with one's 'mates' at work, or in shopping- or street-based actual neighbourhoods, making the activity less vicarious than it at first appeared. Consumption is concerned with the internalization of culture in everyday life, but thereby incorporates parties, pubs and holidays as much as do-it-yourself, home-based activities.

In studies of this kind, extensive quotation from oral history often complements the ethnography in showing the satisfaction gained from controlling one particular domain of self-productive activity. It appears that there has been a return, in part, to activities such as performing rather than simply listening to pop music, and also to gardening, home brewing and do-it-yourself, though this is balanced by leisure created through maximizing monetary income and the full use of mass manufactured services. Again, this is because social groups work best as a kind of practical kitsch, amalgamating and juxtaposing a wide range of activities otherwise separated as work and leisure spheres. There are diverse areas which can be selected for emphasis by this kind of productive consumption, often conceived of as small domains or ponds in which one can feel oneself to be a significant fish. This all depends, however, on access to certain cultural and financial resources which provide the means for appropriation. Without such resources, the feeling is simply one of increasing insignificance within a vast sea.

Capitalism itself has had to adjust to such transformations. For the first half of this century, commerce attempted to create larger, more homogeneous, markets for its goods, using advertising to demolish regional, ethnic and other divisions in the consumer sphere (Leiss 1983), and for a considerable period it was predicted that this trend would continue; but since the 1950s it has had to respond to the emergence of a new ethnicity (e.g. Smith 1981) and general social diversity. The major technological advances brought to industrial production by the microchip appear largely to have followed, rather than promoted, these new patterns of consumption, allowing conti-nued profits when these had been threatened by the demand for more diverse products and shorter production runs made for specific social groups. Late capitalism may have had to adapt to, rather than be the cause of, current social trends. The potential benefit to the consumer might also be extended to the worker, allowing for more flexible working hours, if this new technology was harnessed by progressive political forces (Jones and Graves 1986; Murray 1985). Similarly, political theory appears to have followed observation of a new plurality in political practices and positions (Hall 1985).

Consumption cannot be considered in isolation. There exist much more widely discussed parallel arenas, such as the use of state serivces, including the National Health Service and the education system, which are more obvious candidates for the transformation of objective conditions. The stress on consumption is justified partly by its previous neglect, but also by the contention that it is in this area that the strategies of recontextualization are at their most advanced. This is to say that consumption is now at the vanguard of history, and may provide insights into the further transformation of areas such as welfare and the workplace.

Such an approach also implies a limitation to the kind of analysis of consumption offered by authors such as Bourdieu. Although it is a brilliant picture of the nature of cultural practices in industrial society, *Distinction* reduces almost all consumption to the play of social differentiation. Yet, clearly, even the dominant groups in society face the problem of alienation, as shown from certain genres of literary fiction such as nineteenth-century tragedy set amongst the bourgeoisie amongst other sources. Neither is this problem entirely resolved by the kind of close social solidarity often postulated as prevailing amongst dominated groups. If this classism is stripped away, there remain common problems, in response to which consumption practices develop a plethora of projects. As indicated in the discussion of fashion in chapter 9, such projects may include ideas about the proper relationship between individual and society, models of Romantic pasts and utopian futures developed through style, or adherence to certain moral values, such as feminism or conservatism, expressed in developing particular forms of cultural relations.

These projects, which include many domains otherwise treated in terms of religion, philosophy and morality, comprise a whole series of often fantastic possible worlds, partly submerged and implicit, but which find their primary external expression in material form rather than in any other media, and are the means by which possibilities are discovered and commented upon. These are largely mass practices developed in groups ranging from small youth sub-cultures to large class fractions, but with an individual level of expression. Such projects are not best studied, however, by starting with the social individual, since modern material culture is so complex that it often cuts across particular and possibly contradictory aspects of the same individuals, and is best approached from the cultural patterns themselves. Given these characteristics, ethnography may well provide the most satisfactory methodological approach to the study of this phenomenon.

Conclusion

In this book, a concept of objectification, somewhat violently abstracted from Hegel, has been used to characterize a central issue within the general problem of modernity. I have isolated from the themes of the *Phenomenology of Spirit* a particular historical trend towards an increasing abstraction, but also a specificity; and, following Simmel, I have argued that this trend has as one of its most prominent forms of expression an increase in material forms. Contemporary life is situated not only in a nexus of struggles between freedoms, equalities and competing claims towards totality, but more generally within the context of a quantitative advance in the material forms of culture in almost all countries, creating a massive external world whose internal relationships and social implications are extremely complex. The Romantic illusion that the solution to this complexity lies in simplicity has been rejected. Rather, the emphasis has been on the nature of culture as intrinsically contradictory, a contradiction which is unresolvable. The problem has been to elucidate the historical basis of this contradiction and its contemporary nature, attempting to show how it is grounded in the 1980s. Hegel's non-reductionist approach provides a model for understanding a process of development which takes place within such conditions of contradiction. He illustrated a continual process of societal self-creation through objectification and sublation, through which social self-alienation was the instrument for the historical construction of culture, but the subjects of history had always to preserve themselves from the autonomous forces thereby created, whose re-appropriation was the means of their development. Hegel saw philosophy and comprehension as the means of sublation; here, however, the emphasis has been on praxis – that is, material activities or strategies based on objective conditions.

In order to achieve this aim, it has been argued that it is possible to maintain a critical stance in relation to the mass goods which are produced by modern industry, and to attack the contribution of present relationships in the spheres of mass production and property ownership to inequalities and more general social oppression, while at the same time insisting that these mass goods are indeed our own culture. Emphasis has been placed on the implications of mass goods as the product of industrialization and modernity, rather than assuming that any problematic aspects may be dismissed as having arisen within the context of capitalism. Equally, any attempt to construct models based on a separation of a population from its material environment as thereby embodying some prior or more authentic body of pre-cultural 'pure' social relations is based on an illusion concerning the nature of society. Mass goods represent culture, not because they are merely there as the environment within which we operate, but because they are an integral part of that process of objectification by which we create ourselves as an industrial society: our identities, our social affiliations, our lived everyday practices. The authenticity of artefacts as culture derives, not from their relationship to some historical style or manufacturing process – in others words, there is no truth or falsity immanent in them – but rather from their active participation in a process of social self-creation in which they are directly constitutive of our understanding of ourselves and others. The key criteria for judging the utility of contemporary objects is the degree to which they may or may not be appropriated from the forces which created them, which are mainly, of necessity, alienating. This appropriation consists of the transmutation of goods, through consumption activities, into potentially inalienable culture. Again, no solution has been foreseen to this contradictory strategy, through which inalienability is achievable only through societal self-alienation; and no panacea has been proposed to the ordinary human suffering engendered by the loneliness and massivity of modern culture. Rather, there has been the more modest claim that there is much to be learnt from the activities of those who, faced with the same problem on a mundane and daily basis, appear to have developed strategies from which others might gain.

Our difficulty in preceiving progressive possibilities in the consumption activities around us may derive from three factors in particular. First, there is the inherent invisibility (argued in chapter 6) of what otherwise appears to us as the highly visible material culture which is the form increasingly taken by culture's contradictions. Secondly, there is the continued attraction of a simplistic view of the relationship between production and consumption, where the latter is reduced to merely the problem of the reproduction or completion of the former. Thirdly, under present conditions, consumption only rarely amounts to the ideal model developed here, which is based on its potential as evident in certain cases, and is not a description of general practice. Contrary instances naturally abound. What has been shown, however, is that there is evidence that consumption is developing as one of the major sites through which the necessary autonomy of the objects of commerce and of the modern state might be made compatible with the specific demands of dynamic social groups. An analysis of consumption may then once more become a critical theory of the status quo; but rather than through mere utopianism or nihilism, this will be achieved through the detailed analysis of, and differentiation between, positive and negative tendencies in consumption activities as already practised within the otherwise infertile conditions of the class inequalities of contemproary society.

Following Simmel, it has been argued that the trajectory which leads to modernity has revealed with particular clarity the contradictions inherent in the process of objectification. The general claims of the Enlightenment, the development of its mode of thought and activity and the material advantages which have been created through the division of labour, industrialization, the search for objective science and liberation from customary ties, are all accepted as irreversible historical developments, which cannot be offset by utopian totalities. The development of a strong state which alone can provide the instrument with which social agents might bring about the possibilities of equality, and which can control those forces in modernization tending towards autonomous interest and reification, is accepted, while acknowledging the state's own tendencies in this direction.

The nature of state's institutions, their rationalistic, quantitative, abstracted orders, their scale, and their tendency to relate to particular interests, makes them an externality for the mass population which cannot simply be conceptually sublated through some form of identification with their construction, in the original Hegelian sense, as has been attempted is some totalitarian states. Real sublation may be achieved only through a mass materialist practice, by which people directly participate in the reappropriation of their culture. Self-consciousness, self-knowledge about the processes of objectification and a progressive philosophy or political allegiance are not enough; nor, today, are collective curbs on the exploitation by a minority of the advantages and profits of mass production, or a degree of participation in the political processes of adjudication over the allocation of resources, although these laudable aims are themselves far from achieved at present, and remain complementary to the projects discused here. Observation of industrialized societies reveals a search by the mass population for other instruments which might act directly to negate the autonomy and scale of these historical forces, and turn to advantage certain aspects of the very materiality of the object world in consumption. It is this activity which requires further study, elucidation and development.

For this reason, and in order to obtain a greater understanding of these same processes and their limitations and possibilities, it is necesary to pay far more attention to the qualities and consequences of that surprisingly elusive component of modern culture, which, although apparently highly conspicuous, has consistently managed to evade the focus of academic gaze, and remains the least understood of all the central phenomena of the modern age, that is material culture.

Epilogue, 1993

From Theory to Ethnography to Politics in Consumption Studies

An addition to a book written seven years after its composition might attempt various tasks. I do not intend an apologia or to re-write. I will note a few recent works on material culture but will not attempt to cover the voluminous and inter-disciplinary new writing on consumption which is being reviewed elsewhere (Miller in preparation a). I will, however, briefly refer to my own attempts to develop an ethnography of consumption – not to suggest it has any more or less significance than any other new work – but merely because since this book promised such a study it is reasonable to ask how much of this has actually been accomplished.

However the main task attempted here is different. The extensive writings and thinking about consumption over the last few years create a new context which transforms the nature of how this book might be read even if the contents themselves remain constant. I therefore want to concentrate on how the book's implications may have shifted and then address what I see as the new horizons for the kind of studies which were advocated here.

There is considerable evidence for a shift in debates about consumption where the amount of additional writings is prodigious, but this would be less true for the section on material culture but not at all the case for the section on objectification. There has not been, to my knowledge, any extensive new literature on the concept of objectification as such. There are, of course, constant new writings on the work of the main theorists who are discussed in the first section of this book. Wood's (1990) work on *Hegel's Ethical Thought* provides a useful link between these theoretical concerns and the political implications which I wish to draw attention to in this epilogue. Strathern's fascinating account of 'personification' (1988) in New Guinea would provide a compliment to Munn as a point of departure for the ideas discussed in chapter four. Simmel finally seems to be coming into his own within contemporary sociology (e.g. Frisby 1992).

Judging by the prodigious literature on post-modernism that has appeared since 1987 there is as yet little sympathy for the anti-dualistic theory attempted here. The discussion on post-modernism often assumes a transformation in the world such that the humanity of people has been effectively diminished by the rise of commodities but the dualistic relation upon which this criticism is founded remains in the main unchallenged. Indeed, with a few exceptions (e.g. Harvey 1989), I feel the prediction (pp. 163–7) that this debate would be largely parochial and sterile has been amply borne out. These debates refuse to see the consequences of attempts to transform our common sense notions of person and object, whether derived from Mauss (e.g. Carrier 1990) or less directly from Hegel, rather they attempted a repudiation of this tradition which is derided as meta-narrative. Obviously such generalizations are necessarily crass given the sheer extent and inter-disciplinary range of the debate on post-modernism, though it would be largely supported by Habermas (1987) who provides a useful summary of the antecedents and consequences.

The ethnographic approach I have been taking to consumption since writing this book helps provide an additional comparative perspective to this critique of the narrowness of the writings on post-modernism. For example, many of these writings rely upon a concept of 'super-ficiality' which seems to lie at the aesthetic heart of the debate on post-modernism. By examining the use of 'style' in Trinidad (Miller 1994a) it became evident that the relationship between objects and persons may be quite different in another context. The mode of objectification evident in the development of style depends upon the most profound cultivation of being being located at the surface and demonstrates the parochialism of a term such as superficiality as also the assumptions that concept expresses.

There is rather more recent work on material culture. This has been particularly true of the high quality ethnographic studies emergent from the discipline of anthropology including books by Guss (1989), MacKenzie (1991), Thomas (1992), Weiner and Schneider (1989). In addition there are historical and archaeological books of the quality of Orvell (1989), Schama (1988) and Tilley (1991) as well as books on industrial material culture such as media form (Silverstone and Hirsch 1992). There are even novels (e.g. Baker 1989) that pay the kind of atten-tion to material culture that has rarely been seen since Balzac. All of these constitute a sophisticated analysis of the social use of things.

In tandem with these new works are continued developments in areas such as design studies, cultural studies (Hebdige 1988) and museum studies (Pearse 1989) where there is a sustained growth in attempts to address wider issues. Indeed the concept of 'material culture studies' has clearly played an important role in aiding a number of sub-disciplines which previously had focused rather narrowly on their presumed object of study (such as the museum) to develop more critical and thoughtful perspectives. This heuristic role in inter-disciplinary studies is to be welcomed but what is less obvious is any clear advances in theoretical approaches to material culture per se – that is attempts to define the potential and implication of thingness as against speech, thought and other non-material forms.

The new literature on consumption is being reviewed elsewhere (Miller in preparation a), (though see in particular Campbell 1987, Hirschman 1989, McCracken 1988), but it is clearly this third section of the book which has received most comment and which is perhaps most subject to a changing context of readership. The first change has been a considerable increase in books which seem to take a positive view of consumption as a form of creative appropriation in which consumers are somehow resisting capitalism through techniques of pleasure. These range from quite sophisticated attempts to utilise De Certeau's notions of the tactics of the weak, to rather crude assumptions that anything which might be called 'working class popular culture' must fit into this 'pleasure as resistance' generic category. One of the reasons this trend has been criticized has been a possible association between a series of cultural studies which assert the power of consumers and the simultaneous rise of an extreme free market ideology which extols commodity choice as the most efficient means of empowerment such that governments should in no way intervene to diminish the ability of the market to present choices to the public and that this principle should be extended to what might otherwise be state concerns such as health, education and utilities. There are also specific disciplinary implications. In anthropology, for example, this trend may easily lapse into a sense that as long as the 'local' is able to appropriate from global capitalism then the anthropologist may be secured in their defence of imagined small islands of retained diversity and sociability which are not diminished by shifts in the political economy.

These criticisms are certainly pertinent to my work. This book does indeed attempt to assert possibilities of consumer appropriation as a form of sublation. Furthermore since writing this book I have attempted in a series of ethnographic case studies (e.g. Miller 1992, 1993) to provide clear examples of consumption as localization. In both the theoretical and ethnographic case this was in repudiation of specific ideologies which insist that the secondary possession of images in consumption renders the modern consumer inauthentic as compared to the historical producer. In Trinidad where I have been conducting fieldwork this is of extreme importance, since the discourse on 'Westernization' and 'Imperialism' credits all the

advantages (and disadvantages) of modernity as somehow only developed by and properly pertaining to the affluent countries of Western
Europe and North America. As the Trinidadian novelist V. S. Naipaul
demonstrates such discourses renders all Trinidadian uses of such
goods and images as the antics of 'Mimic Men'. In small countries
which can never hope for economic self-sufficiency this ideology is
clearly detrimental to the self-respect of peoples trying to struggle out
of historical and racist denigration. It is important therefore to
acknowledge localizing possibilities in relation to imported goods such
as American Soap Opera (Miller 1992) and Global Christmas (Miller
1993) which in practice may be used to create the very specificity of
modern Trinidad.

In these, and other circumstances where the very possibility of such
processes continues to be denied, an insistence through demonstration
that consumption may represent self-creation through appropriation
remains valid. There is, however, a considerable difference between the
theoretical programme and subsequent ethnography developed here
and the kind of 'pleasure as resistance in popular culture' texts which
were spawned in the same period. This book does not celebrate consumption as 'resistance' to capitalism. Rather it attempts to emphasize
the contradictory nature, not only of capitalism, but all the major institutions of modernity. Consumption is rather understood as an element
in a cultural process that remains dialectical, always a moment of
becoming within contradiction. In practice this may often take the form
of an attempt to ameliorate capitalism's oppressive consequences in
everyday life, but this may include strategies which embrace as well as
refuse the new possibilities of commodities. The point was not that this
is some new domain of choice, but in a sense the contrary – that increasingly people have no choice but to focus upon consumption as the only
remaining domain in which there are possibilities of sublation in the
sense used in this book. Consumption's importance derives from the
state of rupture and alienation that lies at the heart of modernity, such
that this Trinidadian experience of inauthentification partly derived
from well meaning discourses about anti-imperialism is merely one
example of a common condition of increasing separation of peoples
from the objects they must perforce live through. Capitalism here takes
its place alongside bureaucratization and increasing abstraction and
reflexivity as the inevitable contradictory forces of modernity (Miller
1994a). Attempts at appropriation are therefore for an increasing
number of people the only struggle left to them, but they remain a
struggle – not the assumption of the academic.

Morley (1992: 270–89) has recently addressed a similar criticism of
his studies of television audiences as being merely a retreat to the sitting

room. In reply he notes that given the importance of television itself as political and social media it is the sitting room where the local meets the global. The viewer often receives closer coverage of key events than those a few hundred yards away from the event itself. Habermas (1991) provides a very useful account of the 'Structural Transformations of the Public Sphere' leading up to this new role for television, but as with most modern commentators he quite fails the leap of imagination required to comprehend the significance of this new 'private' public sphere. The democratizing process is inevitably decentralizing relying more on the aggregate of the acts of the multitude. There can be no return to the 'polis'. The new technologies of consumption provide direct links between the private household and the widest public domain and at the very least we require an imagination of how we would wish this process to proceed. This must mean positing clear alternatives and constraints to the position of the market as mediating in this new civil society, rather than merely regrets for the loss of face to face interactions that would only be available for small elites.

There is then a considerable difference between projecting 'resistance' onto something defined as popular culture as against an ethnography of the struggles of peoples to locate identity out of the same materials in which their identity must also inevitably be lost. Any worthwhile study of appropriation must retain this sense of contradiction. As Gell (1988) points out in a very helpful review of this book, consumption is also always an act of knowing one's limitations, what one cannot possess and cannot be. I would concede an element of pendulum swinging, however, such that articles which merely show the possibilities of appropriation in adverse conditions might begin to be replaced by more mature works which give equal weight to the contradictions of alienation and rupture that are just as often the outcome of consumption processes. This was the point of the work on kitchens which is referred to in the introduction (published as Miller 1988) where the possibilities are set against the continued sense of stigma and oppression felt when living within a built environment that appears as the presence of an alien institution. These new writings also mean that to be worthwhile future studies of consumption processes may have to do more than merely demonstrate acts of appropriation. They must analyse the specific but potentially diverse forms and values which are constructed out of the consumption process.

The study of consumption could be easily return to the rather narrow concerns from which it sprung that is the vision of the 'individual in the marketplace'. The theoretical structure of this book relates, however, to a much wider problematic in order to address the problems of rupture faced by a state dealing with largely imported goods and also the sense of rupture when, as in the council estate, goods come from and represent the alien presence of the state and not the market. Indeed in many cases sublation may not be manifested in any actual transformation of the position of individuals with respect to goods so much as a coming to consciousness of a state of rupture in modern life which has to be overcome for people to believe that they retain their sense of humanity.

One of the means by which a balance may be returned to the study of consumption is through a closer articulation between production and consumption. Given the fall of many socialist states this is increasingly part of a larger question of the position of consumption within capitalism. Some books e.g. Leopold and Fine (in press) have argued that works on culture have moved so far in the direction of the 'creative consumer' as to ignore the constraints and implications of particular production and distribution (and all other intervening) processes. What they attempt, and I believe future works should emulate, is detailed consideration of particular forms of capitalist production and distribution in relation to particular forms of consumption. If the term 'post Fordism' is to represent a genuine attempt at a scholarly understanding of transformations in the world rather than a glib generalization on a par with post-modernism then this requires considered comparative work on production and consumption together. This is certainly possible in an island such as Trinidad where the smaller scale of capitalist business allows the linkages between production, distribution and consumption to be more easily encompassed than in the metropolitan environment (Miller in preparation a). I hope I now see more clearly that the theoretical position outlined in 1987 implies a comparative study of consumption carried out in tandem with a comparative study of practising capitalism.

But a return to the articulation between production and consumption should not be a return to the assumption that consumption is merely either the arena of reproduction of production structures nor just the passive end point of production aims. We do not need yet another pendulum swing too far in the opposite direction. The debate over post-Fordism alongside more detailed work on the restructuring of the retail trade and the decentralization of transnational companies all point in the same direction. They suggest that a study of consumption is not a retreat to some remnant local and micro level burrowing down to escape the glare of global capitalism. Quite the contrary they suggest that it is consumption itself that has become the commanding heights of the political economy and that any macro economic development that fails to adapt itself to this understanding is becoming highly anachronistic. This may range from the failure of IMF and World Bank structural adjustment programmes to focus on the importance of first world consumption for third world development through to the failures of transnational advertising to realize that global homogenized brands were only meaningful in relation to an equal trend towards extreme localization (Mattelart 1991). Thus the increasing imperative towards the study of consumption is created by history itself. But to study consumption is to investigate its comparative forms as idioms of social life, not as the post-modern debate suggests simply to project upon it some new global homogeneity or superficiality. The premise for this book is that the necessity for the study of consumption is neither one of ideology nor academic fashion but a coming to perspicacity about a fundamental transformation of the world. In many respects this seems still more plausible in 1993 than when the book was originally conceived.

These concerns help direct us towards a new frontier for theories of consumption which must be simultaneously a theoretical and a political frontier. The decline of communism as a political model cannot be disassociated from the failure of Marx's particular translation of Hegel into self-alienation and sublation through production relations as discussed in chapter three. There is a clear line between his theoretical turn and a book such a Drakulic (1992) which documents the humiliation of women living under regimes so inconsiderate to consumer concerns that they could not produce a satisfactory sanitary napkin. But the establishment during the cold war of a clear association between pure market liberalism and the notion of consumer choice is just as disastrous for the development of consumption theory. Unrestrained capitalism has been just as disempowering of ordinary consumers as unrestrained communism. What we lack is concerted attempts at even the imagination of an alternative articulation between ordinary consumption as appropriation and the structures of the political economy and civil society that would facilitate this (though perhaps Scandinavian social welfare policies did provide some guidance see also Hall and Jacques 1989).

Throughout this book I have argued for modernity as a state of intrinsic contradiction. It follows that a future political model can never have the logical simplicity of either Marxism or the Market. The 'third way' political model that should arise out of consumption theory is always rather a sensitivity to consequence which permits a local and pragmatic variation of its fundamental tenets. It is also a repudiation of the given hierarchies of political theory.

At present the degree of seriousness with which a population's actions are taken are often directly linked to the degree to which those actions are said to be 'politicized' (Miller 1993b). What may be required then is a shift in our assertions as to what 'matters', which opens up different realms which clearly matter but are not yet overtly political. As an example, one could consider the case of shopping. An ethnographic approach to a topic such as shopping should be sensitive to what Gell (1988) calls the 'phenomenology of sublation' the emotional concerns of daily decision making and struggles to identify, particularly at present for women. It is not surprising that it has often been feminist studies which have retained a sense of nuance when discussing the consequences of modern consumption (e.g. Wilson 1985). But the idea that such things matter to the individuals and households engaged is still often divorced from the idea of 'mattering' in the political domain. Indeed at present the individual daily shopping choice is understood as trivial precisely in opposition to the much more occasional but highly emphasized choice of an electorate in determining the political regime.

What a vanguard consumption theory might now attempt is to leap this gulf between the aggregate mass only individualized in ethnographic portrayal and the crucial developments in the political economy as they effect the fate of mass populations. It is in this articulation that new configurations for political action might well emerge. Hegel provided a theoretical foundation for a sense of freedom that depended upon the individual of liberal politics being subsumed within the larger ethic goals of the community. The challenge today is perhaps to translate this into the relationship between aggregate private individuals as consumers and a larger sense of civic morality and responsibility.

A pointer in this direction is the rise of the green movement where in some ways an initial attempt to power through conventional political trajectories as in 'Green' political parties has been shown to be often less powerful than a wider de-fetishization of consumer goods. This represents a rise to consciousness of the mass of consumers as to the origins and consequences of the goods they buy about which previously there was neither knowledge nor interest. This may be an as yet modest change but is is based upon some aspects of daily decision making becoming transformed into explicit moral choices that exercise this new knowledge about the sources and consequences of commodities as an act of responsibility. To a degree then a change in consumer consciousness is the self-creation of citizenship. The advantage of this over conventional politics is that it starts to move political moralities back to the daily decision making processes of the public at large rather than relying only on the consumer's single occasional decision made at election time. This green consumer consciousness has been at least as active in questioning decisions as to governmental and state policy as in pushing the market to at least present itself as concerned for such issues. At present this apparent empowerment of consumers may be more a belief than an actuality, but at the very least it provides a radically different perspective on the potential interplay between consumption and politics in the future. When the origins of goods in the third world exploitation arises as a perceived property of those goods then at least some element of the gulf between the daily struggle for identity and the global moralities of political decision making has been reduced. With sufficient expansion this might in turn lead to the kind of restructuring of the notion of politics itself which consumption theory implies. This would be naive optimism indeed if it were addressed as an assumption about the future. The point, however, is not to make predictions but to demonstrate that there are other ways of thinking about the grounding of consumption as sublation which should be encouraged.

To talk of the de-fetishism of goods implies a re-affirmation in the project that writers such as Hegel and Simmel (and in a related fashion Marx) committed themselves to. That is the potential of consciousness in tandem with an acceptance of political responsibility and political change to re-encompass forces which seem otherwise to escape even the possibility of consciousness. There is at least one choice here between the pessimism of the debates over post-modernism which seem to evoke only an aestheticised narcissism as the appropriate response to a no longer imaginable global hegemony of oppressive forces. The alternative is to use consumption as the pivot for precisely an imagination of alternative political realities in which the self-production of consumers becomes also the emancipation of producers.

The central point of this book is that what Mauss argued for the gift is potentially just as true for modern commodities. 'In these total social phenomena, as we propose to call them, all kinds of institutions find simultaneous expression: religious, legal, moral and economic' (1970:1). The agenda of this book and the subsequent ethnographic work is to force us to acknowledge the consequences of this. It implies that key moral and political choices can be made through transforming our consciousness of consumption as tantamount to the possibilities of sublation within modernist conditions of intrinsic rupture. I continue to believe that this remains one of the most important and challenging academic projects of our times.

References

Baker, N. 1989 *The Mezzanine*. Cambridge: Granta.
Campbell, C. 1987 *The Romantic Ethic and the Spirit of Modern Consumerism*. Oxford: Blackwell.
Carrier, J. 1990 Reconciling commodities and personal relations in industrial society. *Theory and Society* 19: 579–98.

Drakulic, S. 1992 *How We Survived Communism and Even Laughed.* London: Hutchinson.

Frisby, D. 1992 *Simmel and Since.* London: Routledge.

Gell, A. 1988 Anthropology, material culture and consumerism. *J.A.S.O.* Hilary 43–8.

Guss, D. 1989 *To Weave and to Sing.* Berkeley: University of California Press.

Habermas, J. 1987 *The Philosophical Discourse of Modernity.* Cambridge, Mass: MIT Press.

Habermas, J. 1991 *The Structural Transformation of the Public Sphere.* Cambridge, Mass: MIT Press.

Hall, S. and Jacques, M. 1989 *New Times.* London: Lawrence and Wishart.

Harvey, D. 1989 *The Condition of Postmodernity.* London: Blackwell.

Hebdige, D. 1988 *Hiding in the Light.* London: Routledge.

Hirschman, E. 1989 *Interpretive Consumer Research.* Provo, UT: Association for Consumer Research.

Matterlart, A. 1991 *Advertising International.* London: Routledge.

McCracken, G. 1988 *Culture and Consumption.* Bloomington: Indiana University Press.

MacKenzie, M. 1991 *Androgynous Objects.* London: Harwood.

Mauss, M. 1970 (1925) *The Gift.* London: Routledge and Kegan Paul.

Miller, D. 1988 Appropriating the State on the Council Estate. *Man* 23:353–72.

Miller, D. 1992 The Young and the Restless in Trinidad: A case of the Local and the Global in Mass Consumption. In *Consuming Technologies.* Eds R. Silverstone and E. Hirsch. London: Routledge 163–82.

Miller, D. 1993 'Christmas against Materialism in Trinidad.' In Miller, D. Ed. 1993 *Unwrapping Christmas.* Oxford: Oxford University Press.

Miller, D. 1994a *Modernity - An Ethnographic Approach.* Oxford: Berg.

Miller, D. 1994b Could Shopping Ever Really Matter. *Consumer Cultures in Global Perspective.* Ed. V. de Grazia. Workshop papers for the Rutgers Center for Historical Analysis.

Miller, D. Ed. in preparation a *Consumption - New Studies.* London: Routledge.

Miller, D. in preparation b *Capitalism - An Ethnographic Approach.*

Morley, D. 1992 *Television Audiences and Cultural Studies.* London: Routledge.

Orvell, M. 1989 *The Real Thing.* Chapel Hill: The University of North Carolina Press.

Pearce, S. Ed. 1989 *Museum Studies in Material Culture.* Leicester: Leicester University Press.

Schama, S. 1988 *The Embarrassment of Riches.* London: Fontana.

Silverstone, R. and Hirsch, E. Eds 1992 *Consuming Technologies.* London: Routledge.

Strathern, M. 1988 *The Gender of the Gift.* Berkeley: University of California Press.

Thomas, N. 1991 *Entangled Objects.* Cambridge, Mass: Harvard University Press.

Tilley, C. 1991 *Material Culture and Text: The art of ambiguity.* London: Routledge.

Weiner, A. and Schneider, J. Eds 1989 *Cloth and Human Experience.* Washington: Smithsonian Institution Press.

Wilson, E. 1985 *Adorned in Dreams.* London: Virago.

Wood, A. 1990 *Hegel's Ethical Thought.* Cambridge: Cambridge University Press.

References

Abercrombie, N., Hill, S. and Turner, B. 1980 *The Dominant Ideology Thesis.* London: Allen and Unwin.
1986 *Sovereign Individuals of Capitalism.* London: Allen and Unwin.
Althusser, L. 1969 *For Marx.* London: New Left Books.
Anderson, P. 1983 *In the Tracks of Historical Materialism.* London: Verso.
1984 'Modernity and Revolution.' *New Left Review,* 144, 96–113.
Andrews, L. 1979 *Tenants and Town Hall.* London: HMSO.
Appadurai, A. 1986 'Introduction: commodities and the politics of value.' In A. Appadurai (ed.) *The Social Life of Things: Commodities in Cultural Perspective.* Cambridge: Cambridge University Press, 3–63.
Arato, A. 1974 'The neo-idealist defence of subjectivity.' *Telos,* 21, 108–61.
Ardener, S. (ed.) 1981 *Women and Space.* London: Croom Helm.
Arthur, C. 1980 'Personality and the dialiectic of labour and property: Locke, Hegel and Marx.' *Radical Philosophy,* 26, 3–15.
1982 'Objectification and alienation in Marx and Hegel.' *Radical Philosophy,* 30, 14–24.
1983 'The Master–Slave Relationship.' *New Left Review* 142, 67–75.
Asad, T. (ed.) 1973 *Anthropology and the Colonial Encounter.* London: Ithica Press.
Barth, F. 1975 *Ritual and Knowledge amongst the Baktaman of New Guinea.* New Haven: Yale University Press.
Barthes, R. 1973 *Mythologies.* London: Paladin.
1977 'The death of the Author.' In *Image–Music–Text.* London: Fontana, 142–8.
Bateson, G. 1973 'Style, grace and information in primitive art.' In A. Forge (ed.) *Primitive Art and Society.* Oxford: Oxford University Press, 235–55.
Baudrillard, J. 1975 *The Mirror of Production.* St Louis: Telos Press.
1981 *For a Critique of the Political Economy of the Sign.* St Louis: Telos Press.
1983 'The Precession of Simulacra.' *Art and Text,* 11, 3–46.
Bayley, S. 1979 *In Good Shape.* London: Design Council.

Bayly, C. A. 1986 'The Origins of Swadeshi (Home Industry): cloth and Indian society 1700–1930.' In A. Appadurai (ed.) *The Social Meaning of Things*. Cambridge: Cambridge University Press, 285–321.

Bendict, B. (ed.) 1983 *The Anthropology of World Fairs*. London: Scolar Press.

Benjamin, W. 1973 'The work of art in the age of mechanical reproduction.' In *Illuminations*. London: Fontana, 219–53.

1983 *Charles Baudelaire. A lyric Poet in the Era of High Capitalism*. London: Verso.

Benton, T. and Benton, B. (eds) 1975 *Form and Function*. London: Crosby Lockwood Staples.

Berger, P. and Luckmann, T. 1967 *The Social Construction of Reality*. London: Allen Lane.

Berman, M. 1983 *All That's Solid Melts Into Air*. London: Verso.

1984 'The Signs in the Street.' *New Left Review*, 144, 114–23.

Bigsby, C. (ed.) 1976 *Approaches to Popular Culture*. London: Edward Arnold.

Binford, L. R. 1972 *An Archaeological Perspective*. New York: Seminar Books.

1978 *Nunamiut Ethnoarchaeology*. New York: Academic Books.

Birmingham, J. 1975 'Traditional potters of the Katmandu valley.' *Man*, 12, 370–86.

Boas, F. 1955 *Primitive Art*. New York: Dover.

Bottomore, T. and Frisby, D. 1978 Introduction to the translation in G. Simmel *The Philosophy of Money*. London: Routledge and Kegan Paul, 1–49.

Bourdieu, P. 1968 'Outline of a sociological theory of art perception.' *International Social Science Journal*, 20.4, 589–612.

1971 'The Berber house or the world reversed.' In J. Pouillon and P. Maranda (eds) *Echanges et Communications*. Le Hague: Mouton, 151–69.

1977 *Outline of a Theory of Practice*. Cambridge: Cambridge University Press.

1984 *Distinction: A Social Critique of the Judgement of Taste*. London: Routledge and Kegan Paul.

1985 'The social space and the genesis of groups.' *Theory and Society*, 14, 723–44.

Bourdieu, P. and Passeron, J–C. 1977 *Reproduction in Education, Society and Culture*. London: Sage.

1979 *The Inheritors*. Chicago: University of Chicago Press.

Braudel, F. 1981 *The Structures of Everyday Life*. London: Collins.

Brown, R. 1958 *Words and Things*. New York: The Free Press.

Burke, P. 1978 *Popular Culture in Early Modern Europe*. London: Temple Smith.

Campbell, S. F. 1983 'Attaining rank: a classification of shell valuables.' In J. Leach and E. Leach (eds) *The Kula: New Perspectives on*

Massim Exchange. Cambridge: Cambridge University Press, 201–28.

Castells, M. 1977 *The Urban Question: A Marxist Approach.* London: Edward Arnold.

Castoriadis, C. 1984 *Crossroads in the Labyrinth.* Brighton: Harvester Press.

Chapman, W. R. 1985 'Arranging ethnology: A. H. L. F. Pitt Rivers and the typological tradition.' In G. Stocking (ed.) *Objects and Others.* Madison: University of Wisconsin Press, 15–48.

Chaudhuri, K. N. 1978 *The Trading World of Asia.* Cambridge: Cambridge University Press.

Chiodi, P. 1976 *Sartre and Marxism.* Brighton: Harvester Press.

Clarke, D. 1968 *Analytical Archaeology.* London: Methuen.

Collins, R., Curran, J., Garnham, N., Scannell, P., Schlesinger, P. and Sparks, C. (eds) 1986 *Media, Culture and Society.* London: Sage Press.

Colquhoun, A. 1981 *Essays in Architectural Criticism.* Cambridge, Massachusetts: Opposition Books.

Coward, R. and Ellis, J. 1977 *Language and Materialism.* London: Routledge and Kegan Paul.

Crimp, M. 1981 *The Marketing Research Process.* New Jersey: Prentice-Hall.

Csikszentmihalyi, M. and Roshberg-Halton, E. 1981 *The Meaning of Things.* Cambridge: Cambridge University Press.

Curren, J. 1986 'The impact of advertising on the British mass media.' In R. Collins, J. Curran, N. Garnham, P. Scannell, P. Schlesinger and C. Sparks (eds) *Media, Culture and Society.* London: Sage Press, 309–35.

Damon, F. H. 1980 'The Kula and generalised exchange. Considering some unconsidered aspects of the Elementary Structures of Kinship.' *Man,* 15, 269–92.

1983 'What moves the Kula: opening and closing gifts on Woodlark Island.' In J. Leach and E. Leach (eds) *The Kula: New Perspectives on Massim Exchange.* Cambridge: Cambridge University Press, 309–42.

Deetz, J. 1977 *In Small Things Forgotten.* New York: Doubleday.

Donne J. B. 1978 'African Art and the Paris studios 1805–1820.' In M. Greenhalgh and V. Megaw (eds) *Art in Society.* London: Duckworth, 105–20.

Douglas, M. 1967 'Primitive rationing.' In R. Firth (ed.) *Themes in Economic Anthropology.* London: Tavistock, 199–47.

Douglas, M. and Isherwood, B. 1979 *The World of Goods.* London: Allen Lane.

Dubinskas, F. and Traweek S. 1984 'Closer to the ground: a reinterpretation of Walbiri iconography.' *Man,* 19.1, 15–30.

Dumont, L. 1977 *From Mandeville to Marx.* Chicago: University of Chicago Press.

Dupré, L. 1983 *Marx's Social Critique of Culture*. New Haven: Yale University Press.

Durkheim, E. 1965 *The Division of Labour in Society*. New York: The Free Press.

Durkheim, E. and Mauss, M. 1963 *Primitive Classification*. London: Cohen and West.

Dyer, A. 1982 *Advertising as Communication*. London: Methuen.

Earnshaw, S. 1984 'Advertising and the media: the case of women's magazines.' *Media Culture and Society*, 6, 411–21.

Eco, U. 1976 *A Theory of Semiotics*. Bloomington: Indiana University Press.

Elias, N. 1978 *The Civilizing Process*. Oxford: Basil Blackwell.

Engel, J., Kollat, D., and Blackwell, R. 1973 *Consumer Behaviour*. Illinois: Holt, Reinhardt and Winston.

Ewen, S. and Ewen, E. 1982 *Channels of Desire*. New York: McGraw-Hill.

Fabian, J. 1983 *Time and the Other*. New York: Columbia University Press.

Faris, J. 1972 *Nuba Personal Art*. London: Duckworth.

Fenton, W. 1974 'The advancement of Material Culture studies in modern anthropological research.' In M. Richardson (ed.) *The Human Mirror*. Baton Rouge: Louisiana State University Press, 15–36.

Ferguson, M. 1983 *Forever Feminine*. Exeter: Heinemann.

Firth, R. 1957 *Economics of the New Zealand Maori*. Wellington: R. E. Owen.

1983: Magnitudes and values in Kula exchange. In J. Leach and E. Leach (eds) *The Kula: New Perspectives on Massim Exchange*. Cambridge: Cambridge University Press, 89–102.

Forde, D. 1934 *Habitat, Economy and Society*. London: Methuen.

Forge, A. 1973 'Style and Meaning in Sepik Art.' In A. Forge (ed.) *Primitive Art and Society*. Oxford: Oxford University Press, 169–92.

Forty, A. 1986 *Objects of Desire*. London: Thames and Hudson.

Foster, H. (ed.) 1983 *The Anti-Aesthetic*. Port Townsend: Bay Press.

Foucault, M. 1977a 'What is an author.' In M. Foucault *Language, Counter-Memory, Practice*. Oxford: Basil Blackwell, 113–38.

1977b *Discipline and Punish*. New York: Vintage Books.

1981 *The History of Sexuality*. Harmondsworth: Penguin.

Frankovits, A. (ed.) 1984 *Seduced and Abandoned: the Baudrillard Scene*. Glebe, Australia: Stonemoss.

Fraser, W. 1981 *The Coming of the Mass Market*. London: Macmillan.

Freenberg, A. 1981 *Lukács, Marx and the Sources of Critical Theory*. Oxford: Martin Robertson.

Freud, S. 1984 *On Metapsychology*. Harmondsworth: Penguin.

Friedman, J. and Rowlands, M. 1977 'Notes towards an epigenetic model of the evolution of civilisation.' In J. Friedman and M. Rowlands (eds) *The Evolution of Social Systems*. London: Duckworth.

Friedrich, M. 1970 'Design structure and social interaction.' *American Antiquity*, 55, 332–43.

Frisby, D. 1984 *Georg Simmel*. London: Tavistock.

Frosh, S. 1987 *The Politics of Psychoanalysis*. London: Macmillan.

Fry, T. 1982 'Unpacking the typewriter.' *Block*, 7, 36–47.

Furth, H. G. 1969 *Piaget and Knowledge*. New Jersey: Prentice-Hall.

Galbraith, K. 1969 *The New Industrial State*. Harmondsworth: Penguin.

Gans, H. 1967 *The Levittowners*. London: Allen Lane.

Gathercole, P. 1978 'Hau, Maori and Veu: A re-examination.' *Mankind*, 11, (3), 334–40.

Geertz, C. 1979 'Suq: The Bazaar Economy in Sefrou.' In C. Geertz, H. Geertz, and L. Rosen *Meaning and Order in Moroccan Society*. Cambridge: Cambridge University Press, 123–310.

1980 *Negara*. Princeton: Princeton University Press.

Gell, A. 1986 'Newcomers to the world of goods: consumption amongst the Muria Gonds.' In A. Appadurai (ed.) *The Social Meaning of Things*. Cambridge: Cambridge University Press, 110–40.

Gellner, E. 1959 *Words and Things*. London: Gollanz.

Gershuny, J. I. 1978 *After Industrial Society*. London: Macmillan.

1983 *Social Innovation and the Division of Labour*. Oxford: Oxford University Press.

1985 Economic development and change in the mode of provision of services. In N. Redclift and E. Mingione (eds) *Beyond Employment*. Oxford: Basil Blackwell, 128–64.

Giddens, A. 1971 *Capitalism and Modern Social Theory*. Cambridge: Cambridge University Press.

1979 *Central Problems in Social Theory*. London: Macmillan.

1984 *The Constitution of Society*. Cambridge: Polity Press.

Gidri, A. 1974 'Imperialism and archaeology.' *Race*, 15.4, 431–59.

Gilsenan, M. 1982 *Recognising Islam*. London: Croom Helm.

Glassie, H. 1975 *Folk Housing in Middle Virginia*. Knoxville: University of Tennessee Press.

Godard, F. 1985 'How do ways of life change?' In N. Redclift and E. Mingione (eds) *Beyond Employment*. Oxford: Basil Blackwell, 317–37.

Godelier, M. 1972 *Rationality and Irrationality in Economics*. London: New Left Books.

Goffman, E. 1975 *Frame Analysis*. Harmondsworth: Penguin.

1979 *Gender Advertisements*. London: Macmillan.

Goldman, I. 1975 *The Mouth of Heaven*. New York: Wiley.

Goldthorpe, J. H., with Llewellyn, C. and Payne, C. 1980 *Social Mobility and Class Structure*. Oxford: Clarendon Press.

Gombrich, E. 1963 *Meditations on a Hobby Horse*. London: Phaidon.

1979 *The Sense of Order*. London: Phaidon.

Gortz, A. 1982 *Farewell to the Working Class*. London: Pluto Press.

Gould, R. (ed.) 1978 *Explorations in Ethnoarchaeology*. Albuquerque: University of New Mexico Press.

Gould, R. A. and Schiffer, M. B. (eds) 1981 *Modern Material Culture: The Archaeology of Us*. New York: Academic Press.

Graburn, N. H. (ed.) 1976 *Ethnic and Tourist Arts*. Berkeley: University of California Press.

Greenberg, J. and Mitchell, S. 1983 *Object relations in Psychoanalytical Theory*. Harvard: Harvard University Press.

Gregory, C. 1983 'Kula gift exchange and capitalist commodity exchange: a comparison.' In Leach, J. and Leach, E. (eds) *The Kula: New Perspectives on Massim Exchange*. Cambridge: Cambridge University Press, 103–17.

Gullestad, M. 1984 *Kitchen-Table Society*. Oslo: Universitetsforlaget.

Habermas, J. 1972 *Knowledge and Human Interests*. London: Heinemann.

1970 'Technology and science as ideology.' In *Towards a Rational Society*. Boston: Beacon Press, 81–122.

1979: 'Towards a reconstruction of historical materialism.' In *Communication and the Evolution of Society*. London: Heinemann, 130–77.

Haddon, A. C. 1895 *Evolution in Art as Illustrated by the Life Histories of Designs*. London: Scott.

Hall, E. T. 1966 *The Hidden Dimension*. London: Bodley Head.

Hall, S. 1985 'Realignment – For What? *Marxism Today* 29.12, 12–17.

Hall, S., Clarke, J., Jefferson, T., and Roberts, B. (eds) 1976 *Resistance Through Rituals*. London: Hutchinson.

Halsey, A. H., Heath A. and Ridge J. 1980 *Origins and Destinations* Oxford: Clarendon Press.

Hanson, F. and Hanson, L. 1983 *Counterpoint in Maori Culture*. London: Routledge and Kegan Paul.

Haug, W. F. 1986 *Critique of Commodity Aesthetics*. Cambridge: Polity Press.

Hebdige, D. 1981a 'Towards a Cartography of Taste 1935–1962.' *Block*, 4, 39–56.

1981b 'Object as image: the Italian scooter cycle.' *Block*, 5, 44–64.

1983 'Travelling light: one route into material culture.' In D. Miller (ed.) 'Things aint what they used to be.' *Royal Anthropological Institute News*, 59, 11–13.

Hegel, G. 1952 *Philosophy of Right*. Oxford: Clarendon Press.

1975 *Aesthetics*. Oxford: Clarendon Press.

1977 *Phenomenology of Spirit*. Oxford: Oxford University Press.

Hillier, B. and Hanson, J. 1984 *The Social Logic of Space*. Cambridge: Cambridge University Press.

Hindess, B. and Hirst, P. 1975 *Pre-Capitalist Modes of Production*. London: Routledge and Kegan Paul.

Hinton, W. 1972 *Fanshen*. Harmondsworth: Peguin.

Hodder, I. 1982a *The Present Past*. London: Batsford.

1982b *Symbols in Action*. Cambridge University Press.

Hodder, I. (ed.) 1982 *Symbolic and Structural Archaeology*. Cambridge: Cambridge University Press.

Horkheimer, M. and Adorno, T. 1979 *Dialectic of Enlightenment*. London: Verso.

Humphrey, C. 1971 'Some ideas of Saussure applied to Buryat magical drawings.' In E. Ardener (ed.) *Social Anthropology and Language*. London: Tavistock.

1985 'Barter and Economic Distintegration.' *Man*, 20, 48–72.

Hyppolite, J. 1969 *Studies on Marx and Hegel*. London: Heinemann.

1974 *Genesis and Structure of Hegel's Phenomenology of Spirit*. Evanstom: Northwestern University Press.

Inwood, M. 1983 *Hegel*. London: Routledge and Kegan Paul.

Irwin, J. and Brett, K. 1970 *The Origins of Chintz*. London: HMSO.

Jackson, A. 1973 *Semi Detached London*. London: Allen and Unwin.

James, S. 1979 'Confections, Concoctions and Conceptions.' *Journal of the Anthropoligical Society of Oxford*, 10, 83–95.

Jameson, F. 1984 'Postmodernism, the Cultural Logic of Late Capitalism.' *New Left Review*, 146, 53–92.

Jay, M. 1984 *Marxism and Totality*. Berkeley: University of California Press.

Jencks, C. 1977 *The Language of Post-Modern Architecture*. London: Academy.

Joachim, I. 1979 *Alienation from Marx to Modern Sociology*. Brighton: Harvester.

Jones, D. and Graves, A. 1986 'The race for pole position: revolution in the car industry.' *Marxism Today*, 30.1, 28–32.

Kahn, J. and Llobera, J. (eds) 1981 *The Anthropology of Pre-Capitalist Societies*. London: Macmillan.

Kellner, P. 1984 'Are markets compatible with socialism?' In B. Pimlott (ed.) *Fabian Essays in Socialist Thought*. London: Heinemann.

Kempton, W. 1981 *The Folk Classification of Ceramics*. New York: Academic Press.

King, A. 1976 *Colonial Urban Development*. London: Routledge and Kegan Paul.

1980 (ed.) *Buildings and Society*. London: Routledge and Kegan Paul.

1984 *The Bungalow*. London: Routledge and Kegan Paul.

Klein, M. 1975 *Envy and Gratitude and Other Works*. London: Delacourte Press.

Kolakowski, L. 1978 *Main currents of Marxism Volume I*. Oxford: Oxford University Press.

Kramer, C. (ed.) 1979 *Enthnoarchaeology*. Albuquerque: University of New Mexico Press.

Krause, R. 1978 'Towards a formal account of Bantu ceramics.' In R. Dunnell and E. Hall (eds) *Archaeological Essays in Honour of Irving B. Rouse*. The Hague: Mouton.

Kriedte, P. Medick, H. and Schlumbohm, J. 1981 *Industrialisation Before Industrialisation*. Cambridge: Cambridge University Press.

Kroeber, A. L. 1939 'Cultural and natural areas of native north America.' *University of California Publications in American Archaeology and Ethnology*, 38, 1–242.

Langer, S. 1942 *Philosophy in a New Key*. Harvard: Harvard University Press.

Larrain, J. 1979 *The Concept of Ideology*. London: Hutchinson.
1982 'On the character of ideology: Marx and the present debate in Britain.' *Theory, Culture and Society* 1.1, 5–22.

Lasch, C. 1979 *The Culture of Narcissism*. New York: Norton and Co.

Le-Grand, J. 1982 *The Strategy of Equality*. London: George Allen and Unwin.

Leach, E. 1954 *Political Systems of Highland Burma*. London: Athlone Press.

Leach, J. and Leach E. (eds) 1983 *The Kula: New Perspectives on Massim Exchange*. Cambridge: Cambridge University Press.

Lehrer, A. 1983 *Wine and Conversation*. Bloomington: Indiana University Press.

Leiss, W. 1983 'The icons of the marketplace.' *Theory, Culture and Society*, 1.3, 10–21.

Leiss, W., Kline, S. and Jhally, S. 1986 *Social Communication in Advertising*. London: Methuen.

Leone, M. 1984 'Interpreting ideology in historical archaeology: The William Paca Garden in Annapolis, Maryland.' In D. Miller and C. Tilley (eds) *Ideology, Power and Prehistory*. Cambridge: Cambridge University Press, 25–36.

Levinson, S. 1983 *Pragmatics*. Cambridge: Cambridge University Press.

Lévi-Strauss, C. 1969 *The Elementary Structures of Kinship*. London: Eyre and Spottiswoode.
1972 *The Savage Mind*. London: Weidenfeld and Nicolson.
1982 *The Way of the Masks*. Seattle: University of Washington Press.
1987 *Introduction to the Work of Marcel Mauss*. London: Routledge and Kegan Paul.

Levy-Bruhl, L. 1966 *The Soul of the Primitive*. London: George Allen and Unwin.

Lowrie, R. 1937 *The History of Ethnological Theory*. New York: Rinehart and Company.

Lukács, G. 1971 'Reification and the consciousness of the proletariat.' In *History and Class Consciousness*. London: Merlin Press, 83–222.
1975 *The Young Hegel*. London: Merlin Press.

Lyons, J. 1977 *Semantics*. Cambridge: Cambridge University Press.

McKendrick, N. 1983 'Commercialisation and the Economy.' In N. McKendrick, J. Brewer and J. Plumb *The Birth of a Consumer Society*. London: Hutchinson, 9–194.

MacKenzie, D. and Wajcman, J. 1985 'Introductory Essay.' In MacKenzie, D. and Wajcman, J. (eds) *The Social Shaping of Technology*. Milton Keynes: Open University Press, 2–25.

McCarthy, E. D. 1984 'Towards a sociology of the physical world. George Herbert Mead on physical objects.' In *Studies in Symbolic Interaction*, 5, 105–21.

Malinowski, B. 1922 *Argonauts of the Western Pacific.* London: Routledge and Kegan Paul.

Marcuse, H. 1964 *One Dimensional Man.* London: Routledge and Kegan Paul.

Marx, K. 1973 *Grundrisse.* Harmondsworth: Penguin.

1974 *Capital.* London: Lawrence and Wishart.

1975 *Early Writings.* Harmondsworth: Penguin.

Marx, K. and Engels, F. 1967 *The Communist Manifesto.* Penguin: Harmondsworth.

Mauss, M. 1954 *The Gift.* London: Cohen and West.

1979 'A category of the human mind. The notion of person, the notion of 'self'.' In *Sociology and Psychology.* London: Routledge and Kegan Paul.

Miller, D. 1980 Archaeology and Development. *Current Anthropology,* 21, 709–26.

1984 'Modernism and suburbia as material ideology.' In D. Miller and C. Tilley (eds) *Ideology, Power and Prehistory.* Cambridge: Cambridge University Press, 37–49.

1985 *Artefacts as Categories: a study of ceramic variability in Central India.* Cambridge: Cambridge University Press.

1986 Alienation and exchange in the Jajmani system. *Journal of Anthropological Research*, 42.2, 535–56.

forthcoming 'Primitive art and the necessity of primitivism for art.' In S. Hiller (ed.) *Primitivism.*

Miller, D. and Tilley, C. (eds) 1984 *Ideology, Power and Prehistory.* Cambridge: Cambridge University Press.

Miller, G. 1978 'Practical and lexical knowledge.' In E. Rosch and B. Lloyd (eds) *Cognition and Categorisation.* New Jersey: Lawrence Erlbaum Associates.

Miller, G. and Johnson-Laird, P. 1976 *Language and Perception.* Cambridge: Cambridge University Press.

Miller, M. B. 1981 *The Bon Marché.* London: George Allen and Unwin.

Mitter, P. 1977 *Much Maligned Monsters: European Reaction to Indian Art.* Oxford: Clarendon Press.

Mingione, E. 1985 'Social reproduction of the surplus labour force: the case of Southern Italy.' In N. Redclift and E. Mingione (eds) *Beyond Employment.* Oxford: Basil Blackwell, 14–54.

Moeran, B. 1984 *Lost Innocence.* Berkeley: University of California Press.

Mort, F. 1986 The Texas chain store massacre. *New Socialist*, 35, 15–19.

Mukerji, C. 1983 *From Graven Images.* Columbia University Press.

Munn, N. 1969 'The Effectiveness of symbols in Murngin rite and myth.' In R. Spencer (ed.) *Forms of Symbolic Action.* Seattle: University of Washington Press, 178–207.

1971 'The transformation of subjects into objects in Walbiri and Pitjantjatjara myth.' In R. Berndt (ed.) *Australian Aboriginal Anthropology*. Nedlands: University of Western Australia Press, 141–63.

1973a *Walbiri Iconography: Graphic Representation and Cultural Symbolism in a Central Australian Society*. Ithica: Cornell University Press.

1973b 'The spatial presentation of cosmic order in Walbiri iconography.' In A. Forge, (ed.) *Primitive Art and Society*.

1977 Spatiotemporal transformations of Gawa canoes. *Journal de la Société des Océanistes*, 33, 39–52.

1983 'Gawan Kula: spatiotemporal control and the symbolism of influence.' In J. Leach and E. Leach (eds) *The Kula: New perspectives on Massim Exchange*. Cambridge: Cambridge University Press, 277–308.

1986 *The Fame of Gawa*. Cambridge: Cambridge University Press.

Murray, R. 1985 'Benetton Britain: the new economic order.' *Marxism Today*, 29.11, 28–32.

Muthesius, S. 1982 *The English Terraced House*. New Haven: Yale University Press.

Myers, K. 1982 'Tu: A cosmetic case study.' *Block*, 7, 48–58.

New Socialist 1986 Special issue on style, 38.

Nove, A. 1983 *The Economics of Feasible Socialism*. London: George Allen and Unwin.

1985 Beyond the market: Comments on Boris Frankel. *Radical Philosophy*, 37, 24–7.

Offe, C. 1984 *Contradictions of the Welfare State*. London: Hutchinson.

Oliver, P., Davis, I. and Bentley, I. 1981 *Dunroamin : the Suburban Semi and its Enemies*. London: Barrie and Jenkins.

Ollman, B. 1971 *Alienation: Marx's Conception of Man in a Capitalist Society*. Cambridge: Cambridge University Press.

Pahl, R. E. 1984 *Divisions of Labour*. Oxford: Basil Blackwell.

Pahl, R. E. and Wallace, C. 1985 'Household work strategies in economic recession.' In N. Redclift and E. Mingione (eds) *Beyond Employment*. Oxford: Basil Blackwell, 189–227.

Panofsky, E. 1957 *Gothic Architecture and Scholasticism*. New York: World Press.

Parker, T. 1983 *The People of Providence*. London: Hutchinson.

Parry, J. 1986 'The gift, the Indian gift and the "Indian gift".' *Man*, 21, 453–473.

Perlin, F. 1983 'Proto-Industrialization and pre-colonial South Asia.' *Past and Present*, 30–95, 98.

Piaget, J. 1932 *The Moral Development of the Child*. London: Routledge and Kegan Paul.

1962 *Play, Dreams and Imitation in Childhood*. London: Routledge and Kegan Paul.

1971a *Biology and Knowledge*. Edinburgh: Edinburgh University Press.

1971b *Structuralism*. London: Routledge and Kegan Paul.
1972 *The Principles of Genetic Epistemology*. London: Routledge and Kegan Paul.
Plant, R. 1973 *Hegel*. London: George Allen and Unwin.
1977 Hegel and Political Theory 2. *New Left Review*, 104, 103–13.
Plato 1984 'Crito'. In *The Dialogues of Plato*. New Haven: Yale University Press.
Plumb, J. 1983 'Commercialization and Society.' In N. McKendrick, J. Brewer and J. Plumb (eds) *The Birth of a Consumer Society*. London: Europa, 265–334.
Preteceille, E. and Terrail, J–P. 1985 *Capitalism, Consumption and Needs*. Oxford: Basil Blackwell.
Roberts, R. 1973 *The Classic Slum*. Harmondsworth: Penguin.
Rosch, E. 1978 'Principles of Categorisation.' In E. Rosch and B. Lloyd (eds) *Cognition and Categorisation*. Hillsdale: Lawrence Erlbaum Associates, 27–48.
Rose, G. 1978 *The Melancholy Science*. London: Macmillan.
Rosen, M. 1982 *Hegel's Dialectic and its Criticism*. Cambridge: Cambridge University Press.
Rubin, L. 1972 *Essays on Marx's Theory of Value*. Detroit Black and Red.
Rustin, M. 1985 'English conservatism and the aesthetics of architecture.' *Radical Philosophy*, 40, 20–8.
Ryan, A. 1984 *Property and Political Theory*. Oxford: Basil Blackwell.
Sahlins, M. 1974 *Stone Age Economics*. London: Tavistock.
1976a *Culture and Practical Reason*. Chicago: University of Chicago Press.
1976b *The Use and Abuse of Biology*. London: Tavistock.
Said, E. 1975 *Orientalism*. New York: Pantheon Books.
Salisbury, R. 1962 *From Stone to Steel*. Cambridge: Cambridge University Press.
Sartre, J-P. 1969 *Being and Nothingness*. London: Methuen.
1976 *Critique of Dialectical Reason*. London: New Left Books.
Schmidt, A. 1971 *The Concept of Nature in Marx*. London: New Left Books.
Schmidt, J. 1975 'The concrete totality and Lukács' concept of proletariat bildung'. *Telos*, 25, 2–41.
1985: *Maurice Merleau-Ponty: between Phenomenology and Structuralism*. London: Macmillan.
Schultz A. 1970 *On Phenomenology and Social Relations* (ed. H. Wagner). Chicago: University of Chicago Press.
Scoditti, G. with Leach J. 1983 'Kula on Kitava.' In Leach, J. and Leach E. (eds) *The Kula: New Perspectives on Massim Exchange*. Cambridge: Cambridge University Press, 249–73.
Scruton, R. 1979 *The Aesthetics of Architecture*. London: Methuen.
Segal, H. 1979 *Klein*. London: Fontana.
Sennett, R. 1976 *The Fall of Public Man*. Cambridge: Cambridge University Press.

Shennan, S. 1983 'Monuments: An example of the archaeologist's approach to the massively material.' In D. Miller (ed.) 'Things aint what they used to be.' *Royal Anthropological Institute News*, 59, 9–11.

Silk, J. 1980 Adoption and Kinship in Oceania. *American Anthropologist*, 82, 799–820.

Simmel, G. 1950 *The Sociology of Georg Simmel* (ed. K. H. Wulf). Glencoe: The Free Press.

1957 'Fashion'. *American Journal of Sociology*, 62, 541–58.

1968 *The Conflict in Modern Culture and other Essays*. New York: New York Teachers College Press.

1978 *The Philosophy of Money*. London: Routledge and Kegan Paul.

Smith, A. D. 1981 *The Ethnic Revival*. Cambridge: Cambridge University Press.

Smith, B. 1960 *European Vision and the South Pacific*. Oxford: Clarendon Press.

Sombart, W. 1967 *Luxury and Capitalism*. Ann Arbor: University of Michigan Press.

Sperber, D. 1975: *Rethinking Symbolism*. Cambridge: Cambridge University Press.

1979 'Is symbolic thought pre-rational?' In M. LeCron Foster and S. Brandes (eds) *Symbol as Sense*, 25–44.

Sperber, D. and Wilson, D. 1986 *Relevance: Communication and Cognition*. Oxford: Basil Blackwell.

Spooner, B. 1986 'Weavers and dealers: the authenticity of an oriental carpet.' In A. Appadurai (ed.) *The Social Meaning of Things*. Cambridge: Cambridge University Press, 195–235.

Srinivas, M. N. 1966 *Social Change in Modern India*. New Delhi: Orient Longmann.

Steadman, P. 1979 *The Evolution of Designs*. Cambridge: Cambridge University Press.

Strathern, M. 1979 'The self in self-decoration.' *Oceania*, 44, 241–57.

1985: Kinship and economy: constitutive orders of a provisional kind. *American Ethnologist*, 12.2, 191–208.

Sturrock, S. (ed.) 1979 *Structuralism and Since*. Oxford: Oxford University Press.

Tambiah, S. 1984 *The Buddhist Saints of the Forest and the Cult of the Amulets*. Cambridge: Cambridge University Press.

Taussig, M. 1977 'The genesis of capitalism amongst a South American peasantry.' *Comparative Studies in Society and History*, 19, 130–55.

Taylor, C. 1975 *Hegel*. Cambridge: Cambridge University Press.

1979 *Hegel and Modern Society*. Cambridge: Cambridge University Press.

Thirsk, J. 1978 *Economic Policy and Projects*. Oxford: Clarendon Press.

Thomason, B. 1982 *Making Sense of Reification*. London: Macmillan.

Thrift, N. 1977 'Time and theory in human geography.' *Progress in Human Geography*, 1, 65–101.

Torrance, J. 1977 *Estrangement, Alienation and Exploitation.* London: Macmillan.

Turner, T. 1973 'Piaget's structuralism.' *American Anthropologist*, 75, 351–73.

Tylor, E. B. 1881 *Anthropology: An Introduction to the Study of Man and Civilisation.* London: Macmillan.

Vastokas, J. 1978 'Cognitive aspects of North-West coast art.' In M. Greenhalgh and V. Megaw (eds) *Art in Society.* London: Duckworth, 243–66.

Veblen, T. 1970 *The Theory of the Leisure Class.* London: George Allen and Unwin.

Venturi, R., Scott-Brown, D. and Izenours, A. 1972 *Learning From Las Vegas.* Cambridge, Massachusetts: MIT Press.

Vygotsky, L. S. 1978 *Mind in Society.* Harvard: Harvard University Press.

Waites, B., Bennett, T. and Martin, G. 1982 (eds) *Popular Culture: Past and Present.* London: Croom Helm.

Walens, S. 1981 *Feasting with Cannibals.* Princeton: Princeton University Press.

Wallerstein, I. 1979 *The Capitalist World Economy.* Cambridge: Cambridge University Press.

Wallman, S. (ed.) 1982 *Living in South London.* London: Gower.

1984 *Eight London Households.* London: Tavistock.

Weber, M. 1947 *The Theory of Social and Economic Organisation.* New York: Free Press.

Weiner, A. 1976 *Women of Value, Men of Renown.* Austin: University of Texas Press.

1983 '"A world of made is not a world of born": doing kula in Kiriwina.' In J. Leach and E. Leach (eds) *The Kula: New perspectives on Massim Exchange.* Cambridge: Cambridge University Press, 147–70.

1985 'Inalienable Wealth.' *American Ethnologist*, 12.2, 210–27.

Wheatley, P. 1971 *The Pivot of the Four Quarters.* Edinburgh: Edinburgh University Press.

White, L. 1959 *The Evolution of Culture.* New York: McGraw-Hill.

Williams, E. 1985 'Art and Artifact at the Trocedero: *Ars Amerciana* and the primitivist revolution.' In G. Stocking (ed.) *Objects and Others.* Madison: University of Wisconsin Press, 146–66.

Williams, R. 1961 *Culture and Society.* Harmondsworth: Penguin.

1980 'Advertising: the Magic System.' In *Problems in Materialism and Culture.* London: Verso, 170–95.

Williams, R. H. 1982 *Dream Worlds.* Berkeley: University of California Press.

Williamson, J. 1986a *Consuming Passions.* London: Marion Boyars.

1986b 'The problems of being popular.' *New Socialist*, 41, 14–15.

Willis, P. 1978 *Profane Culture.* London: Routledge and Kegan Paul.

Wilson, E. 1985 *Adorned in Dreams.* London: Virago.

Winnicott, D. W. 1971 *Playing and Reality*. London: Tavistock Press.
Winship, J. 1983 'Options. For the way we live now. Or a magazine for superwoman.' *Theory, Culture and Society*, 1.3, 44–65.
Wolf, E. 1982 *Europe and the People without History*. Berkeley: University of California Press.
Wolff, J. 1981 *The Social Production of Art*. London: Macmillan.
Worsley, P. 1957 *The Trumpet shall Sound*. London: MacGibbon and Kee.
Young, R. and Willmott, D. 1957 *Family and Kinship in East London*. London: Routledge and Kegan Paul.
    1973 *The Symmetrical Family*. London: Routledge and Kegan Paul.

The following list represents a few of the most relevant publications which have come out since this book was originally written and might be read in conjunction with it.

Campbell, C. 1987 *The Romantic Ethic and the Spirit of Modern Consumerism*. Oxford: Basil Blackwell.
Culture and History 7, Special issue on Consumption.
Hall, S. and Jacques M. (eds). 1989 *New Times*. London: Lawrence and Wishart.
Hirschman E.C. (ed). 1989 *Interpretive Consumer Research*. Provo U.T: Association for Consumer Research.
McCracken, G. 1988 *Culture and Consumption*. Indiana University Press.
Miller, D. 1988 Appropriating the State on the Council Estate. *Man*, 23. 2, 353–72
Miller, D. (forthcoming) The Young and the Restless in Trinidad. A Case of the Local and the Global in Mass Consumption.
Otnes, P. (ed). 1988 *The Sociology of Consumption*. New Jersey: Humanities Press.
Rutz, H. and Orlove, B. (eds). 1989 *The Social Economy of Consumption*. Lanham: University Press of America.

Index

absolute knowledge, 14, 24, 25–6,
  27, 90, 181
Adorno, T. 45, 167
advertising, 97, 143, 168–9, 171–2,
  203, 205, 212
aesthetics, 14, 80, 97, 98, 100, 113,
  117, 149–50
alienation, 27, 40–4, 62, 76, 78,
  79, 118, 126, 156
Althusser, L. 38–9
America, 119, 148–9
American history, 140–2
American sociology, 68, 78
ancestors, 54–9, 124
Anderson, P. 165, 166
Annales, historians, 135
anthropology, 9, 11, 13, 50–1, 54,
  57, 60, 64, 66–7, 71, 72–3, 96,
  102–3, 110–12, 118–20, 125,
  143–4, 145–6, 157, 167, 169
  of consumption, 18, 145–6, 185,
    207–8, 214
  Marxist, 60
Appadurai, A. 52, 120, 147
archaeology, 111–12, 115, 122,
  124–6, 140, 143
  ethno-archaeology, 112, 143
architects, 159–60, 165, 175, 198
architecture, 97–8
  see also housing styles
art, 8, 10, 28, 32, 101, 111, 113,
  123, 127, 130, 149, 151–2,
  165, 166, 187
Arthur, C. 27, 41–2
arts and crafts, 114, 140
asceticism, 72, 174

Australian aboriginals, 13, 50,
  53–8
authenticity, 10, 174, 193, 211,
  215

Barth, F. 126
Barthes, R. 145, 164
  Mythologies, 164
Baudelaire, 139
Baudrillard, J. 46–8, 96, 117, 129,
  164–5, 189, 206
  For a Critique of the Political
    Economy of the Sign, 46
  The Mirror of Production, 46
  The Precession of Simulacra,
    165
  critique of Marx, 46–8, 117
Bauhaus, 129, 159
behaviourism, 87, 104, 105
Benjamin, W. 9, 121, 124, 139,
  155
Bergen, 198–9
Berger, P. and Luckmann, T.
  64–5, 81
Berman, M. 121, 166, 208
Block, 142
Boas, F. 113–14
Bourdieu, P. 9, 15, 52, 93, 102–6,
  107, 146, 147, 149–57, 165,
  167, 168, 172, 182, 197, 207,
  213, 158
  Distinction, 15, 147, 149–57,
    158, 166, 167, 213
  Outline of a Theory of Practice,
    146, 156
  on class, 150–6

criticisms of, 154–6
on education, 104, 150–2
on habitus, 93, 103–5, 130,
    150–5
and Kantian aesthetics, 149–50
on material culture, 103–5
methodology of, 155
Braudel, F. 135, 137
British history, 134–9, 182–4
British society, 3, 4, 11, 133,
    158–61, 168–70, 173, 178,
    186, 193–4, 196–8, 203,
    210–12
built environment, 160–1, 170,
    187
    see also housing styles
bureaucratic institutions, 186–7,
    195
business studies, 143–4

capitalism, 9, 10, 11, 16, 17, 50,
    68, 73, 76, 79, 115, 116, 119,
    136, 144, 165, 167, 176, 178,
    180, 181, 183, 184, 185, 186,
    192, 193, 195, 196, 199, 200,
    206, 212–13
categories, cognitive, 174
categorization, 103–5, 112, 116,
    127–8
Chicago, 146–7
children's sweets, 168–9, 191
Chintz, 123
Chomsky, N. 96
churinga, 59, 124
cognitive order, 146
colonialism, 67, 137
Colquhoun, N. 96–7, 98
commerce, 143, 185–6, 190
commodities, 51–2, 71, 115, 120,
    129, 164, 189, 192
communism, 14, 75
    see also Marx
consciousness, 65, 99–100, 107
consumer cooperatives, 139, 201
consumer protection, 144
consumer psychology, 110, 143
consumption, 3, 4, 9, 16, 17, 18,
    44, 47–9, 70, 76, 133, 140,

144, 158, 168–9, 171, 176,
    182, 185, 189, 190–3, 195–217
conspicuous, 170, 199
and equality, 196–203
history of, 135–42
and inalienability, 17, 190–2,
    204
neglect of, 3, 48, 133, 140
as projects, 213–14
socialism of, 144
studies of, 142–57
as sublation, 191
as work, 190–2
constructivism, 87, 93, 104
contradiction, 14, 17, 33, 42–3,
    68, 72, 79–80, 82, 91–2, 164,
    177, 184, 185, 188, 193, 194,
    202–3, 208, 209, 214, 216
Coronation Street, 197
cosmetics, 193–4
cotton trade, 137–8
council estate, 159, 160
craft production, 185
critical theory, 216
Csikszentmihalyi, M. and
    Rochberg-Halton, E. 146–7
culture, 4, 8, 9, 11, 13, 14, 20, 32,
    33, 42, 60, 66–7, 76, 79–81,
    180, 192–3, 194, 204, 214–15
definition of, 33
as process, 11, 214
tragedy of, 79–81

Damon, F. 62
Death of the Author, 106, 176
Deetz, J. 140–1
Delhi, 122
department stores, 139
Descartes, R. 20
design, 9, 116, 117, 138, 169
design history, 142
dialectic, 24, 92–3, 178
diffusion, 111
discursive penetration, 170
diversity, 6–10, 32, 77–8, 81, 175,
    179, 181, 195–6, 208–9, 212
do-it-yourself activities, 210

dominant ideology, 115, 162, 163, 168
Douglas, M. 168
Douglas, M. and Isherwood, B. 143, 145–6, 157, 173–4
dreamtime, 54–7
Duchamp, M. 5
Durkheim, E. 6, 9, 44, 64, 128, 146, 181, 185, 192
dyeing technology, 123, 137

Eastern Europe, 206
economics, 143, 145, 146, 157
education, 149, 151–2, 183
efficiency, 116, 117, 129
Elias, N. 152, 182
emulation, 126, 136, 139, 147
Engels, F. 181, 182, 197
Enlightenment, 20, 135, 216
epigenetic, 87, 89
equality, 17, 73–6, 79, 186, 198–202, 211
ethnicity, 17
ethnography, 4, 154, 198, 199, 208, 210, 211
   see also anthropology
evolutionary studies, 110–11
Ewen, S. and Ewen, E. 164
exchange, 51, 53, 61–4, 70–2, 120
   spheres of, 135
externalization, 4, 12, 21, 23, 28, 30, 32, 40, 56–7, 62–5, 79, 180, 195

false consciousness, 162–3
fantasy, 172, 175
fashion, 126, 136, 138, 174–5, 209, 213
feminism, 7, 46, 174
fetishism, 18, 39, 44, 77, 103, 143, 204–6
Feuerbach, L. 35, 44
Fichte, J. 19, 20, 30
film, 134–5
food, 153
fort-da game, 95
Forty, A. 106, 138, 141

Foucault, M. 162–3, 164
fragmentation, 16, 208–9
framing, 5, 100–2, 208
France, 139, 149, 201
Frankfurt school, 6, 10, 45, 160
freedom, 73–6, 77, 181, 185
Freud, S. 6, 91, 95, 100
function, 47, 115–18
functionalism, 111, 206
Furth, H. 94

Galbraith, K. 169
Gawa, 60–3, 66
gender representation, 54–6, 107, 169, 171, 174–5
Georgian style, 141
Gershuny, J. 210
Giddens, A. 41, 170
gifts, 50–2, 71, 120, 204
Glassie, H. 141
Goffman, E. 101, 172
   Frame Analysis 101
Gombrich, E. 100–1
   Sense of Order, 100
Gortz, A. 167, 210
Gramsci, A. 162
gravestones, 141
Greater London Council, 203
Gullestad, M. 198

Habermas, J. 45, 82, 160
habitus, see Bourdieu
Hall, S. 173
Harlow, 198
hau, 50–2, 119
Haug, W. 164, 169
health, 172
Hebdige, D. 167, 169–70, 173, 175
hedonism, 136
Hegel, G. 4, 5, 12, 14, 19–45, 48, 65, 66, 67, 68, 69–71, 78, 79, 82, 89–90, 93, 115, 178, 179, 180, 181, 189, 192, 193, 214, 216
   Aesthetics, 28–9
   Logic, 21, 38

Phenomenology of Spirit, 4, 12, 19–35, 37, 69, 178, 179, 214
Philosophy of Right, 29
on absolute knowledge, 24, 25–6, 27, 18
on art, 28–91
use of history, 20, 22, 24–5
on material culture, 28–9, 31
on objectification, 27–33, 45, 179–80, 214
on philosophy, 19, 20, 22, 25–6, 30
on property, 29
on rationality of the actual, 22, 26
use of theology, 19, 30
hegemony, 162
history, 20, 125, 134
   Marxist, 139, 144–5
hi-tech, 117, 187
Hodder, I. 127, 143
hospice movement, 203
household, 7–8, 210–12
household furnishing, 7, 8, 102, 198, 208
housewives, 198–9
housing styles, 6, 141, 159–61, 163, 175
Hyppolite, J. 42

ideology, 16, 45, 81–2, 117, 160, 161–3, 205
impersonal relations, 73–5
import-substitution, 138
inalienability, 17, 51–2, 126, 190, 193, 204, 208, 215
inauthenticity, 11
India *see* South Asia
individualism, 64–6, 73–5, 81, 106, 118–21, 130, 141–2, 147, 159, 160, 174, 176, 194–5, 196, 199, 214
   see also self
industrial society, 4, 6, 16–17, 183–7, 195, 216–17
industrial revolution, 46, 74, 114, 134–42, 181, 182, 185

industry, 175, 185–6, 196, 215
infant development, 86–95
informal economy, 210–11
initiation rituals, 55, 126
introjection, 178
Israel, 125, 201

Jackson, A. 159
James, A. 168
Jameson, F. 165–6
Japan, 114, 119

Kant, I. 20, 22, 70, 75, 87, 112, 179
Kantian aesthetics, 70, 100, 149–59
kibbutz, 201–2
King, A. 159, 161
kinship, 53–4, 73
kitomu, 51, 62
kitsch, 11, 166, 208, 212
Klein, M. 14, 87, 90–3, 94–5
   on introjection, 90–3
   paranoid-schizoid position, 91–2
   phantasy, 92–3
   play technique, 94
   on play, 94–5
   on projection, 90–3
Kolakowski, L. 32
Kroeber, A. 143
Kula, 13, 51–2, 53, 60–3, 113
Kwakiutl, 114, 128, 129

Lacan, J. 99
Langer, S. 96–7, 105
language, 15, 86, 94, 95–8, 102, 105, 107
Lasch, C. 164
   The Culture of Narcissism, 164
Leach, B. 114
Lehrer, A. 98
leisure, 196–7
   see also Veblen
Lévi-Strauss, C. 52, 59, 64, 124, 128
   The Elementary Structures of Kinship, 52

The Savage Mind, 59
Levy-Bruhl, L. 119
liberalism, 75, 79, 181
linguistics, 3, 95–6, 102, 103, 127, 130
Locke, J. 120
London, 138
Lukács, G. 19, 38, 44–5, 68, 76, 162, 164

McKendrick, N. 135, 136, 138
Malinowski, B. 61, 63
  The Argonauts of the Western Pacific, 61
manufacture, 112–14, 134, 138
Maori, 50
Marcuse, H. 45, 164, 167
  One Dimensional Man, 164
market, 120, 125, 126, 193, 196, 199–201, 203
Marx, K. 6, 13, 19, 34–49, 50, 53, 64, 70, 75–8, 93, 114, 115, 117, 134, 140, 146, 154, 162, 164, 178, 179, 180–5, 189, 190, 192, 205–6
  Capital, 34, 39, 44, 162
  Economic and Philosophical Manuscripts, 34–41
  Grundrisse, 48, 183
  on communism, 14, 35, 37, 43, 45
  as conservative thinker, 46–8
  consistency of views, 38–9
  on consumption, 48–9, 181
  on culture, 36, 42, 48–9
  on fetishism, 39, 44, 205–6
  on Hegel, 27, 30–1, 34–45, 48, 181
  as modernist, 75
  on objectification, 36, 37, 39–43, 45, 47
  on philosophy, 35
  on production, 35–9, 46–8, 183
  on property, 120
  on reification, 44
  on rupture, 36–7, 39
Marxism, 6, 10, 13, 43–5, 162, 207

Western, 68, 72, 76
Marxism Today, 203
Masks, 128
mass consumption, *see* consumption
mass culture critique, 166–7, 173, 174, 176
material culture, 3, 4, 13, 14–15, 59–60, 69, 76–8, 85–6, 95–130, 141–2, 143, 154, 167, 170, 171, 174, 177, 208, 215, 217
  contrasted with language, 95–8, 100, 102
  and function, 115–18
  and manufacture, 112–15
  in ontogenesis, 86–95
  in play, 93–5
  properties of, 59, 99–102, 105, 107–8, 109–10, 129–30, 170
  as propositional, 98
  quantitative rise of, 3, 13, 76–8, 162, 181, 215
  and the self, 118–21
  and space, 121–4
  and style, 127–9
  study of, 15, 85–6, 110–12
  and time, 124–7
  and the unconscious, 100–2, 107–8
Mauss, M. 51–2, 53, 62, 63, 64, 118, 120, 204
  The Gift, 52
Mead, G. 31, 85
media, 7, 97, 133, 161, 168
merchants, 139
Merleau-Ponty, M. 31
Mesopotamia, 122
miners strike (1984–5), 203
mode of production, 113
modernization, 141, 180
modernism, 7, 10, 117, 129–30, 159–61, 166, 174–5, 187, 210–11
modernity, 4, 6, 8, 10, 16, 67, 68–9, 74–5, 80, 179, 209
  defined, 69

money, 7, 71–6, 77, 136, 185, 189
monuments, 124–5
Morris, W. 114, 140, 167, 200
motor scooter, 169, 175
Mukerji, C. 136
Munn, N. 13, 14, 52–67, 106
  criticisms of, 66
  on Gawa, 60–3
  influences on, 53, 65
  subjectivism and objectivism in,
    63–7
  on Walbiri, 53–60
museums, ethnographic, 116
Muthesius, S. 159
myth, 56, 145

National Childbirth Trust, 203
National Health Service, 173, 213
needs, 144, 150, 164, 188
New Guinea, 60, 126, 193, 194
New Socialist, 203
nihilism, 10, 165, 176, 179
Nove, A. 199–201
  The Economics of Feasible
    Socialism, 199

object-relations, 90–3
objectification, 12, 13, 18, 19,
    27–33, 39–43, 47, 56–7, 64–7,
    70–1, 80–2, 95, 104, 105, 108,
    118, 121, 129, 153, 156, 162,
    178, 179, 189, 192, 194, 204,
    205, 214–16
  and alienation, 41–3
  definitions of, 28, 40–1, 43,
    81–2, 179–80
  Marx's transformation of, 39–43
  origins of, 27, 30, 178
  relativity of, 82
  as theory of consumption,
    190–2, 214–16
  as theory of culture, 33, 56–8,
    62, 65–6, 80–1
objectivation, 65, 81
objective culture, 77–8, 189, 209
objectivism, 64–5, 102–3, 106,
    108, 163–5, 167, 168, 174,
    176

Offe, C. 201
Oliver, P. 159, 160
ontogenesis, 82, 86–95
Options, 171
oriental style, 123
orientalism, 122–4

Pacific, 119, 122
Pahl, R. 210–12
Paris studios, 123
parlour, 197–8
Parry, J. 120
phenomenology, 19, 53, 63–4
philosophy, 4, 85, 214
photography, 150
Piaget, J. 5, 10, 82, 87–90, 93–4,
    95
  Play, Dreams and Imitation in
    Childhood, 87–9
  on accommodation, 88–90
  on assimilation, 88–90
  operational thought, 88, 90
  on play, 89, 94
play, 15, 89, 93–5, 99
Plumb, J. 138
politics, 152, 213
popular culture, 11, 136, 150, 173,
    207
populism, 166, 175, 207
positivism, 45
possession, 75, 133
post-modernism, 10, 11, 16, 152,
    165–6, 175, 189, 206
post-structuralism, 6, 15, 64, 145,
    152, 165, 176, 194
potlach, 52
pottery, 114, 126, 140–1
poverty, 197, 203, 211
power, 163
pragmatics, 102, 127
praxis, 35, 42, 66, 107, 129, 182,
    196, 207, 214
pre-capitalist societies, 50, 60, 67,
    75
prestige goods, 122, 136
Preteceille, E. and Terrail, J-P,
    144

primitivism, 67, 122–4
production, 17, 61, 133, 134, 136,
    140, 168, 169, 181, 182, 192,
    210, 215
projection, 178
property, 75, 118, 119, 120–1,
    199, 201
proto-industrialization, 134, 139
proxemics, 100
Prussia, 179
psychology, 87–90, 103, 110, 208
psychoanalysis, 87, 90–3, 94–5

racism, 123
recontextualization, 174–6, 190,
    196, 208–9, 212, 213
reification, 44–5, 58–9, 204
relativism, 109
religion, 129
representation *see* signification
resistance, 162, 173
Return of the Jedi, 134–5
revolution, 162
Roberts, R. 197
    The Classic Slum, 197
Romanticism, 14, 20, 26, 31, 32,
    43, 45, 70, 73–4, 79, 80, 118,
    119, 122, 156, 166, 181,
    206–7, 214
Rustin, M. 97

Sahlins, M. 48, 51, 145–6
Said, E. 123
Salford, 197–8
Sartre, J-P. 19, 30, 44, 120
Saussure, F. 96, 97
Schultz, A. 31, 101
scientific revolution, 71, 74, 183,
    185, 187
Scruton, R. 31, 96–7
self, the, 93, 95, 118–21
    see also individualism
self-alienation, 12, 56, 63, 189,
    192, 214
self-decoration, 193–4
semantics, 95, 97, 102, 127, 128
semiotics, 126, 145

Sheppey, Isle of, 210
shopping, 116, 190, 212
signification, 46–7, 54–8, 61, 89,
    92, 94, 95, 105–6, 113–14,
    115, 128–9, 161, 164–5
Simmel, G. 5, 9, 13, 14, 19, 33,
    42, 60, 68–92, 120, 121, 139,
    147, 155, 174, 180, 181, 182,
    185, 187, 188, 189, 193, 209,
    214, 216
    The Philosophy of Money, 13,
        68–76
    on alienation, 76–9
    on blasé attitude, 78
    on cynical attitude, 78
    on desire, 70
    on fashion, 174
    on growth in abstraction, 71–6,
        78, 81
    on material culture, 70, 76–80,
        180
    on metropolis, 78
    on modernity, 68–9, 74–5, 121,
        187
    on purpose, 70–2
    relation to Hegel, 19, 69–71, 79,
        80–1, 181
    relation to Marx, 75–8, 181
    Romanticism of, 70, 79–80
    on state, 74
Smith, B. 122
soap operas, 7
socialism, 6, 17, 75, 79, 115, 140,
    159, 166, 176, 183, 184, 186,
    187, 188, 193, 203, 206, 207,
    211
    market, 199–201
society, 11–12, 73–4, 146, 154,
    177, 193, 215
sociology of art, 176
Solomon Islands, 116, 125
South Asia, 114, 116, 122, 123,
    126, 137, 139, 183, 209
spatial order, 121–4
state, 124, 186–7, 189, 190, 192,
    195, 200, 212, 216
    allocation, 133

state monopoly capitalism, 145
Stonehenge, 126
Strathern, M. 193
structuralism, 59, 70, 90, 102, 103,
    112, 128–9, 145, 156, 207
style, 8, 117, 127–30, 138, 174,
    191, 206
subjectivism, 20, 31, 64–5, 168
sublation, 12, 17, 28, 30, 40, 77,
    79, 191, 202, 214, 216
suburbia, 159–61
sumptuary laws, 135–6
super-ego, 92–3
symbolism, see signification

Tambiah, S. 119
taste, 150–3, 182, 197
technology, 74, 76, 111, 112–15
television, 7, 8, 212
textiles, 123
texts, 176
Thailand, 119
time, 122, 124–7
third world, 182
tools, 117
totality, 130, 164, 209
    of person, 208–9
trade, 137, 139
trade unions, 183
transitional object, 95

unconscious, 99, 102, 105, 107
unhappy consciousness, 24, 36,
    178, 184, 188, 204
USA, see America
use value, 47–8, 164, 206
utopian models, 182

Veblen, T. 9, 147–9, 151, 156,
    197, 199

on conspicuous consumption,
    148
on leisure class, 118, 147–8
Victoria and Albert museum, 117,
    123
Vygotsky, L. 94, 95

wage labour, 189, 210
wages, 7, 184, 188, 202
Walbiri, 53–9, 63, 67, 80
    ancestors, 54–9
    iconography, 54–8
    relation to environment, 53–8
    rights over representations, 54
Wallerstein, I. 137
Weber, M. 6, 71, 136, 147, 181,
    187
Wedgwood, J. 138
Weiner, A. 52, 63
welfare state, 183, 186
West Africa, 123
Williams, Raymond 176
Williams, Rosalind 139, 201
Williamson, J. 173
Wilson, E. 174, 194
wine, 98
Winnicott, D. 95
Winship, J. 172
Wolff, J. 176
women's magazines, 138, 170–2
Words and Things, 85
workplace, 197, 201, 210
working-class life, 150, 197–8
world fairs, 139

youth cultures, 169

Zimbabwe, 125
Zola, E. 139